New York
CURIOSITIES

Help Us Keep This Guide Up to Date

Every effort has been made by the author and editors to make this guide as accurate and useful as possible. However, many things can change after a guide is published—establishments close, phone numbers change, facilities come under new management, and so on.

We would appreciate hearing from you concerning your experiences with this guide and how you feel it could be improved and kept up to date. While we may not be able to respond to all comments and suggestions, we'll take them to heart, and we'll also make certain to share them with the author. Please send your comments and suggestions to the following address:

GPP
Reader Response/Editorial Department
PO Box 480
Guilford, CT 06437

Or you may e-mail us at:
editorial@globepequot.com

Curiosities Series

New York CURIOSITIES

Quirky characters,
roadside oddities &
other offbeat stuff

Second Edition

Cindy Perman

Guilford, Connecticut

The prices, rates, and hours listed in this guidebook were confirmed at press time. We recommend, however, that you call establishments to obtain current information before traveling.

To buy books in quantity for corporate use or incentives, call **(800) 962–0973** or e-mail **premiums@GlobePequot.com.**

All photos by the author unless otherwise noted.

Maps by Daniel Lloyd © Morris Book Publishing, LLC

Text design: Bret Kerr

Layout artist: Casey Shain

Editor: Tracee Williams

Project editor: Lauren Brancato

ISBN 978-0-7627-6984-1

Printed in the United States of America

10 9 8 7 6 5 4 3 2 1

For my mom—my top salesperson, PR person, therapist, and favorite travel companion

New York

LONG ISLAND

NORTH COUNTRY

SOUTHEAST

CENTRAL

WESTERN

contents

★ ★

acknowledgments

An enormous thank-you goes to my mom for always believing in me—and promoting me shamelessly! You are always there to hit me with a high five when things go right, give me a big hug when things go wrong, and make me laugh—even when I think it's not possible! I can't imagine this book, first *or* second edition, without you.

A huge thank-you to my work family at CNBC.com. This book wouldn't have been possible without you guys. From giving me time off to work on the book to making me laugh on a daily basis, you guys rock—and not just in Rocktober!

To all of my family and friends—especially Cheryl, Gennine, Christina, Amy, Andy, Ann, Dora, Jenn, Karolina, Christiane, Jamie, Rianna, and my orange slices—Heidi, Joy, Ashley, and honorary man slice Scott—thank you for your love, support, big belly laughs, and bacon.

My deepest gratitude to all the people I met in my travels, for letting me sit in your office, your kitchen, and on the front porch. Thank you for sharing your stories and trusting me to tell them in this book.

This has been an amazing journey. I am truly grateful to every person who has handed me a cup of Gatorade, a shot of espresso, or a slice of bacon along the way.

introduction

What Is a Curiosity?

Great question. I like you already!

A curiosity is anything you wouldn't find in a typical guidebook. So, if you're searching these pages for a good hotel room in Niagara Falls, you've bought the wrong book. If you want to know the scientific reason why they call Niagara Falls the "Honeymoon Capital of the World," keep reading. If you want to know how to get to the Statue of Liberty . . . um . . . do you still have your receipt? But if you're curious about who's waving back to Lady Liberty from the Brooklyn side, congratulations! You're gonna love this book.

It includes everything from a house shaped like a group of mushrooms in Rochester, to a man who will teach you to walk on fire in Ithaca, the Loch Ness Monster's long-lost cousin in the Adirondacks, a man who built his own castle with found objects in the Hudson Valley, and a human car wash in New York City.

It's meant to be part guidebook, so, where possible, I'll tell you where you can go to see some of these cool things. Other stories are about private people doing cool things, such as the guy in Brooklyn who missed his home country so much that he built a replica of the Greek island he came from in his backyard. Please use your discretion with those stories; don't stand in the yard and gawk!

I'm going to give you a ton of material for your next cocktail party or water cooler show, and perhaps a few more reasons to get out there and see New York State. So, sit back in your coziest armchair and come along for the ride. Then, get in your car and drive.

Welcome to New York

Before we hop in the car and start meeting people, I thought we could take a little helicopter ride to get you acquainted with the state.

Ready? Headphones on, seatbelts fastened.

introduction

New York is the nation's twenty-seventh-largest state, clocking in at 54,471 square miles. I fear you won't be able to concentrate if I don't tell you the top three largest states, so here goes: Alaska is number one, at more than 650,000 square miles, followed by Texas, which is half that size, and California.

OK, back to New York.

You see over there in the west? That's Niagara Falls, which pumps out forty million gallons of water per minute! Over here, in central New York, are the Finger Lakes; despite the name, there are actually eleven. *The Wonderful Wizard of Oz* author L. Frank Baum was born here in Chittenango, and some say, central New York *is* Oz. Up there

I Love Moo York!

introduction

are the Thousand Islands. Not to split hairs, but there are, um . . .
1,864 of them. We've got four mountain ranges, including the famous
Adirondacks and the Catskills. And down there are the bright lights of
New York City, one of the largest cities in the world.

Nearly half of the state's 19.4 million people live in New York City.
On the other side of the state, Wyoming County has more cows than
people, and in the Adirondacks' Lewis County, there are *twice* as many
cows as people.

Not only are there more cows here than you realized, but there are
also more castles than you may have expected. You'll read about five of
them in this book.

The state flower is the rose, and the state insect is the ladybug. Our
official bird is the bluebird; our fish is the trout. The state animal is the
beaver, a shout-out to our European fur-trader founders.

Milk is the official state beverage, as New York is the third-largest
dairy-producing state. (Aha! That explains all the cows.) The state fruit is
the apple, introduced by European settlers in the 1600s, and, thanks to
some elementary schoolkids in Syracuse, the state muffin is also apple.

Our state motto is *Excelsior,* Latin for "Ever upward." And, of course,
the state song is "I Love New York."

So, grab an apple muffin and splash some milk in your coffee. Make
a wish on a ladybug and get ready because . . . you're gonna love New
York, too!

Western New York

1

Western New York

Land of Talking to the Dead and Chicken Wings

When you think of western New York, you think: Kodak. Niagara Falls. Buffalo wings. But there's so much more to learn—and eat! In this chapter, we'll sample the region's other culinary delicacies, including bread made by monks and Rochester's famous garbage plate. (Hey, if my mom tried it, so can you!)

Once you've had a chance to digest all that, we'll visit with some avant-garde artists, including Surapa, the elephant who paints at the Buffalo Zoo! We'll tour museums devoted to everything from Jell-O to kazoos. We'll have tea in a storybook house in Forestville, attempt to communicate with the dead in Lily Dale, and take a walk on the ocean floor in Olean. (Did you pack your bathing suit? Never mind. You won't need it.)

Oh, but do bring an extra pair of old shoes! Writing your name on the bathroom stall is so 1984—we're going to leave our mark on western New York by flinging our old footwear up in the Shoe Tree!

★ ★

The Sauce Beneath Their Wings
Buffalo

For years, cooking chicken meant breasts, thighs, and drumsticks, with the wings tossed aside as scraps for soup.

But in 1964, something magical happened at the Anchor Bar in Buffalo. Some of Domenic Bellissimo's friends stopped by late one Friday night to visit the bartender. They were ravenously hungry, so Bellissimo asked his mother Teressa, who was back in the kitchen, to

Some runners limber up for the running of the "chickens."

whip up something for his friends. Ever the improviser, Teressa fried up a bunch of those chicken-wing scraps, smothered them with a secret sauce, and served them with blue cheese and celery.

And with that, the buffalo wing was born.

Fast-forward to 2001 and the debut of *Osmosis Jones,* starring Bill Murray as a compulsive junk-food eater who dreams of attending the fictitious National Buffalo Wing Festival. After seeing the movie, local newspaper columnist Donn Esmonde asked readers, "Yeah, why don't we have a Buffalo Wing Festival?" Well, entrepreneur Drew Cerza heeded the call and in 2002 launched the annual Buffalo Wing Festival.

The event opens with a "Running of the Chickens," though you may be surprised to learn that it doesn't involve actual chickens—it's people dressed as chickens. There's an International Federation of Competitive Eating–sanctioned chicken wing–eating contest, a Miss Buffalo Wing pageant, a Cheesiest Couple contest, and the Blue Cheese Bowl, which is like bobbing for apples only it's bobbing for wings in a kiddie pool full of blue cheese.

An estimated 85,000 people attended the 2011 festival and consumed more than half a million (or thirty-seven tons) of wings. The vendors, who take the competition for best sauce very seriously, serve up wings in all kinds of creative flavors, including Jamaican jerk, garlic Parmesan, and, for the adventurous, suicidal and atomic. There's also a variety of other wing-inspired foods, including wing-flavored pretzels, chicken-wing meatballs, and even chicken-wing soup.

There's even a "Hall of Flame" on the festival's website to honor those who "who have advanced the wing's climb from an unwanted chicken part that usually ended up in a Dumpster to a much-devoured favorite and national food icon."

For more information visit www.buffalowing.com or call (716) 565-4141.

★ ★

A Wing a Weck, a Wing a Weck
Buffalo

Where's the beef?

Why, it's right here in western New York! Thanks for asking.

With no disrespect to the chicken wing, which will forever remain tucked in western New York's heart, there's another delicacy from the Buffalo area—and, some foodies say, it's the real reason to visit western New York.

It's called beef on weck. Sure, other cities have roast beef sandwiches, but what sets this sandwich apart is the "weck," short for *kummelweck,* which is a crusty roll topped with rock salt and caraway seeds. Inside is a heaping pile of thinly sliced, juicy, rare roast beef with a dollop of freshly grated horseradish.

This local delicacy has been served in Buffalo-area restaurants and bars for more than one hundred years and is thought to have been brought to the region by German immigrants. Apparently, the reason why it hasn't taken flight outside of Buffalo the way the wing has is—not for lack of an aerodynamic structure, but—because the weck is hard to bake and it doesn't have a long shelf life.

One of the best places to try beef on weck is Schwabl's (www .schwabls.com), a 150-year-old family-owned business in West Seneca. The cozy, tavern-style restaurant bills itself as a "step back in time," with homemade German potato salad, over fifty homemade soups, and cocktails "made the old-fashioned way with all fresh ingredients—no mixers used here." Plus, over twenty different beers, a dozen wines, and birch beer on tap.

Some of the other places for beef on weck that are popular with the locals include Charlie the Butcher's Kitchen (www.charliethe butcher.com) with several locations around the city and Bar-Bill (www .barbill.com) in East Aurora.

There are even variations on the beef on weck—Schwabl's offers "surf and turf" a roast beef dinner with yellow pike or haddock. For a

few bucks extra, you can get the turf part (the roast beef) on a weck.
And at Seabar (www.seabarsushi.com), a sushi place in downtown
Buffalo, they even have a beef on weck sushi roll—the inside of the
roll has carved roast beef and the outside has caraway seeds and
salt—just like the weck.

Where's the beef? It's in western New York.

★ ★

A Wing, a Weck, a Wipe
Buffalo

Buffalo has solidified its place in the culinary history books with the buffalo wing and the beef on weck. But there is another invention from Buffalo that is, dare I say, more important than the wing or weck.

It's the windshield wiper.

It was a dark, rainy night in 1917. Buffalo theater owner J. R. Oishei was driving his car when he collided with a bicyclist. Both lived, and the cyclist wasn't seriously injured. But Oishei was so shaken up that he vowed to figure out a way to improve visibility when driving in bad weather.

In 1920 he formed the Tri-Continental Corporation, which introduced the world's first windshield wiper, called the Rain Rubber. You know, for safe, um . . . driving.

The Rain Rubber was basically a handheld squeegee, a rubber blade on a wooden handle, so drivers could clean their two-piece windshields, popular on cars at that time. There was an opening between the upper and lower sections that drivers could stick the squeegee through to remove the water from the windshield.

World War I put windshield and wiper technology on hold for a few years, but thankfully, when the war ended, automakers were back on the case and finally developed a one-piece windshield. Trico, as the company later called itself, followed suit and made the first automatic windshield wiper.

After wooing Henry Ford, Trico had enough money to gobble up the competition. It came out with the first dual windshield wiper in 1929, and windshield-wiper fluid debuted in 1936.

So, the next time you're choking on your own road rage about the pouring rain or that truck in front of you that just kicked up a tsunami on your windshield, remember it could've been a lot worse if you had to squeegee it off by hand.

Go home, order a bucket of wings, and forget about the whole thing.

⋆ ⋆

The Da Vinci of Da Zoo

Buffalo

You know the saying "An elephant never forgets"? It's true. Elephants are really smart and can do much more than hold each other's tails and stand on each other's backs.

At the Buffalo Zoo, their elephants do all kinds of things to keep busy—they play instruments, have scavenger hunts, and even have watermelon-eating contests.

They do activities together but, like their human counterparts, not all of them are interested in the same thing, so the trainers work to find each girl's strength. (The boys are a little too aggressive, so most zoos have girls.)

Surapa, an elephant who's around thirty years old and trainers describe as a "bit of a diva," has found her hidden talent—painting.

Trainer Melissa King says Surapa has two main styles: a circular swirl and an up-down motion they've dubbed "blades of grass" because that's what it looks like. King finds Surapa doesn't have a favorite color but, when left to her own devices, she often chooses yellow. They reward her with small food items such as jelly beans, whole loaves of bread, corn on the cob, and apples.

They tried painting with their other elephants—one tried to eat the paintbrush and the other just stood there with the brush in her trunk. Some of the other animals at the zoo have dabbled in art, like the lizards, monkeys, and giraffes, but mostly that means they just run or slither across the canvas. Or, in the case of the giraffe, lick it. (Don't worry, it's all nontoxic paint!)

Surapa is the real Picasso of pachyderms—the da Vinci of da zoo. (Well, her style may be closer to messy Matisse!)

She paints year-round, and her pieces are sold in the gift shop for about forty dollars. At the holidays, she also paints wineglasses and Christmas ornaments. Wineglasses are twenty-five dollars a pair, and the ornaments sell for anywhere from ten to fifteen dollars, depending on the size. The zoo says she paints several hundred items per year.

Where do I draw my inspiration from? It can come from anywhere, really—jelly beans, apples, corn on the cob . . .
COURTESY OF THE BUFFALO ZOO

And, in case you're wondering—no, she hasn't broken any yet!

"Actually, the only broken ornaments are from us keepers when we hang them up to dry!" King says. "Surapa has never broken a single glass or ornament."

"With the smaller stuff like wineglasses and ornaments, it requires a little more focus, a little more finesse," King explains. "Instead of using her elephant strength, she has to focus on the task at hand! And she really seems to enjoy it."

She doesn't paint every day—you know how moody artists can be! Some days, all the jelly beans in the world can't inspire you . . .

If you're lucky, you might catch her at work when you visit. One of the best times to stop by is for Elephantastic Weekend in June, when all the girls show off their mad elephant skillz.

For more information visit www.buffalozoo.org or call (716) 837-3900.

The Secret Sidewalk
Charlotte

Most of us don't have a million dollars to shell out for a waterfront mansion on Lake Ontario's Beach Avenue. But there *is* a way we can step into the fairy tale of lakeside luxury. It's called the Secret Sidewalk.

Once upon a time, a trolley ran through here, curving around the resort community between the houses and the lake. When it was

Leave the glass slippers at home and take a stroll on the Secret Sidewalk. But make sure you're back before midnight!

removed, the city put a sidewalk in its place. It's called the Secret Sidewalk because not too many people know about it, and just by looking at this stretch of Beach Avenue, you wouldn't even see it was there. There are six entrances to the sidewalk between the houses, some camouflaged with hedges, others running so close to the driveways, you'd think you were trespassing.

The mansions were built in a variety of styles, with gigantic porches, well-manicured lawns, and charming gardens that line the sidewalk. Between the sidewalk and the lake, resident-owned decks feature rows of pristine Adirondack chairs and even dining-room sets. Now *that* is dining on the lake—you can't get much closer than that!

My mom and I enjoyed a stroll along the sidewalk, chattering like a couple of little girls at a tea party about which house we'd want and why. Once we'd made our final selections, we picked out our favorite outdoor dining set. You know, for our first sunset dinner at the manse.

And they lived happily ever after. ~ The End. ~

The Secret Sidewalk runs from 490 to 720 Beach Avenue in Charlotte, but the best starting point is between nos. 490 and 510, near the intersection of Clematis Street.

Made in the Kazoo.S.A.
Eden

So, you go to New York, you buy a souvenir. You flip it over, and it's made in China. Welcome to the twenty-first century.

Today, so many things—especially small trinkets—are made in China. But don't go outsourcing your next vacation just yet. Good news, America! The metal kazoo is still made in the good ol' USA, right here in Eden, just a few miles southeast of Buffalo.

There are eighteen parts to a metal kazoo, made by an assembly line of human-operated die-press machines, the same way they were produced in 1916. You can actually watch this fascinating process at the Kazoo Museum & Factory in Eden. Or, you can try your hand at making one yourself. (Don't worry, you won't need seventeen friends.)

★ ★

Also on display is a collection of historical kazoos (yes, there is such a thing), including wooden kazoos; kazoos in the shape of various instruments such as trumpets and saxophones; kazoos in the shape of planes, trains, and tractors; and even liquor-bottle-shaped kazoos (to "kazelebrate" the end of Prohibition in 1934).

At the museum, you'll learn about Kazoophony, once an eighty-piece orchestra, which prompted *Playboy* magazine to declare: "If you ain't heard Mozart on the kazoo, you ain't heard nothing yet." In the gift shop, you can buy everything you'll need to start your own kazoo band.

If you're worried that maybe you don't have the gift of music, never fear: The museum touts the kazoo as "the most democratic of instruments because anyone can play."

Now if that's not all-American, I don't know what is.

For more information visit www.edenkazoo.com or call (716) 992-3960.

Kazoos come in all shapes and sizes—even planes, trains, and automobiles!

The Crunch Starts Here

I've got news for you, California. Granola was ours!

James Caleb Jackson co-owned an abolitionist newspaper and lectured on the cause, but poor health forced him into early retirement. He was near death when he decided to visit a spa for a "water cure," a popular alternative-medicine treatment in the mid-nineteenth century. His miraculous recovery made him a believer in the healing power of water—so much so that he went to medical school and then bought a spa of his own in 1858.

The Dansville Water Cure, which Jackson renamed Our Home on the Hillside, became one of the largest spas in the world under Jackson's management. Of course, the first step of any water program is to drink more water, but there were also baths, wet-sheet wrappings, and yes, even water douches. Jackson, whom you might call a historical health nut, took it a step further, encouraging his patients to eat healthier. He had them cut out the bad stuff—red meat, sugar, coffee, alcohol, and tobacco—and eat more fruits, vegetables, and unprocessed grains.

In 1863, Jackson made his most lasting contribution to society, one that lives on in almost every American household today: He invented the first cold breakfast cereal, and the predecessor of granola. It was called "granula."

So, how did we get to granola?

Well, Kellogg caught wind of this new breakfast fad, and crunched out a knockoff of granula, one that was tastier and easier to make. The company changed the name to "granola," to avoid being sued by Jackson.

Dude, are you listening?

Lana's the Little House
Forestville

There once was a lady named Lana.
Lana lives in the Little House.
The house has lots of nooks and crooks,
Even some painted-on books!
The shutters go clickety-clack.
There are fresh scones on the baker's rack.
The teapot goes woo! woo!
The piano upstairs will play a tune for you.
The garden is full of flowers,
And some milkweed for the butterflies.
Berries are ripe for the picking—
Strawberries, raspberries, and blueberries for pies.
There's a cat named Barney,
And a bullfrog named Charley.
Charley lives in a pond the shape of a heart.
Look closer, it's the turtle, George Burns, in that part!
They croak and they plop and they swish—
Oh, look! Here come Frank Sinatra and Dean Martin,
   the koi fish!
There's Milton Berle the bumble bee.
I'll see you all soon, I'm heading inside for a spot of tea!

The Little House isn't a fairy tale, though it feels like it what with all those characters on your trail. (OK, that's enough with the rhyming.) It's a real place, built in 1980 in Forestville by a couple of guys who wanted to create a real-life storybook house. Buffalo native Lana Lewis bought it in 2001, and before long, there were knocks at the door from curious neighbors.

Well, Lana knew how special the place was, and she decided to open it for tours and teas. As you wander around the gardens and through the house, she'll tell you the charming story of the place, while calling out hello to all of the animals she's named.

Once upon a time, in a land far, far away. . . . Actually, scratch that. It's right here in Forestville!

The price per person is twenty-five dollars for a tour or thirty-two dollars for the tour and afternoon tea. Lana tries to make it a truly special experience, with scones, butter tarts, and "world-class tea" in flavors like chocolate strawberry and coconut almond. She adds: "I don't make any of it, which is why I know it's good!"

I can't vouch for her baking skills, but I can tell you that she's a wonderful host to guide you through this fairy tale of an afternoon. For more information visit www.lanasthelittlehouse.com or call (716) 965-2798.

The Star-Spangled Store

Elma

Having a hard time finding products that are made in America anymore?

Mark Andol thought so, too. So in April 2010 he opened a store that sells nothing but things that are made in America—"down to the packaging."

The store sells hundreds of items, including lawn chairs, wigwam socks, a US Marine Corp blanket, candles, wind chimes, the original "Slinky," classic Coca-Cola tin signs, and the original Anchor Bar buffalo wing sauce—just to name a few.

"The recession, the trade imbalance, and unfair trade practices have met their match in Mark Andol!" the MIA website declares. He's made it his personal mission to bring manufacturing jobs—and dollars—back into the US economy.

Why should you support their mission?

If you listen carefully, you can hear the faint chant of "U-S-A! U-S-A!" coming from aisle 9.
PHOTO BY CHERYL PERMAN

"Because China is a long drive to work!" the website quips.

You gotta love a patriot with a sense of humor.

Made in America has become so rare, like a breed of panda you only find in a zoo, that more than fifty tour buses now make the store a stop on their routes!

If this town outside of Buffalo isn't on your itinerary, you can also shop online at www.saveourcountryfirst.com.

I Love Lucytown

Jamestown

Do you love Lucy?

From the minute she entered America's living room in 1951, there was a lotta love for Lucille Ball. There was something very real about her and her relationship with real-life husband Desi Arnaz in the *I Love Lucy* show. She wasn't trying to present a perfect image like so many icons of that time. She took situations everyone could relate to and showed us the absurdity of it all.

So many people loved *I Love Lucy* in the 1950s that telephone companies reported a "substantial reduction" in calls when the show was on and department stores changed their late shopping night to Thursday from Monday, so it wouldn't conflict with the broadcast. It was only produced until 1957, but by the time of Lucille Ball's death in 1989, the show was airing in syndication in more than eighty countries.

Nowhere else is she more popular than in Jamestown, the hometown of Lucille Ball as well as her Lucy character. Here, you'll find the Lucy-Desi Museum and the Desilu Playhouse featuring costumes, personal items, television clips, and recreated sets from the show. You can visit a replica of the Tropicana nightclub, where Arnaz's Ricky character performed, and try your hand at Lucy's famous Vitameatavegamin commercial. (It's got vitamins, meat, vegetables, and minerals!)

You can visit her childhood home and the cemetery where her ashes are interred. The local theater is named after her, as is the local park. Sprinkled along 3rd Street in downtown Jamestown are three murals of scenes from the show. And, in one of the museum's two gift shops, you can buy every imaginable *I Love Lucy* product ever made, including a *Lucy*-themed Monopoly game, a *Lucy* bingo dabber, and a reproduction of her famous pink candy-factory chef's hat.

Every August, the month in which Ball was born, Jamestown hosts a Lucille Ball Festival of Comedy, featuring well-known comedians from all across the country as well as a kids' comedy show.

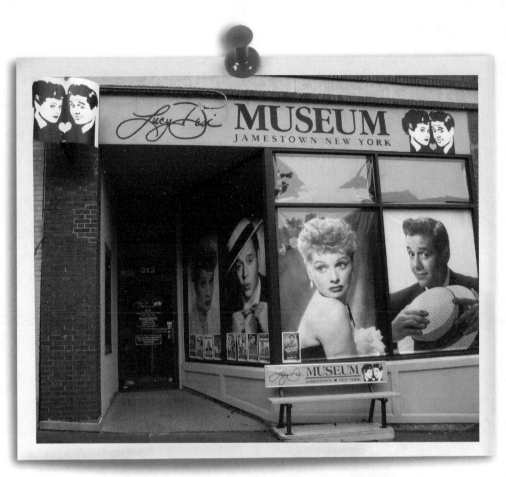

The Lucille Ball museum—it's got vitamins, meat, vegetables . . . and everything Lucy!

"Comedians sort of play Jamestown on their way to the top at the Lucille Ball Festival of Comedy," says Journey Gunderson, executive director of the Lucille Ball-Desi Arnaz Center for Comedy.

So, head over to Jamestown and say, "Lucy, I'm home!" If you don't, you got some 'splaining to do.

For more information visit www.lucy-desi.com or call (877) LUCY-FAN (582-9326).

★ ★

Jell-O and Welcome to America

Le Roy

You already know that the human head weighs eight pounds (thank you, Jonathan Lipnicki and *Jerry Maguire*), but did you know that Jell-O and the human brain register exactly the same on an EEG machine?

Did you also know that there is such a thing as a gelometer, a device used to measure the "jiggliness" of gelatin?

It's more than Jell-O—it's fine art!

These are just a couple of the fascinating facts that you'll learn at the Jell-O Gallery in Le Roy, which is a half hour southwest of Rochester, toward Buffalo.

Jell-O was invented in Le Roy in 1897 by a carpenter who also made cough medicine. After a few false starts and one well-placed ad in *Ladies' Home Journal,* Jell-O finally caught on, and today we can all claim to have watched it wiggle and, yes, seen it jiggle.

The Jell-O Gallery was created in 1997 for the jiggly dessert's one-hundredth anniversary. A museum devoted to gelatin might have the potential to be a small-town "eh," but this one is worth the trip. It's chock-full of fun Jell-O trivia such as which fruits float or sink in Jell-O, as well as great Jell-O paraphernalia including old advertisements by well-known illustrators such as Maxfield Parrish and Norman Rockwell. You haven't really lived until you've seen a Norman Rockwell–like painting incorporating Jell-O, or, for that matter, a still-life portrait of Jell-O.

You'll also learn about Jell-O geography. In the United States, red is always the favorite flavor, but in Japan, it's coffee. From 1910 to 1920, Jell-O was served to immigrants at Ellis Island to welcome them to America. Utah, sometimes called "the Jell-O State," even made the jiggly treat its state snack. (There was apparently a countermotion for ice cream, but it was declared "unsexy" because it wasn't "wiggly and jiggly.") FYI: If you're ever attending a party in Utah and are asked to bring a "green salad," that means lime Jell-O with shredded carrots.

Oh, and in case you're wondering (you were, right?), fresh fruits such as apples and bananas float in Jell-O, while seedless grapes and canned fruits in syrup sink.

I could go on, but I don't want to take all the fun out of it for you. For more information visit www.jellogallery.org or call (585) 768-7433. While you're there, be sure to pick up a brain mold for your Jell-O!

Living with the Dead
Lily Dale

A woman walks down the street, past the small sherbet-colored Victorian homes, dragging one foot behind her and announcing to the air that she just got off the mother ship. Dracula jumps out from behind a tree.

This is what most people expect from Lily Dale, a small, gated community of Spiritualists in southwestern New York. "A strange little village . . . " one guidebook entry starts. "You have to be a psychic to live there!" a friend advised with a gleam of the bizarre in her eye.

Ms. Mother Ship and Count Dracula did indeed visit Lily Dale, but they were freaks there just as they would be in your town, giving all the residents a good laugh. They aren't what Lily Dale is about.

Lily Dale is an idyllic community one hour south of Buffalo, tucked between the placid Lake Cassadaga and the Leolyn Woods, a rich, old-growth forest. You have to be a Spiritualist to live there, but the community's gate is always open to visitors.

So, what is Spiritualism? The basic tenet of the religion, which was founded in western New York more than one hundred years ago, is the continuity of life after death. You can believe in God, Allah, Buddha, or no god, but the common thread is that you don't believe that life stops when you die; the spirit continues on infinitely. Spiritualist practice hinges on communicating with the spirit world.

Susan Glasier, the executive director of the town's governing body, the Lily Dale Assembly, once described Spiritualists this way: "We're just like everyone else, except we talk to dead people!" (That's an explanation for us laymen, because Spiritualists don't think of it as death, rather a transition of the spirit to the next level.)

It may sound somewhat fantastical, but if you go to Lily Dale, the one thing you'll notice is how completely normal it seems—and, how open-minded the people are. They welcome skeptics and the most devout believers with the same hospitality.

★ ★

There are more than thirty registered mediums in Lily Dale, but not all Spiritualists are mediums. And, to clear up the psychic issue, the late Donna Riegel, who was a medium in Lily Dale, once explained: "Every medium is a psychic, but not every psychic is a medium."

In the summer months, you'll pay a gate fee of ten dollars per person to enter Lily Dale, and there are plenty of free events such as meditation, healing, and "message" (as in, from the other side) services, but you'll have to share the mediums with everyone else. You can have a private reading with a medium, starting at around forty dollars. There is also a library, a museum, and a hotel that offer no shortage of fascinating Spiritualist artifacts and books. Not to be missed is the charming pet cemetery; it's worth the gate fee to just wander around.

For more information visit www.lilydaleassembly.com or call (716) 595-8721.

Lily Dale, the town that welcomes the living as well as the dead!

Burnt Offerings

Spiritualism started in Hydesville, New York, in 1848, when the famous Fox sisters, Kate and Margaret, allegedly made contact with the spirit of a peddler who'd been murdered in their house years earlier. The spirit would knock to answer their questions.

Spiritualism was one of a whopping seven religions founded in New York State around that time. The religious wave was so immense that western New York was later dubbed the "Burned Over District," meaning there was no one left to convert.

Praise Jesus!

The seven religions are: the Free Methodist Church, Millerism, Mormonism, Perfectionism, Spiritualism, Universal Friends, and the Wesleyan Church.

The Wesleyan Church was founded in 1843 in Utica by Reverend Orange Scott as a splinter of the Methodist Church on the principles of abolition of slavery and women's rights. The Free Methodist Church, founded in Pekin, New York, in 1860 by Benjamin T. Roberts, took equality a step further, believing that the church shouldn't discriminate against the poor by charging for prime pew seats. (Hence, the "free" part.)

Speaking of "free" thinking, that brings us to Mormonism, founded in 1827 in Palmyra, New York, when then-fourteen-year-old Joseph Smith found a set of golden plates from an ancient civilization on a hill and became a modern-day prophet. Smith wrote the Book of Mormon and, in his spare time, started the whole polygamy thing, personally taking on thirty-three wives.

Way to go, Joe.

Perfectionism took creative marriage to a whole new level. John Humphrey Noyes, who founded the religion in Oneida, New York, in 1848, decided that every member of the congregation should be married to every other member of the opposite sex. Well, the idea never quite caught on in the broader community, so the group said, what the heck—let's make silverware.

Now, it's going to get a little crazy. Can I get a hallelujah?

Millerism, which was the precursor to the Seventh-day Adventist Church, was founded by William Miller in Low Hampton, New York, in the 1840s. It was based on the notion that Jesus Christ would return to earth in 1844. You can imagine that Millerism sort of fizzled when 1844 came and went with nary a Jesus spotting.

In the 1700s, Jemima Wilkinson had a near-death experience and decided that—no, not that she was waiting for Jesus Christ—she was the incarnation of Jesus Christ. And so, in the town of Penn Yan, New York, the religion known as Universal Friends was born. Another key tenet was abstinence. (That makes sense. I mean, who has time for recreational activities, when you've got Jesus Christ in front of you?) When Wilkinson actually died, her body wasn't buried for years because everyone was standing around waiting for her to rise from the dead, like J.C. the First. Needless to say, this religion fizzled, too.

And now, for the awards. I'm going to give the award for "Least Likely to Win a Following on Wall Street" to the Free Methodists. Mormonism wins for "Most Likely to Get Divorced," and Perfectionism takes home the coveted "Most Likely to Succeed (at Something Else)" award.

Congratulations to everyone. Can I get an Amen?

Amen!

★ ★

A Tree for Lost Soles

Lyndonville

Ever wonder what to do with that favorite pair of shoes that's past its prime? You hate to throw them away, but the Smithsonian won't return your calls.

Well, if you live in the village of Lyndonville, the answer is simple: You toss them up in a tree, where they will be immortalized until the next strong wind.

Locals call it "the Shoe Tree," but it's actually four trees (there were five but one died), with hundreds of shoes dangling from the branches, lounging in the surrounding field, and crawling up the tree trunk, as if making a break for higher ground. They come in all shapes, colors, and sizes—sneakers, soccer cleats, work boots, cowboy boots, moccasins, and sandals.

There are many local myths about how the Shoe Tree started. One story goes that a man didn't like his wife's shoes and tossed them up in the tree. Another suggests it was a high school prank.

One online poster reports that nailing shoes to trees is a tradition among the cottage community in Canada, just across the lake from Lyndonville.

We're getting warmer.

The tree was started by Diane Bane, a local factory worker, in October 1986. She saw something on TV about those shoe trees in Canada and thought it would be neat to make one in Lyndonville. She was cleaning out her closet and had a bagful of shoes. She told then-boyfriend Earl Baun to find her a tree so they could start one.

They hopped in Bane's truck with about eight to ten pairs of shoes. Bane kept watch while Baun tossed the shoes up in the tree. "Then, we went around begging neighbors, relatives, and friends—'Hey, you got any shoes?' They'd say, 'What are you going to do with them?' We'd say, 'Oh, throw them up in a tree!'" Bane says, giggling.

Several newspapers and TV stations have reported on the tree over the years but only once, in a 1995 *Rochester Democrat & Chronicle*

You always knew those sneakers of yours were legendary. Now, you can put them in this outdoor museum for old footwear!

article, has Bane been mentioned. Meanwhile, she lives right around the corner.

Why the mystery?

"We kept it quiet for a long, long time because we had a con-servation officer that didn't like Earl," Bane says. "He said he was going to find out who started it and arrest him for littering!" Like a real-life Rosco P. Coltrane, that conservation officer was bound and determined to find out who did it. ("A gu gu gu!") Bane says he'd even harass the local hunters who gathered near the tree. "He'd say, 'I know you guys know who did this!'" Bane explains, "but nobody would ever tell him!"

★ ★

Now, the tree has become such a landmark, Bane says, even the sheriffs use it to give directions.

For the record, Bane, now a grandmother, has never thrown a pair of shoes in the tree. She admits it was her idea, but Baun, who has since passed away, did all the shoe flinging. Now, more than twenty years later, she's thinking about it. "I'm going to have to find a pair of shoes," Bane says. "I'll go over there and just wing one up there!"

Bane is retiring from her factory job soon and thinks when she retires, that might be the time. "We have to wear these stupid, uncomfortable steel-toe shoes. I can't think of a better place for 'em!" she opines. "That's my goal—to throw these stupid shoes up in those trees!"

The great thing about the Shoe Tree is that anyone can toss shoes up there and become part of a local landmark. The Orleans County tourism board says local custom is to make a wish as you toss your shoes in the tree.

I know what I'm going to wish for: a new pair of shoes! Well, that, and that I don't get busted by Rosco and Flash. Yeeeeeeehaw!

The Shoe Tree is located at the T intersection of Lake Shore and Foss Roads in the village of Lyndonville, town of Yates.

Social Studies in the Outhouse
Mumford

Living history museums make for a wonderful class field trip. Inside of beautiful old buildings, people in period costumes show you how to churn butter, resole shoes, and stamp your own wallpaper.

Mumford is home to the largest living history museum in the state, and one of the largest in the United States. The Genesee Country Village & Museum is a lovely historic village, with trellises draped with purple wisteria, a trolley that runs around it, and a couple of oxen lounging back in the oxbow.

It may not be as big as Colonial Williamsburg, but the Genesee Country Village & Museum has a national distinction all its own: It has the most outhouses of any living history museum in the United States!

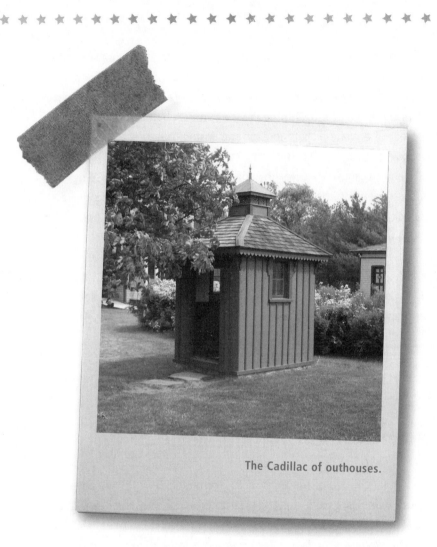

The Cadillac of outhouses.

The thirteen outhouses aren't clustered in one place, nor are they noted on the village map. (Perhaps so you don't get them confused with the modern-day facilities.) But, as you wander around the village, they pop up here and there, offering insight into the people who once used these now-historic holes in the ground.

Each one is distinct and is often trimmed to match the house or building it belongs to. The outhouse tucked between the bushes near the Brooks Grave Methodist Church is a modest white four-seater with a wood-shingled roof. An outhouse between the schoolhouse and land office has separate privies for men and women.

Out by the oxbow and nearby garden, there's a humble two-seat shack, the wood showing the wear of time. A blue two-seater in the corner of a white picket fence on the Foster-Tufts property screams middle class.

James Livingston, a wealthy entrepreneur, had an in-house out-house, meaning the three-seat outhouse was attached to his white Greek Revival mansion, which had giant columns and wide porches on both floors.

The octagonal-shaped Hyde House has one of the classiest com-modes I've ever seen. It's not octagonal, but still pretty fancy. It's lime green, to match the house, with teal stripes and lime-colored scalloped trim on the roof and matching cupola. Built for a farmer-turned-doctor, it has four seats.

Now that's outhaute couture!

For more information on the Genesee Country Village, visit www .gcv.org or call (585) 538-6822.

Power to the People

Niagara Falls

Niagara Falls, one of the seven natural wonders of North America, is more than just a tourist attraction—it's a power source for both the United States and Canada.

The power of the falls, which pump out more than 1.5 million gallons of water per second, has been harnessed to generate actual power for residents and businesses since 1881. In those days, it ran the local mills and a few streetlights. Today, hydroelectric power plants at the falls generate more than 4.9 million kilowatts of energy—enough to run nearly four million homes. (The US side uses just over half—2.7 million kilowatts—of that capacity.)

In all, Niagara Falls supplies one quarter of the power used in New York State and Ontario.

Pretty powerful, eh? I mean literally, it makes power.
COURTESY OF NIAGARA TOURISM & CONVENTION CORP.

Now, the thing about water is, it freezes. So, if you're relying on it for a power source year-round, you have to ensure that the flow is uninterrupted.

The falls have never completely frozen over due to the depth and speed of the water, but there are some pretty massive chunks of ice that form in the winter which can be fifty feet thick or more. In 1848, the flow of water was stopped completely for several hours due to an ice jam. So much so, that people walked out into the riverbed to retrieve artifacts!

As amazing a sight as that must've been, the powers that be (literally, the power authorities in New York and Ontario) started using an "ice boom" in 1964 to prevent further ice jams. An ice boom is a giant floating chain (nearly two miles wide) that is stretches across the mouth of the Niagara River at Lake Erie to prevent frozen buildup. It is set in place every year in December and removed in March. The chain keeps any ice from clogging the river and shutting down the water flow—and the power. Think of it like a snake for your drains—only on a massive scale!

Apparently the removal of the boom in the spring is a pretty spectacular site—it releases the hounds, or the remaining melting ice chunks, as it were, which then go cascading over the falls.

Throughout the winter, both power authorities deploy ice-breaker boats, small vessels that help crunch up bigger chunks into more digestible pieces.

High on the power of the falls? Visit the Power Vista, located four and a half miles downstream (still a pretty scenic place), which has more than fifty interactive exhibits on Niagara Falls' hydroelectric power operation. For more information, visit the website www.nypa.gov/vc/niagara.htm.

Over the Falls in a Barrel

Niagara Falls

Everyone makes jokes about going over Niagara Falls in a barrel, but how did that whole thing start? Who was the first guy to do it?

Actually, that first guy was a lady.

It was 1901, and her name was Annie Taylor. It wasn't the comedic head-sticking-out-the-top-type stunt—Taylor actually crawled inside a wooden barrel and had it sealed airtight with a bicycle pump. She was a little banged up—but lived.

The next few tries weren't quite as pretty: In 1911, Bobby Leach took the plunge in a steel barrel. He broke both kneecaps and his jaw in the fall, though he also survived. In 1920, Englishman Charles Stephens took to the falls in a wooden barrel. He tied himself to an anvil inside the barrel, with the idea that adding such weight would give him more stability and control. Alas, the only thing left in the barrel at the bottom was his right arm.

Eesh.

In 1928, "Smiling Jean" Lussier tried it in a rubber ball. He survived. In 1930, a Greek waiter named George Statakis went the barrel route and survived the descent but suffocated to death after his barrel got stuck behind the falls for more than fourteen hours.

Perhaps beginning to doubt the merits of the barrel, in 1961, Nathan Boya of Jamaica, New York, also went the ball route, though his was made of steel and rubber and also included an oxygen tank. He hit the rocks on the way down, but the biggest casualty was a dent to the ball. Boya survived.

In 1984, Canadian Karel Soucek survived a trip in a barrel. And in 1985, there were two more successful barrel runs: Rhode Island bartender Steven Trotter survived a trip in one wrapped in inner tubes, while Canadian mechanic John Munday pulled it off in a plain barrel.

In 1989, the first duo went over the falls—Canadians Peter DeBernardi and Jeffery James Petkovich.

Not to be outdone, John Munday decided to give the falls a second run—this time, with a partner, Lori Martin, a caterer from Georgia. He then had the distinction of not only surviving a trip over the falls twice but also being in the first man-woman duo to do so.

I'll drink to that. Bartender! Another round, please.

In 2003, Michigan resident Kirk Jones took the plunge wearing nothing but the clothes on his back—and lived.

Of course, pulling a stunt like that—in a barrel or otherwise—is illegal in both the United States and Canada. The fines can run up to $25,000, though in recent years they have been in the $2,000 to $6,000 range.

For what it's worth, fish have a much better success rate than their human counterparts. Many go over, few die. The reasoning goes that their bodies are just more pliable, plus they're cushioned by all the bubbles. It's "nothing more than a big elevator for the fish," retired Niagara Falls detective sergeant Rick Berketa wrote in his Thunder Alley blog (www.niagarafrontier.com/faq.html#fish). The bigger risk than dying in the fall is actually being picked off by a seagull at the bottom if they are stunned when they first land and drift toward the surface.

If you really want to know what it's like to go over Niagara Falls in a barrel, check out the *Legends & Daredevils* movie at the Niagara IMAX Theater (www.imaxniagara.com). Their tagline is, "Only IMAX puts you in a barrel." There's also a Daredevil Gallery there, where they have many of the barrels and other contraptions used by the Niagara thrill seekers.

OK, hang on. Whoooooooooooooooooooooooooa!

Something in the Air

There's a scientific reason why they call Niagara Falls the "Honeymoon Capital of the World."

No, I didn't say physiological reason, so get your mind out of the gutter, OK?!

Niagara Falls is known in the scientific community as the "Negative Ion Capital of the World." Negative ions—which you can't see, taste, or touch—clean the air, dragging dust and other pollutants to the ground. When they reach your bloodstream, they boost the chemical serotonin your body produces, relieving stress, boosting energy, and even creating a feeling of euphoria.

Mass marketers have picked up on the negative-ion effect, which is why you're increasingly seeing products with ionizers—everything from air purifiers to hair dryers. The idea is that they alleviate allergens in the air and keep dust particles out of your hair, but hey, if you feel euphoric about drying your hair, who's a marketer to stop you?!

The average household has dozens or hundreds of negative ions, while a beach, a forest, or a mountain may have tens of thousands of them. So, while the view may be spectacular, that breathtaking feeling you get just may be the negative ions talking! You'll also feel the effects after a good rainfall. Ions get their charge when molecules are broken apart by catalysts such as sunlight or moving water. That refreshed, awake feeling you get in the shower? It's not psychological; it's the negative ions created by the falling water.

If your shower is dispensing a few gallons of water per minute and you feel that good, imagine how that is amplified at Niagara Falls, which pumps out 37.4 million gallons of water per minute. Some people say the falls' effect is more than euphoria, it's an aphrodisiac!

So, the next time you hear about some crazy guy trying to go over Niagara Falls in a barrel or your best friend went there for a vacation and came back married, you know what to blame: negative ions!

All I want to know is: How can something so negative feel so good?

★ ★

Take a Walk on the Ocean Floor
Olean

Imagine hiking through giant rock formations that were once part of the ocean floor, without getting wet.

Imagine doing it in western New York, more than 300 miles from the Atlantic Ocean.

Rock City Park, located just this side of the Pennsylvania border, is the world's largest formation of quartz conglomerate. It's like cement with small white pebbles mixed in, just the way the ocean jumbles

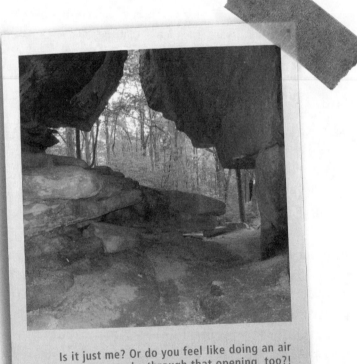

Is it just me? Or do you feel like doing an air breaststroke through that opening, too?!

everything up. The formations are massive—some three or four stories tall—creating canyons with nooks, crannies, and gaps where the rocks overlap. The formation resembles a bunch of giant aquarium rocks, just waiting for a fish—or a human—to swim through.

The rock was created 320 million years ago, and the formation was the result of the tectonic plate shift that pushed up the Appalachian mountain chain. "Remember, much of the continent used to be covered in ocean," explains Dale Smith, who co-owns Rock City Park with his wife, Cindy. As the ocean receded and the earth eroded, it exposed these stunning rock canyons.

You might've guessed that glaciers played a part in the rock formation, but here's another *Jeopardy!* question you and I would've gotten wrong. "The glaciers passed as close as seventy-five miles away, but not here," Dale says.

Once you've completed your walk on the ocean floor, take some time to enjoy the breathtaking thirty-five-mile view from the tops of the rocks.

I think I'm still going to need some time to get my head around the fact that the ocean was once in western New York, and that I just went deep-sea diving without an oxygen tank! But, that's to be expected, I guess. As Cindy Smith explains, this was all a very long time ago, B.C. (Before Cindy!)

Rock City Park is located at 505A Rock City Road off of Route 16, a few miles south of Olean. For more information visit www.rockcitypark .com or call (866) 404-ROCK.

Secret Ingredient: Monks
Piffard

You go to the grocery store and pick up a loaf of bread without giving it much thought. But have you ever had bread made by a monk?

The monks at the Abbey of the Genesee, tucked in the rolling hills of the Genesee River Valley, have been baking bread for more than fifty years.

It started with a recipe one of the monks, Brother Sylvester, picked up while he was in the Navy, stationed in the Mediterranean, during World War II. He would bake the bread for the other monks at mealtime, but guests enjoyed it so much, they started asking for an extra loaf to take home.

This is where it comes in handy to be quiet and listen to what God is telling you to do. Brother Sylvester got himself a patent on that bread recipe, the monks built a bakery, and, like the bread in the oven, the business rose from there.

Today, the monks crank out about 40,000 loaves of Monks' Bread a week, and they've added cakes to their repertoire. They sell them via an on-site store; grocery stores in Buffalo, Rochester, and Syracuse; and their website, www.monksbread.com.

So, does Monks' Bread taste different? Absolutely. It's fresh, yet hearty, with a yeast-y twang. Brother Sylvester tweaked the recipe to make it richer, since eight months out of the year, the monks aren't allowed to put butter or anything on their bread. However, butter isn't the key ingredient—or even an ingredient. The monks are a peace-loving people and refuse to engage Enemy No. 1: trans fats. They use soy oil.

Every monk takes a shift in the bakery, from the abbot on down. "Some of our ingredients are more quality ingredients than other companies because their overhead is more expensive than ours," says Father Stephen, the bakery's production manager. "Monks don't cost much for upkeep!"

Michael Rizk, who used to help out in the bakery when visiting on retreat, says working with monks was very different from your average nine-to-five job. "Monks aren't competing," Rizk says, "they're cooperating." And even though they're not getting paid, they work with a smile on their faces.

Rizk added that the monastic environment helps to make the work more like a meditation. "You focus on the present moment," he explained. "It's God's work."

Five-six-seven-eight some yeast . . . some soy oil . . .
Monks and bread incorporated! We're gonna do it!
Give us any bread we'll make it . . .
PHOTO BY FATHER STEPHEN MULLER

In the calm center of my bread-loving place, the secret ingredient has become apparent to me—monks!

I think I have the recipe now: Mix a bushel of wheat, a cup of sugar, a pinch of yeast, and a splash of soy oil. Stir in three dozen mindful monks, a handful of smiles and cooperation, to God's taste. For more information on the monks, visit www.geneseeabbey.org or www.monksbread.com.

★ ★

The House That Grew from a Bottle

Pittsford

Everyone calls it the "Mushroom House" because it looks like a group of mushrooms to scale. But here's a little secret: It was never meant to look like mushrooms at all.

The house was built in 1970 for lawyer Robert Antell and his wife, Marguerite, a sculptor. They told architect James Johnson that they wanted him to "surprise them" with something really unusual.

So, Johnson, who also designed Rochester's famous Temple Sinai, started looking for inspiration. He knew the house had to be raised because it was on a ravine. "I went into the shop where [the model] was being built—really, just our garage," Johnson recalls. "A fellow working on it had gone into the field next to the house and picked some wildflowers. I saw the Queen Anne plant and said, 'Whoa!' and pulled it out of the Coke bottle."

The stem of the Queen Anne plant became the basis for Johnson's design. It's not clear who started calling it the "Mushroom House," but I guess it was just easier than saying the "Stem of the Queen Anne's Lace Plant House."

The house, which is more than 4,100 square feet, has three bed-rooms and three bathrooms. It consists of five interconnected pods: four are enclosed for the main house, including one "kids' pod"; the fifth is an open-top deck. The pod floors are covered in 9,000 earth-toned ceramic tiles made—literally made and fired—by Marge Antell. The walls are stucco. Tentacle-like stems sprout from columns up into the ceiling.

"We're twenty-five feet up off the ground," said Chris Whitman, who owned the home with her husband for about thirteen years before selling it in 2012. "Because you're up high, you're living with the birds." Another nice feature, she described, is that, with all the windows, "when the seasons change, it's like the house is full of paintings. And they change every season."

The Whitmans, who are cousins of the original owners, recruited Johnson to design an addition when they bought the house. It was

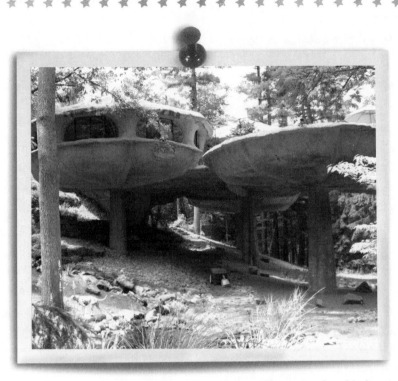

Man, they grow 'em big here!
PHOTO BY STEVE WHITMAN

tricky because the house's landmark status meant they couldn't alter the exterior. So, Johnson and his team chose the obvious solution: an underground pod!

To access the underground pod, or as the Whitmans call it, "the cave," you take a stairwell that descends from the middle of the living-room floor, where a fireplace used to be. There's a tunnel, which Johnson calls a "time tunnel," with mosaic on the floor that creeps up the cave-like walls. "My idea was to connect the old with the new, since there was a time warp of thirty years or so" between the two projects, Johnson says.

The Mushroom House is off Park Road in Powder Mill Park. It's a private home so you can't just pop in, but if you want a peek, check out the real-estate listing at www.mushroomhouse.us.

Never Put a Horse in Reverse

Rochester

You know George Eastman for his contributions to photography. Frankly, if it weren't for him, your camera might still be the size of a microwave.

Eastman quit school at the age of fourteen to help support his family. When he was in his early twenties, Eastman became obsessed with making photography simpler, and he started mixing chemicals in his mom's kitchen after work. From those cauldrons sprang the Eastman Kodak Company.

That's all tremendously impressive, but while you were busy trying to figure out what to point your nano-camera at next, here are a few things you might've missed about the man behind the camera.

Eastman created the name Kodak because he wanted a distinctive word that didn't violate any foreign trademarks. The less scientific reason was that his mother's maiden name was Kilbourn, and the guy just really liked the letter *K*.

Eastman's obsession with convenience wasn't limited to photography. In the garage of his dream home, built in 1902, he had a giant lazy Susan–type device installed so that he never had to drive his horse and carriage—and later, his car—out backward. (Maybe the neighbors complained when he pulled the horse out you-know-what side first.)

In the conservatory of his home, a nine-by-eleven-foot replica of an elephant head—one of his African safari conquests—towers overhead. That same room contains an organ that once had 7,200 pipes. Each morning, an organist would play while Eastman, a lifelong bachelor, ate breakfast.

Sure, we all have organists for our Cheerios, but here's one thing you probably can't top: After one performer complained of poor acoustics in the conservatory, in 1919 Eastman invented a hydraulic-lift system to literally slice the house in half and extend that room by nine feet without disturbing any of his precious gardens.

Soon after his African safari, Eastman was diagnosed with an irreversible spinal disease. He took his own life in 1932. But true to form, he left this note: "To my friends: My work is done. Why wait?—GE."

Today, Kodak is one of the most recognizable brand names in the world. Eastman's mansion is a landmark. The attached museum contains the camera that shot the flag raising at Iwo Jima, alongside the famous photograph, as well as the NASA lunar orbiter, used to photograph the surface of the moon, a camera used to photograph Marilyn Monroe and a Technicolor camera used on the sets of *The Wizard of Oz* and *Gone with the Wind*. There are more than 400,000 photos and negatives, and more than 25,000 film titles— including the personal collections of Ken Burns, Spike Lee, and Martin Scorsese.

George Eastman. Now there's a Kodak moment!
COURTESY OF THE GEORGE EASTMAN HOUSE

Whether you're interested in a master's degree in photo preservation or just want a peek at that elephant head, check out the George Eastman House at 900 East Avenue in Rochester. For more information call (585) 271-3361 or visit www.eastmanhouse.org.

Red or White?

Rochester

Every Rochesterian knows the answer to the question, "Red or white?"

If you attend a backyard barbecue in Rochester and opt for a hot dog, it's one that will surely be put to you. It means, do you want the standard red hot dog or Rochester's hometown dog, the white hot.

There are two main differences: 1) the color and 2) the taste. Red dogs are a little sweeter, while white hots tend to be richer, meatier, and mildly spicy. They often contain a dairy component, like nonfat dry milk, and mustard, which gives them a little kick.

They consist of unsmoked pork, beef, and veal and get their white color because they're not smoked or cured.

The white hot was introduced to Rochester in the 1920s by its significant German population. At the time, white hots were offered as a cheaper alternative, but today they are made with high-quality meats and cost a little more than regular hot dogs.

What'll it be: Red or white?

White hots are sold at area stores, like Wegmans, and at all the major sports stadiums in western New York, including those of the Buffalo Bills football team, Rochester Amerks hockey team, and Rochester Rhinos soccer team. If you want to do your own taste test, Wegmans sells a sampler pound pack of four reds and four whites.

OK. So now the only thing left is for you to answer the question, "Red or white?"

I know what I'd say!

★ ★

Toni Eckmair's Bowl-Y Grail
Rochester

Antoni Eckmair's motto is: "All materials are art materials and all projects are art projects," which he adopted from the late Stanley Czurles, who was an art professor at the State University College at Buffalo (where Eckmair's father taught). Eckmair, also an artist, is the kind of guy who goes to the kitchen to get a sandwich and leaves a trail of art in his wake.

He has a deep appreciation for famous works like the Mona Lisa, but he doesn't appreciate when they're put behind velvet ropes and glass cases. "They lock up the really good art because it's dangerous!" Eckmair quips.

As a result, his chosen gallery is his front yard on Hayward Avenue in downtown Rochester, near the public market. Here, large, metal birds are suspended from trees. Toy carousel horses scale the fence as if fleeing a merry band of children demanding one more bounce on the horsey. His metal shop is a glass box made of old shower doors. There's a totem pole of papasan chairs. There's a pile of flat rocks in the shape of a man, which Eckmair explained is an inukshuk, a man-made landmark used by the Inuit people in the Canadian arctic tundra, where there are few natural landmarks. (That's not a problem here on Eckmair's lawn.) Nearby is a tree made of blue glass, a giant hand protruding from the ground, and what appears to be a collection of bowling balls.

Bowling balls?

Eckmair says he's actually become something of a bowling-ball magnet after creating a bowling-ball machine along his fence. The ball travels down a wire alley overhead, hits a lever, drops down, winds around, and somewhere along the way it crushes fresh herbs such as mint, thyme, and sage.

People are always looking to unload their stuff—and their guilt for simply throwing it away. So, if you haven't bowled in fifteen years and it's time to send the ball on its way, you go, "I know, the bowling ball

You won't have a hard time figuring out which house is Antoni Eckmair's. Even the gate is like *Bam! Pow! Hizzah!*

guy!" Eckmair estimates that, thanks to such donations, his inadvertent bowling-ball collection is around 200 and counting. "I use them for mulch!" Eckmair quips.

It's not just bowling balls, either: Eckmair finds all kinds of things dropped on his doorstep. He calls it the "inanimate-object breeding program," which has provided a lot of raw materials for his art.

The *Rochester Democrat & Chronicle* once referred to him as "a wizard of unwanted things."

When he's not in the garage—I mean, "Secret Lab"—creating art, you might find him off jousting with other members of his medieval fight club, the Society for Creative Anachronism. ("We dress up in armor and hit each other with sticks," Eckmair explains.) He even makes his own armor in the Secret Lab. One of his favorite self-made toys is a "jousting machine" comprised of two knight dolls on horses rigged to garage-door openers.

Now, if you could just stand right there and clack these coconut halves together for me . . .

The Garbage Plate
Rochester

It all started with two hot dogs, cold beans, and french fries. That was the main dish served at Alex Tahou's restaurant when the Greek immigrant opened it in 1918 in a former train station in downtown Rochester.

Nick Tahou took over his father's restaurant in the 1940s, and it still carries his name today. Ask anyone from Rochester—they know Nick Tahou Hots. And it's all because of the "garbage plate," which is to Rochester what the cheesesteak is to Philadelphia.

The origin of the name "garbage plate" dates back to the 1980s, when Nick's became popular with college students—especially those sobering up after a night of heavy drinking—since it was open twenty-four hours. Nick's offered comfort food at its finest: Meat, potatoes, beans, and macaroni all piled up on one plate and smothered in a deliciously spicy, greasy concoction infused with ground beef.

★ ★

Gimme one of those plates with all the garbage on it!

The students, in an act of either fatigue or rebellion, snubbed the standard—"I'd like two hot dogs, cold beans, and french fries, please"—in favor of "Gimme one of those plates with all the garbage on it!"

"We hated that!" says Nick's son—also named Alex—who now runs the family business. "We would say, 'Don't call it that! It's hots and potatoes, or a cheeseburger plate.'"

But every good businessperson knows when to cash in the chips—or the hot-dog plate—and while the Tahous didn't like those kids calling their food garbage, this is the dish they were coming for and telling all of their friends about. In fact, the word-of-mouth buzz drove so much traffic to the restaurant that it made advertising unnecessary. By the late 1980s, Nick's embraced the crude nickname-turned-phenomenon, tacking on a sign out front that reads HOME OF THE GARBAGE PLATE, and trademarking the "garbage plate" name.

You can get your own garbage plate—with your choice of meat and up to four different side items—for about six dollars at two Nick's locations: 320 West Main Street in downtown Rochester and 2260 Lyell Avenue in the town of Gates. The Gates location is still open twenty-four hours, but the downtown restaurant, which is in a grittier area, closes at 8:00 p.m.

Why Is That Red Elephant Laughing?

Rochester

From the minute you pull into the parking lot of ARTISANworks in downtown Rochester, you get the sense that this is the party where all the cool art hangs out—and you just got invited!

There's a great, big, red elephant who, with a well-placed bench in front of him, looks like he has a great big smile on his face. He's accompanied by a red gorilla, a pair of red giraffes, and a red turtle, who look like they just got off the brightly painted bus nearby (that has a roof deck, by the way) and are now roaming the jungle of plants and metal sculpture—and we haven't even left the parking lot yet!

Inside the giant warehouse it's an explosion of art—a zebra stands next to a classic car, a life-size motorcycle carved out of wood stands next to a real motorcycle, giant paintings slide down the walls, and suspended from the ceiling, a creature with human arms bursts out of a bomb casing and a bridal dress flies through the air on a Victorian-style tricycle.

The 50,000-square-foot space has an electrifying energy—like Night at the Museum, you half expect the place to suddenly come alive.

ARTISANworks functions like a museum or gallery—but without the pretense—as well as an artists' cooperative, an event venue, and a community-outreach center. Housed in the former Farrell factory, which made cannons during World War II, nearly every inch of the massive space is covered in art. Long hallways and high ceilings give

ARTISANworks—where the art is nice enough to step outside and greet you in the parking lot!

visitors tons of breathing room for their artistic interpretations, while all sorts of nooks and crannies allow for intimate contemplation.

ARTISANworks is the brainchild of entrepreneur Louis Perticone, who has an eye for art and a nose for business.

There is a large showroom, used for weddings or other large events, and themed rooms for dinner parties or other small gatherings. Among the small rooms is a Frank Lloyd Wright dining room, a Japanese tatami dining room, a Marilyn Monroe room (where you can do your best dress-blowing impression—ooh!), and a 1950s retro lounge.

For more information visit www.artisanworks.net or call (585) 288-7170.

Lookit Me, I'm Flying!
Rochester

If you've ever wanted to run off and join the circus—wafting through the air on the silks, spinning in the hoop, flying on the trapeze—it's not too late!

Just next door to ARTISANworks is Aerial Arts of Rochester, a massive fitness facility that offers everyone from kids to adults the chance to run off and join the circus for a day or a couple times a week—while working out at the same time.

And, you are cleared for takeoff!
PHOTO BY WILLIAM D'OVIDIO

"I take Cirque du Soleil and break it down for the average individual," says William D'Ovidio, who co-owns the studio with his wife Jennifer. "We wanted to do something that is totally unique and has never been done in Rochester," he explains.

They teach classes in aerial hoop (known as a lyra), static trapeze, hammock, and aerial silks.

Sorry, hammocks? Is there a nap component?!

Actually, that's hammock as in yoga hammock, where you do all kinds of yoga poses suspended in this contraption. Imagine the bragging rights you'd have after doing a downward dog midair!

If you're not sure which one is your favorite, they have an aerial sampler class for one and a half hours on a Saturday.

They also do a lot of parties—everything from kids' birthday parties to adult parties for birthdays, bachelorette parties, you name it.

So what did you do for your birthday?

Ran off and joined the circus!

D'Ovidio says that, in addition to being a great way to work out, it's a unique and fun experience for everyone.

"Everyone brings their cameras and before they leave, they've all got Facebook photos!" D'Ovidio says.

In addition to Aerial Arts, the D'Ovidios have a sister studio called "Vertical Arts Studios," where Jennifer teaches pole dancing classes—for fitness, not to go into the business!

For more information, visit www.aerialartsrochester.com and www .verticalartsstudios.com.

The Lady with the Alligator Purse

Rochester

> Miss Susie had a baby.
> She named him Tiny Tim.
> She put him in the bathtub to see if he could swim.
> He drank up all the water.
> He ate up all the soap.

He tried to eat the bathtub,
but it wouldn't go down his throat!
Someone call the doctor.
Someone call the nurse.
Someone call the lady with the alligator purse!

Do you remember this children's rhyme? Maybe you sang it starring a Miss Lulu. Maybe you jumped rope to it. Maybe you paddy-caked it. (Hey, kids are fickle. They can't be trusted to precisely relate oral history.) One thing we can all agree on: It was a solid parenting decision to call for the doctor. Ditto the nurse. But, have you ever wondered who that lady was with the alligator purse? No matter how that rhyme has changed, she always seems to be in there.

Next time your kid eats the soap, stop the first person you see with one of these!

Well, the people at the Susan B. Anthony House in Rochester claim that that lady was, in fact, Miss Anthony, who was known for carrying a large alligator purse in her suffragist travels during the second half of the nineteenth century.

So, wait. Let me get this straight. Your kid just tried to eat the bathtub, is currently digesting soap, and you need a suffragist?!

Apparently, it wasn't so much that they needed a suffragist as it was the suffragist being in the right place at the right time. That rhyme traces its origins to California, where Miss Anthony spent several months lobbying for women's right to vote. So, while the kids were jumping rope and making up their rhyme, they saw this woman, day after day, hurrying past with an alligator purse . . . purse rhymed with nurse . . . and there you have it!

A hop, skip, and a vote later, you can buy a jump rope with a copy of that rhyme for three dollars at the Susan B. Anthony House (www .susanbanthonyhouseshop.org). If you go there, you can also see the purse—in person!

The Abandoned Subway
Rochester

Looking at downtown Rochester, it's hard to remember that this recovering casualty of suburban sprawl was once America's first boomtown. But all you have to do is look beneath the surface.

Along Broad Street and South Avenue, below Nick Tahou's restaurant, the Gannett Building, and the Rundell Library, are a series of decrepit tunnels. This was once the Rochester subway system.

It was the 1920s, and Rochester was booming. But the townsfolk were grumbling that the part of the Erie Canal that ran through downtown had become a giant cesspool and they wanted that smelly thing the heck out of their city! So, the canal was rerouted to go around the city. Rochester, meanwhile, had been doing a bit of navel-gazing and realized that it was missing one thing that all the other cool cities had: rapid transit.

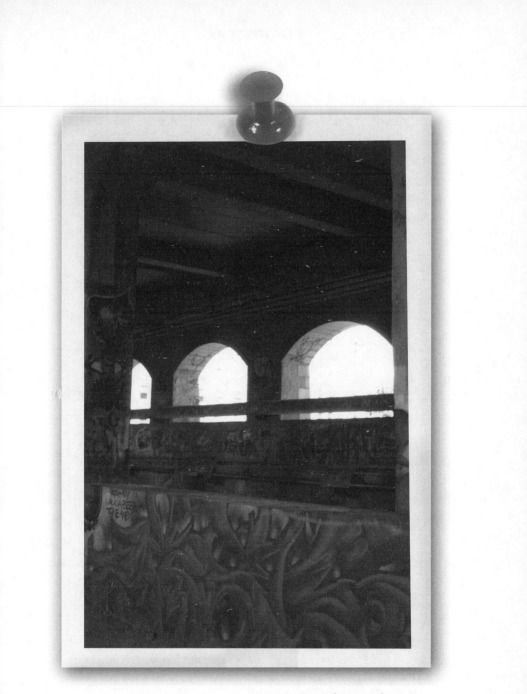

Next stop, underground art.
Please watch your step.

So, out went the water and in went the tracks! Rochester converted that old canal bed into a subway tunnel, and the Rochester Subway opened for business in 1927. "This was one of the biggest public works projects outside of New York City or Boston," explains Tom Hack, chief structural engineer for the city of Rochester. But two years later, the Great Depression hit, and ridership never picked up after that. "It was a great idea, but bad timing," Hack says. The subway was shut down in 1956.

A few parts were filled in, others claimed by the homeless. The part beneath the library was flooded and used as an early air-cooling system. From the outside, you can still see the water rush through the crescent-shaped windows and into the Genesee River below.

Next to the library entrance, as the light begins to fade, a crumbling stairwell descends from the ceiling to a platform that slips off to nowhere. Deeper into the tunnel, a small building sits crumpled in the darkness. In another corner is the "elephant door," used to bring elephants up into the War Memorial (now the Blue Cross Arena) for the circus. A waterfall beneath the library breaks the eerie silence.

Light reappears in the part known as the Broad Street Aqueduct, between the library and the Gannett Building, revealing stunning graffiti on the crash walls between the tracks. It's not your run-of-the-mill, profanity-laced thug art. Brightly colored and painstakingly detailed, it looks to be the work of high-end graffiti artists.

"Most of the graffiti runs in ten-foot sections, and it changes almost weekly," Hack says incredulously. "If you came back next week, this would all be different!" The artists, Hack says, never leave a trail. There are no spray-paint cans littered about, and in twelve years, he's never seen a single artist down there.

The decaying tunnels are dangerous, and trespassing is strictly forbidden. But the city is working on a redevelopment plan for the former subway tunnels, and one day soon you might be able to go down there.

What you can do now—legally—is check out one of the original Rochester subway cars at the New York Museum of Transportation in the Rochester suburb of Rush. Visit www.nymtmuseum.org or call (585) 533-1113.

★ ★

America's First Daredevil and Dare Bear

Rochester

Da da da da! Ladieeeees and gentlemen! I present to you . . . the very first American daredevil . . . Sa-aaaam, Paaaaaaaaatch!

(Hey, look. This was before television got you all razzled and dazzled. That sort of thing used to work to get a crowd going.)

Now, you know about Harry Houdini and Evel Knievel and that time Fonzie jumped the shark. You may not know the name Sam Patch. But you should—he's the guy who first blazed the trail of daredevilism.

Patch's dare of choice was simple but dangerous: He jumped over waterfalls. It started when he was just a boy working in a Rhode Island textile mill and he would jump off the mill dam to entertain the other boys. His first big jump, which catapulted him to fame, was in 1827, when he successfully jumped the eighty-foot Passaic Falls in New Jersey.

Patch, who earned the nickname "The Yankee Leaper," successfully jumped Niagara Falls—twice, no less!—but alas, the life expectancy of a falls jumper isn't very long.

Patch decided to take on the ninety-six-foot High Falls in downtown Rochester. He successfully made the jump during a practice session. For the big show, on Friday, November 13, 1829, there was great fanfare. Patch was said to have a pet bear cub, Chester, who often "jumped" with him. I say this with quotes because in the case of the Rochester show, Patch got caught up in the preshow excitement and tossed Chester off the twenty-five-foot tower built for the jump. So, whether he really jumped—or was pushed—who knows?!

In any case, you probably know where this is going. That Friday the 13th jump would be Patch's last, at the ripe old falls-jumping age of thirty. He apparently dislocated both shoulders in the impact and drowned. His body was recovered the following spring. (Chester lived, by the way.) Patch was buried in Rochester's Charlotte Cemetery with a wooden board that said simply: SAM PATCH—SUCH IS FAME.

Darnit, Chester! Didn't I tell you
Friday the 13th was an unlucky day?
FROM THE COLLECTION OF THE
ROCHESTER PUBLIC LIBRARY LOCAL HISTORY DIVISION

Rochester holds the famous daredevil and his buddy Chester dear
to its historic heart. There's even a sightseeing boat named the *Sam
Patch* that does tours on the Erie Canal.

You can take a stroll around High Falls, but please, no jumping.
Instead, head over to the High Falls Visitors' Center, which features some
cool interactive exhibits, including a replica of a Rochester city street and
a mini–High Falls, as well as unique exhibits from local artists. For more
information visit www.centerathighfalls.org or call (585) 325-2030.

★ ★

Deer Dad, You Were Right!

West Valley

When Lenny Nagel was ten years old, his father gave him a set of deer antlers and said, "These are nature's art and, just like snowflakes, you will never find two alike. Take good care of them."

Like most boys, young Lenny took that as a challenge and set out to prove his father wrong. He picked up deer antlers every chance he got, whether it was in the woods or at a garage sale.

Forty years later, Nagel has more than 4,500 sets of antlers. And you know what? His father was right—no two are alike!

Nagel and his wife, Barb, both avid hunters, have opened the collection to the public in a museum called the Antler Shed that they set up in a barn behind their house.

The first thing you notice when you walk into the barn will be the support pillars, covered in hundreds of antlers. With the antlers spaced less than an inch apart, the poles look like a dinosaur spine or a creature from the movie *Alien*. Each pole, Nagel explains, represents the lifetime collection of one person. The poles are surrounded by mounted deer heads and antlers tacked all over the walls—even on the ceiling!

"What I really enjoy doing is, if it's an older person's collection—and the kids have no interest in keeping it—getting all of their information and writing a story about it and putting it in the museum," Nagel says.

For example, there's the story of Carl W. Hey. Hey's favorite venue to hunt deer was in a place called the Muck Farms, swamps that were drained and converted to potato farms. The deer "love swamps and they love taters," Hey used to say, "makes 'em grow big horns!" He also admitted, "I missed my wedding by one hour, I missed two of my kids' births. I missed lots of bank payments and always missed my mother-in-law's birthday. But never an opening day of deer season!"

And while the price of antlers has increased significantly—Nagel used to be able to buy an entire box of antlers at a yard sale for five to ten dollars, but now antlers sell for anywhere from twenty to four

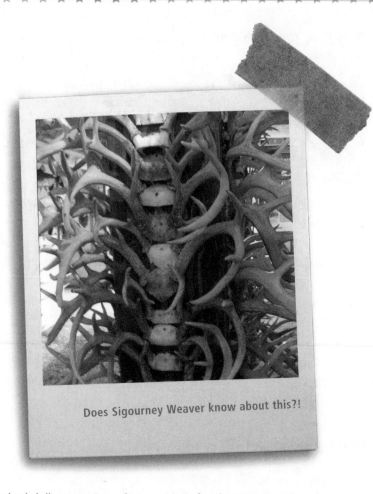

Does Sigourney Weaver know about this?!

hundred dollars on eBay—he's not in it for the money. "Once something goes up there, it's in the collection," Nagel says.

In addition to the antlers, the museum has a collection of knives and other household objects, such as a manicure set and a curling iron, with deer-antler handles. Some of the utensils date back to the 1700s.

The museum has many taxidermy trophies, some part of personal collections, some mounted by Nagel himself. On the second floor is a black bear standing on its hind legs, which Nagel shot in Minnesota. In the corner, Nagel built a small hunting cabin, complete with a mannequin dressed as a hunter. "That's my taxidermied brother!" Nagel exclaims.

You gotta love taxidermy humor.

The Antler Shed Taxidermy and Whitetail Museum is located at 8558 Hebdon Road in West Valley. For more information call (716) 699-4427.

The Electric Cow-Pany
Wyoming County

New York State is home to New York City, one of the most densely populated cities in the world.

On the other side of the state, life is pretty different. In Wyoming County, there are more cows than people. By the numbers, that's about 52,000 cows and 43,000 people.

Most of the pop-moo-lation consists of Holsteins, those iconic black-and-white dairy cows. New York is, after all, the third-largest dairy-producing state in the nation, and Wyoming County is the top milk-producing county in New York State.

So, what's it like living in a place where there are more cows than people?

Diane Johnson-Jaeckel of the Wyoming County Tourism Agency says you have to be pretty resourceful to live in a place this rural. "People here are multitalented. They can take care of livestock, fix machinery, make repairs, do electricity, and even pull cars out of ditches in the winter!"

Sounds like a pretty great place to build life skills. But I know what you're thinking: What about the smell?

I'm not gonna lie to you. Cows are adorable, but they do stink. Though, if you live around them long enough, you don't notice it. During an interview on the Emerling family farm, Mike Emerling said matter-of-factly: "I don't smell anything right now."

Fortunately for those of us passing through who do smell something, Emerling and three other farms have teamed up to test new technology called a manure digester. Essentially, it extracts methane gas (the stinky part) from the manure and converts it to electricity used to power the farm.

Emerling said his annual electric bill used to be about $92,000. The manure digester pumps out twice that amount of electricity, which might impress you more if you realize it's enough to light up seventy-five homes!

You can take a tour of Emerling and other farms in Wyoming County, but consider yourself warned: They haven't quite worked out the stink yet. Hey, things just don't become ex-stinked overnight!

So, did you hear about Mabel? Girl, that man milked her for all she was worth!

★ ★

They also have a dairy festival every year in June, called Agri-Palooza. It's held at a different farm each year and includes tours of the farm, plus fun family events such as a pedal tractor race, an ice cream–eating contest, and more.

"It's a celebration of agriculture, one of our main industries," says Meghan Stearns, the current director of Wyoming County Tourism.

For more information on the farm tours, visit www.wyomingcounty ny.com and for details on the next Agri-Palooza, visit www.facebook .com/agripalooza.

Going for the Gold in New York
Western and Central New York

Just about everything west of Albany in this state is snow country, thanks to weather-meddling Lake Ontario. Shoveling is a way of life. Here, you're just as likely to overhear odds-making on a white Easter as you are a green Christmas.

You would think that if you're the city that gets the most snow, you lose. But in 1970, a former meteorologist for the National Weather Service in Rochester decided to turn that around and started the Golden Snowball Awards (www.goldensnowball.com). Each year, the snow is tallied in the regions' largest cities, and the *winner* is the city with the most snow.

The cities that compete are Albany, Binghamton, Buffalo, Rochester, and Syracuse. New York City doesn't compete because it averages only two to three feet per year—something the other cities might log on their lunch break.

Syracuse dominates the competition—it's won the last eight years in a row. And, since 1950, Syracuse has recorded the most snow of the five cities more than 70 percent of the time.

In the 2008–9 season, one of the snowiest in recent years, Syracuse logged nearly 150 inches of snow. That's about twelve and a half feet, which is enough to cover you and all of your friends, even if you're sit-ting on each other's shoulders having a chicken fight. Rochester came

And the winner is . . . Syracuse! (Try to act surprised.)
COURTESY OF THE CITY OF SYRACUSE, MEDIA CENTER

in second with 103.7 inches; that's more than eight and a half feet, which would bury even Andre the Giant, who was seven feet, four inches tall.

Syracuse not only dominates the New York contest but also the national contest, the Golden Snow Globe awards (www.goldensnow globe.com), which pits the nation's largest cities with a population of over 100,000 against each other. Syracuse comes in first place just about every year, and Rochester and Buffalo often round out the top three, beating other great snowy cities like Erie, Pennsylvania; Green Bay, Wisconsin; Anchorage, Alaska; and Denver, Colorado.

Back to New York—a word about the little guys. The Golden Snowball Awards focus on the state's biggest cities, but some smaller communities such as Oswego scoff at all the attention their urban counterparts get for snowfall. Oswego averages about 180 inches per season. These people eat a foot of snow for breakfast. Oswego has been known to get 300 inches in a single season; that's twenty-five feet, which would cover you and your friends, even if you were all having a chicken fight on the shoulders of Andre the Giant.

And so, while the ladies on Fifth Avenue are wearing their full-length fur coats as winter armor, and the Orange men and women of Syracuse are getting all the glory, the people of Oswego shovel smugly, knowing that they are New York's true winter Olympians.

Does all this weather talk make you want to get outside and measure some snow? The National Weather Service trains weather spotters all over the country. Every year, they have training sessions in New York State. Capture some of that powdery glory for yourself! For more information, visit www.nws.noaa.gov/skywarn.

Rattlesnake Pete

Rochester

His name was Pete Gruber, but everyone called him Rattlesnake Pete. When he was a boy growing up in Oil City, Pennsylvania, his Native American friends taught him how to catch snakes. And he was pretty darn good at it.

Most boys outgrow their creepy-crawly phase at some point. Not Pete. He grew up to be a snake-oil salesman and the northeast's go-to guy for any sort of snake emergency. When Pete moved to Rochester in 1893, he opened a saloon that doubled as a museum for his collection of live snakes. He decorated the walls in snakeskin.

Billed as "The Greatest Curiosity in the City," Rattlesnake Pete claimed other oddities in his collection, including a four-legged chicken, the first electric chair, and "the stony corpse of a petrified female." Many of the bizarre exhibits, along with more common items such as saddles, guns, and ropes, hung from the ceiling like a butcher shop. All the bric-a-brac around the saloon is probably why he has been mistaken as the founder of the Cracker Barrel restaurant chain. (He wasn't, but that little historical blooper should make your next visit to a Cracker Barrel that much more entertaining.)

Pete provided the townsfolk with snake oil, thought at the time to be a pain reliever for arthritis and other joint problems. He also took some of the locals out with him when he went on a snake hunt, wearing his rattlesnake-skin vest and driving a Rambler with two brass snakes for a hood ornament.

But perhaps Rattlesnake Pete's most curious use of snakes was in treating goiters, which are caused by a swollen thyroid gland. Instead of simply applying snake oil to the goiter or developing some sort of cream as you might expect, Pete would actually wrap the

All of a sudden, a goiter doesn't sound so bad. Get this thing offa me!

entire snake around the victim's—I mean, patient's—neck! The snake didn't cure the goiter per se, but the constricting process apparently brought some relief.

No word on what he used to treat the anxiety caused by having a snake around one's neck.

Central New York

2

Central New York

A Visit to Oz and Walking on Fire

Central New York *is home to the Finger Lakes, an enchanting area of rolling hills, canopies of trees, and, of course, rippling lakes. It's the countryside that inspired L. Frank Baum to pen the tale of* The Wonderful Wizard of Oz *and some say Central New York is Oz. (Quick, check the bushes for Munchkins!) There's also cause to believe that the real Bedford Falls, the idyllic snow-capped town from* It's a Wonderful Life, *is here, too!*

Not to be missed is the two-story outhouse in Phelps. (That should give you plenty of material for your car jokes.) You can also spend a day digging for diamonds in Herkimer and learn to walk on fire in Ithaca.

You know what they say, "When in Naples," . . . *you do as the Naplese and order up a slice of grape pie because this is the self-proclaimed "Grape Pie Capital of the World!" Hang on to the fork, though, because we're headed to Oneida, where we're going to investigate cutlery's sexy past.*

Finally, we'll cap the evening off with dinner at a castle that is said to be haunted. Or, we could just go down to the dungeon for some drinks.

Eek! What was that noise?

Woo! Woo! Yes, I Need a Room, Please.
Avoca

Sick of the standard-issue hotel room? Looking, maybe, for a few more bells and whistles?

At the Caboose Motel in Avoca, you can rent a caboose for the night. Built in 1916, the now-retired cabooses were overhauled with a fresh coat of red paint, and each was branded for a different US rail line: Nickel Plate Road (short for the New York, Chicago & St. Louis Railroad), New York Central System, Great Western, Pennsylvania Railroad, and Erie Railroad.

Grab your jammies and hop aboard!

✦ ✦

Inside, the cabooses were renovated and equipped with a shower, bathroom, seating area, heat and air-conditioning, cable TV, telephone, and sink. Each caboose sleeps five or six people: Two upper bunks are part of the original sleeping area, and on the main floor, there's one single and one double bed. One caboose even has some of the original lime-green train seats.

You thought I was kidding about the bells and whistles, but each caboose also has a speaker that pumps out train sounds. Woo woo! But don't worry; you can control the volume, so you won't actually feel like you're sleeping on the tracks.

The motel also offers standard hotel rooms and welcomes curious passersby who just want to come in for a tour. I'm holding you to the honor system—don't go buying the "I slept in a caboose!" trucker hat, unless you actually did.

If you do spend the night, don't forget to walk through the aisle and demand tickets from your family members.

All aboard! Please watch your step and stand clear of the closing bathroom door!

For more information on the Caboose Motel, visit www.caboose motel.net or call (607) 566-2216.

You Are Now . . . Entering . . . the Horsey Zone
Binghamton

Touring Binghamton can be a little dizzying. That's because the area is home to not one, not two, but six carousels! The region even refers to itself as the "Carousel Capital of the World."

The carousels were gifts from local shoe manufacturer George F. Johnson, donated between 1919 and 1934. "George F," as they called him, was big on incentives to improve the quality of life of his workers and the community. He felt that the carousels made for a happier life and would contribute to young people becoming more productive citizens.

Johnson also felt strongly that there should be no charge for admission to the carousels, a policy that stands today. However, the city likes to say that the price is one piece of litter—that is, please find and dispose of one piece of litter in exchange for the free ride!

The carousels were all manufactured by Allan Herschell, another famous New Yorker, and two even have the original Wurlitzer band organs. If you ride all six, you get a commemorative button.

A fun bit of trivia: The carousel at Binghamton's Recreation Park was featured in an episode of the *Twilight Zone*. (Doo dee doo doo . . .)

I feel like someone—or something—is following me.
Anyone there? Doo dee doo doo . . .

★ ★

That's because Zone creator Rod Serling grew up here and used to ride this carousel as a child. The episode is called "Walking Distance."

As you lock the door to your rental car . . . unlock your imagination. . . . Beyond it is another dimension . . . a dimension of bright lights, bouncing animals, and tinkling organ music. . . . You've just crossed over into . . .

the Horsey Zone.

For more information visit www.visitbinghamton.org/whattosee/carousels.php and www.rodserling.com/binghamton.htm.

Make It Spiedie, I'm Hungry!
Binghamton

Buffalo's got the wing and Rochester has the garbage plate, but when you're in Binghamton, make it spiedie!

(I'm going as fast as I can—stop rushing me!)

The spiedie is Binghamton's local delicacy, likely brought over by Italian immigrants in the 1920s. It consists of cubed chicken, lamb, or another meat, marinated overnight or longer in a concoction of olive oil, vinegar, Italian spices, and mint. It's then grilled on skewers and served on Italian bread or a roll, which you use like an oven mitt to pull the meat off the skewer!

The name spiedie comes from the Italian *spiedo,* which means "kitchen cooking spit." (Not a small, often inappropriate men's bathing suit.)

In 1983 a couple of local families got to talking about who had the best spiedie recipe. So, they decided to put their spits to the test and held a cook-off. After a couple of years, the cook-off ballooned into a festival and now, every year, the area holds a Spiedie Fest and Balloon Rally—as in giant balloons in the sky.

David Pessagno, the festival's coordinator, fondly recalls his grandfather talking about how he and his friends would leave the Endicott Johnson Factory and head to Augie's after work to help their friends sell lamb spiedies on the corner for five cents.

★ ★

Pessagno, who has been with the festival for more than twenty years, has a friend who is a hot-air balloonist, which is how the whole balloon thing entered the spiedie picture.

Today, the August festival features the signature spiedie cooking contest.

"This is the event that started it all, a salute to marinated meat on skewers, the pride of Broome County!" the Spiediefest website proclaims.

Trivia

That's Ms. Rudolph, to You!

OK, fellas. The buck stops here.

I've just received this dispatch from Candor, and I'm taking it all the way to the North Pole.

Martha Goodsell of the Fallow Hollow Deer Farm explains that, in the winter, male reindeer shed their antlers first; the ladies keep their antlers longer to protect the winter food supply.

So, while we've all been dazzled by Rudolph's bright nose and brawn and the antler-clad machismo of Dasher, Dancer, Prancer, Vixen, Comet, Cupid, Donner, and Blitzen (we should've known by the names), they were frauds!

"At Christmas, when you see the [antlered] reindeer pulling Santa's sleigh, they couldn't have been males," Martha says, with an enlightened smile. "At that time of year, they're all ladies!"

I demand a remake of the movie. I was robbed of some of Christianity's most famous female role models!

In the meantime, please join me in song: "Rudolph the red-nosed reindeer / had a very shiny nose. And if you ever saw HER / you would even say it glows. . . ."

There's also music, arts and crafts, and thirty or more hot-air balloons filling the sky overhead. There are even a few tethered balloons in fun shapes, prompting some to call it the "Macy's Thanksgiving Day Parade in the Sky!" They've had balloons in the shape of a dog, an eagle, a dragon—even a monster truck!

So, get spit-fired up and head over to Binghamton—and make it spiedie! For more information visit www.spiediefest.com.

The Night Watchman Is a Donkey

Candor

The Fallow Hollow Deer Farm in Candor is the second-largest fallow deer farm in the United States. (The first is in Texas.) For the uninitiated, fallow deer don't guide Santa's sleigh (those are reindeer); they are raised primarily for venison.

The venison from this farm has been served at some of New York City's finest restaurants, including the Four Seasons, and to some pretty famous people, from the governor to Martha Stewart.

There are 425 hilly acres for the deer to roam, with an eight-foot-high steel fence, in case any of the deer had any ideas of running off to New York City to pursue acting instead of dinner!

Martha and Brian Goodsell are the humans who run the farm, but they can't possibly walk around all 425 acres to guard their herd. So, when they started interviewing for the position of night security guard, they considered dogs, but dogs are small enough to run the risk of getting hurt by the deer's antlers.

Then, they found the applicant with the perfect skill set: the donkey.

Donkeys are herding animals, so you can't have too many or else they just protect the other donkeys, Martha explains. But if you have only one or two, they'll adopt the deer as their social circle and protect the herd, she says. One way to tell if a donkey feels safe: You'll find him lying down, burping up grass balls!

So, what are the big, tough bucks doing while the donkey's keeping an eye on the herd? The bucks usually hang back and send out the ladies to test the waters for danger! The donkey, not one treat a woman like a canary in a coal mine, partners with the lead doe to keep a lookout. And when a predator such as a coyote or fox approaches, the donkey will bite, chase, and stomp it to get it away from the herd.

So, ladies, the next time your man isn't standing up for you and you call him another name for a donkey, be careful! You may be insulting the donkey.

For more information on the farm, call (607) 659-4635.

Getting to the Point
Candor

When Robert Berg makes a point, people pay attention.

That's because Berg makes atlatls.

Of course. Wait, atla—WHO?

An atlatl is a spear-throwing device. It is "essentially, a stick with a handle on one end and a hook or socket that engages a light spear or dart on the other," according to the World Atlatl Association.

"It was the weapon of choice in North America prior to . . . the bow and arrow," Berg explains. (The bow and arrow, incidentally, came on the scene around the same time that Jesus Christ was born.)

"It was used by every ancient culture in the world at one time or another," says Berg. It was used by hunters during the last Ice Age and, some say, was a contributing factor to the extinction of the woolly mammoth. When Columbus arrived in America, he was greeted by the natives, who were—you guessed it—armed with atlatls.

The atlatl was such a powerful weapon, in fact, that it was "the only weapon Cortez and his Conquistadors feared because it easily pierced Spanish armor," Bob Perkins wrote on his website, www.atlatl.com.

Today, the atlatl is still used by some tribes in Australia, Papua New Guinea, and South America, but in North America, it is only for sport and competition.

Berg owns Thunderbird Atlatls, the largest manufacturer of atlatls in the world today. But he doesn't just make atlatls; he also uses them for hunting and fishing. Manning his booth at a Native American Pow Wow in Owego, Berg flashes pictures of wild boars he shot with atlatls

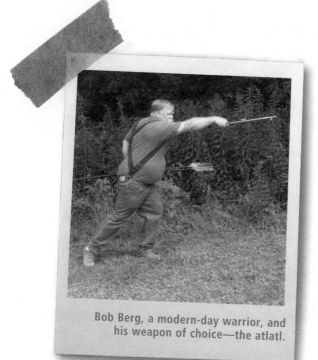

Bob Berg, a modern-day warrior, and his weapon of choice—the atlatl.

in upstate New York and Georgia.

Why not just use a gun?

"I'm a primitivist," Berg explained. "If everyone's goin' that way, I go this way—it's easier goin'!"

And, for all you techno-elitists, Berg says, "It's not unsophisticated. . . . It's all the same technology, brought forward. I twist the cordage to make the atlatl in the exact same ways they twisted the cables to hold up the Brooklyn Bridge!"

If you're looking to beef up your survival skills (you know, should you find yourself stranded on a desert island or on a reality TV show), Berg teaches a primitive survival class as well as atlatl making. Leave the apron at home, though, because this isn't a pottery class—after you learn to make an atlatl, you'll learn to shoot it as well!

Anyone have any good boar recipes?

For more information visit www.thunderbirdatlatl.com or call (800) 836-4520.

Hahhhhhhh. Smell My Breath!

I'll make you a deal. On the count of three, we both eat the garlic, OK? That way no one gets accused of dragon breath. Ready? One . . . two . . .

One festival devoted to garlic is curious enough. As it turns out, there are at least eight garlic festivals right here in New York State!

The largest is the Hudson Valley Garlic Festival (www.hvgf.org) in Saugerties, where nearly 50,000 people come to eat garlic steak sandwiches, garlic mashed potatoes, garlic ice cream, and chocolate-covered garlic cloves. There's also the Mohawk Valley Garlic and Herb Festival in Little Falls (www.littlefallsny.com) featuring a garlic cook-off and the Garlic Queen Pageant; and the Cuba Garlic Festival in Cuba (www.cubanewyork.us), which kicks off with a little dancin' in the streets, followed by a coronation of a Garlic Queen and King.

There's also the Multi-Ethnic Garlic Festival in Binghamton; the Susquehanna Valley Garlic Fest in Milford; the Fox Run Vineyards Garlic Festival in Penn Yan; the Long Island Garlic Festival in River-head; and the Sharon Springs Garlic Festival.

Some people are drawn to garlic for the taste; some eat it because it helps you stay healthy, especially if you feel a cold coming on. But the reason they come to the garlic festivals is for the variety.

Do you know what kind of garlic you buy in the grocery store? Probably not. That's because there's one choice and it's labeled "garlic." In fact, there are more than 200 varieties of garlic!

"There are different types of heat—mild to very hot," Bill Ziese, a garlic grower and organizer of the Sharon Springs Garlic Festival, explains. "Some creep up on you, some burn immediately. There are some where heat forms in the back of your tongue. There's also garlic that's nutty and earthy," Ziese says.

Bavarian garlic, for example, is mild. Music garlic (how cute is that?) is zesty.

Transylvanian garlic (oh yeah, there is such a thing!) is a little hot, and German White garlic is hot with a capital "H!" One grower called it "garlic with attitude."

For all you garlic lovers out there, Ziese has some advice: "If you keep eating garlic every day, your body stops smelling like garlic!"

Hhhhhhey, honey? Good news!

For a full listing of garlic festivals, visit www.garlicseedfoundation .info/festivals.htm.

...ope Valley Farm
Certified Naturally Grown

German White: Garlic with attitude for those who choose to go the limit. Full traditional flavor with lasting zest. Excellent ...rage.

Try me!

Some like it hot. Do you?

The Wonderful Wizard of Chittenango

Chittenango

L. Frank Baum had many jobs, from reporter to fancy-poultry breeder, but he was always a great storyteller.

One day, when he was living in Chicago, Baum was telling a story to some neighborhood kids in his living room. One little girl looked up and said: "Mr. Baum? What's the name of the place where Dorothy and her friends live?"

Baum hadn't yet given it a name, but he didn't want to disappoint the little girl. His eyes raced around the room before settling on a filing cabinet. The bottom drawer was labeled O-Z. He turned to the little girl and replied, "Oz."

His wife, Maud, "thought it was an absurd word," says Kathleen Sorbello Di Scenna, an L. Frank Baum historian. "The children thought it was magical."

Baum, author of *The Wonderful Wizard of Oz* and more than a dozen other Oz-based books, was born in Chittenango, a small village about fifteen miles east of Syracuse.

Every summer, thousands flock to Chittenango for a four-day Oz festival, featuring everything from the Emerald City Classic golf tournament to a spaghetti dinner with some of the original Munchkins; a Wizard of Oz ballet; a parade featuring a slew of Dorothys, Tin Men, Lions, and Scarecrows; a costume contest; and a Wizard's balloon launch. In 2007, the name of the festival was changed to Oz-stravaganza from OzFest so as not to be confused with the Ozzfest heavy-metal music festival founded by Ozzy Osbourne and his wife Sharon.

Those who have studied Baum's life and writing suggest that, in *The Wonderful Wizard of Oz,* Kansas is based on his experience living in drought-ridden South Dakota, while Oz is based on his boyhood in central New York.

"I believe that central New York is the Land of Oz," Di Scenna says.

She points out that, in one of his less-famous works, *Dot and Tot in Merryland,* Baum describes his boyhood home in central New York,

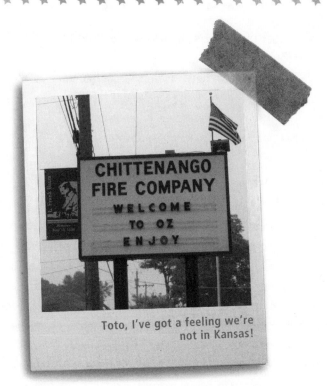

Toto, I've got a feeling we're not in Kansas!

called Rose Lawn, and it sounds and awful lot like Oz. "In my opinion . . . Dorothy is actually walking onto Rose Lawn," Di Scenna explains.

This may not be heavy metal, but man, this is heavy!

Chittenango boasts that it "transforms into Oz" during Oz-stravaganza, but you can visit some of Baum's personal landmarks any time of year to see if you can find little bits of Oz in central New York.

First, there's the yellow brick road Chittenango installed down its Main Street to get you into the Oz spirit. There's an All Things Oz Museum at 211 Genesee Street. In nearby Mattydale, on Route 11 (formerly Plank Road) is where Rose Lawn used to be; the former family property is now home to an action-sports center. There's the Matilda Joslyn Gage house in Fayetteville, where Baum's mother-in-law lived, and the Stanton house, ten miles south, where his mother lived. There's also an old-growth forest near the North Syracuse Junior

High School that the keepers swear was Baum's inspiration for Oz's enchanted forest!

Use your brain. Have a heart. Have courage! And, as you stroll down the Yellow Brick Road, the local shopkeepers would like to remind you, "There's no place like Chittenango!"

For more information visit www.oz-stravaganza.com.

You're a Giant Faker. No, You Are!

Cooperstown

Some people go to war for their religious beliefs. George Hull had other ideas.

Hull, an atheist, thought that the (largely Christian) American public would be gullible enough to believe in giants just because it said so in the Bible. So, in 1868, Hull and a partner secretly commissioned a sculpture of a "petrified man," more than ten feet long, made out of gypsum. To get the statue to look old and authentic, they did every-thing from hammering the "skin" with a block of wood with hundreds of sewing needles to create pores to dousing it with a gallon of sulfu-ric acid.

Hull buried the gypsum giant in a shallow, five-foot grave on a farm in Cardiff, New York, that was owned by a relative. Then, he went back to work as a cigar manufacturer in Binghamton and waited.

Sure enough, about a year later, workers who'd been hired to dig a well on the farm discovered the giant.

Hull wasted no time, quickly pitching a tent over the site and charg-ing fifty cents admission per person to see the great Cardiff Giant!

Within a few months, people began questioning the authenticity of this petrified giant. That didn't really matter, though, because the discovery was provoking something much bigger: a debate about reli-gion versus science that forced people to question their fundamental beliefs.

Visitors flocked to see the giant when it was thought to be a great scientific discovery and even later when it was proved to be a great

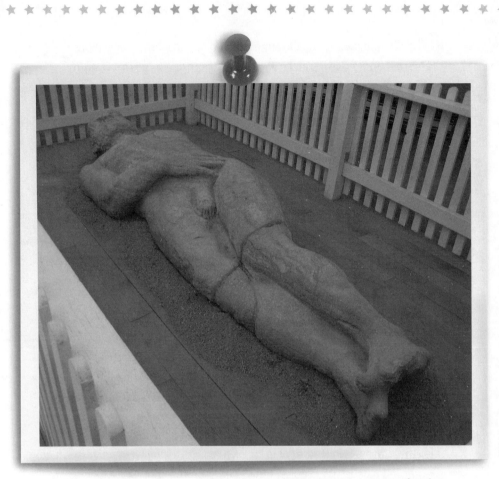

A fake giant is classic. Never goes out of style!

hoax. It was such as success that P. T. Barnum tried to buy it. When he could not, he created a copy . . . of the fake giant! In fact, both fakes were on display in New York City—two blocks apart—at the same time. In a testament to Barnum's showmanship, his fake actually drew more visitors.

The Cardiff Giant was acquired by the New York State Historical Association in 1947, and is currently on display at the Farmers' Museum in Cooperstown.

So, why are people still paying money to see this fake giant, more than one hundred years later? Barbara Franco explains in *The Cardiff Giant: A Hundred-Year-Old Hoax*: "Despite the fact that hoaxes were a common occurrence of the nineteenth century, the Cardiff Giant's extraordinary success sets it apart as a classic in the art of hoaxing."

Oh, man. That is classic.

Finally, Franco writes: "Everyone goes away satisfied that they have seen the great American hoax."

To get in on the hoax, visit www.farmersmuseum.org or call (888) 547-1450.

No Baseball Experience Necessary
Cooperstown

Did you know that, even if you've never played baseball in your life, *you* could be in the Baseball Hall of Fame?

The Cooperstown museum has an exhibit called "Sacred Ground," which honors some of the sport's most beloved ballparks. At the entrance are fabric mâché statues honoring some of the game's most famous fans!

There's Pearl Sandow, who cheered for the Atlanta Crackers—and later the Braves—while attending more than 5,000 games in her sixty-six-year fan career! You couldn't miss her, with a pile of white hair that she described as a "snow-cone style." On her 100th birthday, the Braves even brought the Cooperstown statue to join her at the stadium, where she was named team captain for a day.

Dancing his way to superfan fame was Yoyo, who wore a suit, fedora, and sunglasses, and did the "Mummers Strut" through stadium aisles during Philadelphia Phillies games for more than thirty years! Mummers.com describes the strut this way: "Spread your arms, supporting an invisible cape; pumping your elbows, rocking and bobbing your body, you strut forward and back, sideways and in circles."

And, how can we tawk about supa fans and nawt tawk about Hilda Chesta? A die-hard Brooklyn Dodgers fan, Hilda Chester attended

★ ★

The stats of these superfans are pretty impressive!

nearly as many games as the players did from the 1920s until the Dodgers left Brooklyn in 1957. After a heart attack in 1941, she couldn't yell anymore, so she brought a frying pan and iron ladle to the games to keep making a ruckus for her boys!

And so, my fame-loving friends, you don't have to hit 500 home runs to be in the Baseball Hall of Fame. All it takes is dedication. Cheer, strut, or bang your frying pan until they retire your ladle!

For more information visit www.baseballhalloffame.org or call (888) HALL-OF-FAME.

Round and Round the State

Cooperstown

If you're not sold on paying admission to the Farmers' Museum just to see a fake giant, here's another reason to visit this rural-history museum—the Empire State Carousel.

It's more than a carousel; it's more like a spinning history lesson of New York State. The museum calls it "the museum you can ride on."

The carousel was built over two decades by more than 1,000 artisans—from carvers to quilters, painters, and woodworkers—and assembled on Long Island. It was started in 1982 and found a permanent home at the Farmers' Museum in 2006.

Instead of horses, there are twenty-three hand-carved animals on this carousel. There's Bucky Beaver, representing the state animal and fur-trading roots; Benny Brook Trout, representing the state fish; Daphne Duck, a shout-out to the duck farmers of Long Island; and Louie Loon, a nod to the bird that has captured the imagination—and poetic license—of the Adirondacks.

If you're not an animal person, you can ride in a scallop shell (the state shellfish) or an Erie Canal boat.

There are also paintings of famous New Yorkers from all corners of the state, from Susan B. Anthony and Uncle Sam to P. T. Barnum and daredevil Sam Patch. There's even a little (oh, the irony) Cardiff Giant painted in the P. T. Barnum panel!

Go ahead. Give it a whirl!

Living in Candy Land

Cooperstown

There's a house in Cooperstown, just off Main Street, that stands out from all the rest. Actually, it doesn't just stand out, it sort of jumps out, spins around, pats you on the back, and says, "Hey there, buddy, what's happening?!"

The 3,000-square-foot Greek Revival house is painted in eleven Candy Land colors on the outside—including pink, lavender, teal, and yellow—and thirty-eight colors on the inside!

Rob Lipson, an anesthesiologist with a love for historical restoration, bought the house in 2003 and painstakingly restored and rebuilt it according to historical preservation standards over the next six years. He's also the guy responsible for those paint colors.

Tell us, doctor, how did the house wind up in this . . . condition?!

There's a lot of trim work involved in the Greek Revival style, Lipson explains.

"People just usually paint it white. There are so many different textures—when you do a crown molding, you might have seven different pieces of wood," he says. "I always thought it would be cool to accent it all in different colors."

And that he did! There are seven bedrooms, seven bathrooms, and two and a half kitchens in the house, and each room has about four to five trim colors.

Lipson says the winters can get kind of long and boring in Cooperstown. And, when he bought the house, it was pretty drab. He was inspired by some of the cool paint colors he saw on houses in San Francisco (hey there, Painted Ladies!), Charleston, South Carolina, and Martha's Vineyard.

Of course, the logical question is: What do the neighbors think?

Well, Lipson is a smart man, so you know what he did? He went to each neighbor, explained what he was doing and asked which color they would like to look at every day! The family next door with three kids sat down at the kitchen table with the paint chips and ultimately

★ ★

settled on teal. An older lady across the street chose lavender for the front. And on the other side, the woman had already painted her house pink and said, "Anything but pink." That side is yellow.

One older lady across the street did yell at him. She said it looked like a "[bleep] [bleep] whorehouse." Though she quickly added, "But I'd sure like to work in it!"

Whew! I'd say those colors sure have livened up the neighborhood!

Some of the psychiatrists in town have joked that the house is like a shot of Prozac for passersby. And in the case of at least that one neighbor, you could say it was a shot of something else!

It looks pretty unassuming in black-and-white, but what you're looking at is actually pink, purple, yellow, and blue!

There's a very interesting legal lesson in all of this: There are a lot of rules and regulations you have to comply with while doing historical preservation. But guess what the historical preservation board has absolutely no jurisdiction over? You guessed it—paint colors!

When Lipson brought the woman who would later become his wife to the house for the first time, she said, "I've always wanted to live in a dollhouse!"

She was definitely The One.

The couple has since moved to Cape Cod, and Lipson sold the house to a fellow doctor from the hospital—a surgeon. You might think a Candy Land house would be a tough sell, but the new owner is from Latin America, where the colors are much more vibrant, so he actually enjoys all those bright hues and has left them the same since he bought the house in 2010.

"It's inviting and cozy," Lipson says. "Never boring!"

From Glass Slippers to Atomic Art
Corning

Great news, Cinderella: We've got your glass slipper right here! Now, here's the bad news: It's not very comfortable. Ooh, hey, watch yourself. Look out for that lightning!

The Corning Museum of Glass has a lot of what you might expect—vases, bowls, glass-blowing demonstrations, and glass in technology exhibits—but the museum also has a slew of glass objects you probably didn't even know existed.

In addition to the glass slipper, there's a glass glove and—taking Cinderella to a whole new level—a glass evening gown! There's a set of colored lenses, attached like measuring spoons, which were used by Victorian tourists to view the landscapes through rose-colored glass . . . or yellow or blue . . . (Ooh, wicked stepsister, you're looking a little green today!)

There's a Barbie-size, 3-D glass portrait of an Egyptian pharaoh. It's the oldest known glass portrait, dating back to the 1400s . . . BC!

There's a household iron made of glass, a short-lived design aimed at conserving metal during World War II. The museum also has World War II–era bullets tipped in glass, for the same reason.

The museum has some glass that will bend your definition of glass. There's glass created in 1945 by the test explosion of an atomic bomb in White Sands, New Mexico, as well as glass created by the impact of meteorites (which looks like drumsticks left on the grill too long) and glass created by lightning (which looks like a hollowed-out log).

For all of you "world's largest" lovers—get your checklist ready—the museum is also home to the world's largest paperweight, clocking in at a whopping 100 pounds!

There's a lot to look at in the Corning Museum of Glass—and some of it looks back!

With the world's largest collection of glass—more than 45,000 objects—there's definitely something that'll make you go "Hmmm" at the Corning Museum of Glass.

Was that glass eye looking at me?

For more information visit www.cmog.org or call (800) 732-6845.

How Many Fingers Am I Holding Up?
The Finger Lakes

Given the name, you might guess that there are five Finger Lakes, but in fact, there are eleven. (Though, the large ones do look like fingers.) And, while it's fun to think of their creation as God making His own Hollywood Walk of Fame handprint, the lakes were actually formed by glaciers during the last Ice Age, more than 100 million years ago.

Can you name at least three of the lakes?

I didn't think so.

Allow me. The lakes are, from west to east: Conesus, Hemlock, Canadice, Honeoye, Canandaigua, Keuka, Seneca, Cayuga, Owasco, Skaneateles, and Otisco.

It's hard to stand out in a family of eleven, but here are a few fast facts to help you tell them apart:

Keuka Lake is one of the few Y-shaped lakes in the world, and its water flows both north and south.

The St. Lawrence River must've hogged all the islands (you know, that little place called the Thousand Islands) because there are only two islands in all of the eleven Finger Lakes! The smallest (145 feet long) is Squaw Island in Canandaigua Lake. The 11,000-year-old island is said to be where Seneca women and children hid during the 1779 Sullivan Expedition, an American offensive against the Iroquois. The other is Frontenac Island in Cayuga Lake, and is thought to have been an Algonquin burial ground.

The two deepest lakes are Seneca and Cayuga (618 feet and 435 feet, respectively); their deepest points are below sea level. The deepest part of Honeoye Lake, by contrast, is thirty feet.

★ ★

All but one of the lakes (Hemlock) were named by Native Americans. Canadice Lake means "long lake," but it's actually the smallest of the Finger Lakes at just under four miles long. Cayuga, the longest of the lakes (nearly forty miles), means "boat landing." Seneca means "place of stone." Conesus translates to "always beautiful," which, I'm sure, caused quite a fuss among the other lakes at the time.

Why is it always Conesus, Conesus, Conesus?!

It's Not about Being Wright

Hammondsport

If I say, "Ford," you think automobile, right?
If I say, "Wright brothers," you think airplanes, right?
Now, what if I say, "Glenn Curtiss"? Anything?
Right.

In 1907 Glenn Hammond Curtiss was dubbed "The Fastest Man on Earth," clocking in at more than 136 miles per hour on a V-8-powered motorcycle he built himself. At the urging of early flight enthusiasts such as Alexander Graham Bell (yes, he of telephone fame), Curtiss took his speedy talents to the skies, where he soared to the titles of "founder of the American aircraft industry" and the "Father of Naval Aviation."

It's not Wright, I tell you. It was Curtiss who was issued the first US pilot's license! (The Wright brothers were actually nos. 4 and 5 in the pilot's license pecking order.)

So, why do we know the name Wright, but not Curtiss?

Simple: It's easier to have one name on a multiple-choice test! Well, that and the fact that the Wrights, who worked secretively, spent much of their time suing other aviation pioneers like Curtiss to ensure that it was their name that would forever be the answer to that multiple-choice question. "It was this mentality that they could control aviation by patent," said Trafford Doherty, executive director of the Glenn H. Curtiss Museum in Hammondsport.

Curtiss, meanwhile, was working out in the open—like the Wikipedia of his time—with Bell and others to build better flying machines

The P-40's shark nose became a symbol of America's defiance and resolve during World War II.

and find practical applications. He also got help from Henry Ford, who loaned Curtiss his best lawyer to help fend off the legal advances of the self-righteous Wrights.

While the Wrights were off working in secret, it was Curtiss who made the first preannounced public flight. For those of you keeping score at home, that's "Fastest Man on Earth" in 1907, and first public flight in 1908. Man, time really flies!

Another fun fact: Curtiss was also responsible for early development of the RV. "Curtiss loved to camp, but he hated to sleep on the ground!" Doherty explains.

Take a plane, train, or automobile to the Glenn H. Curtiss Museum in Hammondsport, located at the southern tip of Keuka Lake. For more information visit www.glennhcurtissmuseum.org or call (607) 569-2160.

This Lake's Got Flare

Canandaigua Lake

The Finger Lake known as Canandaigua has some of the most expensive lakefront property in the United States. It's a popular summer-home spot forty miles southeast of Rochester.

You'd think that, with all the golfing, boating, and other activities of the affluent—not to mention, learning to spell Canandaigua—that residents wouldn't have much time for historical appreciation. But they've managed to preserve a pretty spectacular Seneca Indian tradition known as the "Ring of Fire."

Every year, in early September, the Seneca elders would light a fire on top of Bare Hill, located on the southeastern side of the lake in what is

The ring of fire
PHOTO COURTESY VISITFINGERLAKES
.COM/VALERIE KNOBLAUCH

now Middlesex, in order to give thanks for a good harvest. As a symbol of unity, members of the tribe would light smaller fires all along the shore, creating a ring of fire around the lake. They chose Canandaigua for the sacred event because it's where they believe their ancestors first emerged from the earth. In fact, *Canandaigua* means "the chosen spot."

Today, the event is held on the Saturday of Labor Day weekend. A bonfire is lit on Bare Hill—probably not by children, but let's not call them elderly—at dusk. Residents who live on the shores of the sixteen-mile-long lake take that as their cue to light red flares, recreating the Senecas' ring of fire.

Two of the other western Finger Lakes, Keuka and Honeoye, also host rings of fire.

In case you're wondering how you coordinate hundreds of people with flares, local shops, including Wegmans grocery stores, begin selling them in early summer for one dollar so residents have plenty of time to get their flares by Labor Day. However, it's not clear how they remember where they put them!

★ ★

Ancient New York Bling

Herkimer

Did you know there was a diamond mine right here in New York?

OK, it's not the kind of diamonds you're thinking of. They're actually quartz-like objects called Herkimer diamonds. They look a lot like diamonds in the rough. The big difference is that they're not as faceted as their more expensive counterparts, and they're not quite as hard. Diamonds are a ten on the hardness scale; Herkimer diamonds are about 7.5.

Herkimer diamonds, the mine says, are "doubly terminated quartz crystals already faceted by nature." They are unique to the area and—gemistorians, prepare to be dazzled—they're believed to be more than 500 million years old. That was when a shallow, prehistoric sea used to cover much of New York and the east coast.

The diamonds, which can grow up to six inches but are typically less than an inch in diameter, are tucked in elliptical-shaped pockets in dolomite limestone bedrock. Sometimes excavation can turn up a few, sometimes it can pop open a whole pocket!

The mine opened to the public in 1955 and, for a small fee, you can spend the day digging for diamonds. Here's the best part: You get to keep everything you find!

So, let's see, that's more than fifty years and thousands of people who've been digging up these diamonds. Isn't the supply about to run out?

Not anytime soon. The mine consists of 400 acres, less than five of which have been used up in the last fifty years. So, keep digging!

Now, I'm definitely drawn to shiny objects, but I've got to be honest here, when I saw couples and families out there all day, toiling away with their hammers, baking in the summer sun, it seemed more like prison than a vacation. Still, everyone I spoke with absolutely loved digging for diamonds.

What am I missing? Maybe it's all in the marketing. Say "diamonds" and we're there.

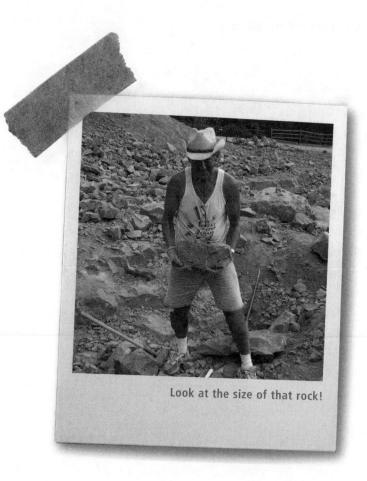

Look at the size of that rock!

Renee Scialdo Shevat, president and owner of the Herkimer Diamond Mines, puts it this way: "When you find a pocket, it piques your interest that you'll find more. It's like the lottery—you might win that million dollars!"

Plus, some people think the crystals have mystical properties—that they "activate the third eye," boost psychic abilities, and aid in general well-being.

They also make a very pretty pendant.

To check out your prospects, visit www.herkimerdiamond.com or call (315) 891-7355.

Eight Brains in Jars

Ithaca

Does having a larger brain make you smarter? Is my brain different from your brain?

These were the questions of Burt Green Wilder, a Civil War surgeon and founder of Cornell University's anatomy department. Well, this was the late 1800s, so his questions were just a smidge less politically correct. What Dr. Wilder really wanted to know was: Were the brains of "educated and orderly persons" (i.e., white men) different in size, shape, or weight from those of women, murderers, blacks, and the mentally ill?

In order to find out the answer to this loaded question, in 1889 Dr. Wilder started a brain collection, the first of its kind in the United States. At its peak, the collection consisted of at least 600 brains (all donated, by the way); today, the collection has dwindled to seventy, though only eight are on display at Cornell because those are the only ones still matched up to their bios.

In case you're wondering how Dr. Wilder got women and African Americans to donate their brains after that introduction, it was to prove Wilder wrong—that their brains were, in fact, no different.

And, you know what? They were right! Six hundred brains later, Dr. Wilder had absolutely no evidence that the brains were any different among races, genders, or varied mental capacities.

The brain collection today is exciting because it contains the brain of Wilder himself, as well as the brain of a convicted murder, Edward Rulloff, who was executed in 1871.

The first thing your critical eye will sleuth up is that Rulloff's brain appears to be slightly greener than the rest. Aha! A difference! Well, yes. But, Barbara Finlay, a psychology professor at Cornell and the curator of the brain exhibit, explains that it's "slightly green due to the fixative that we're using, not anything to do with being a murderer."

The truth is, once you get over being dazzled by seeing actual human brains in jars and inspecting them closely to see if you will be *the chosen*

The murderer, he's right behind me, isn't he?

one who finds the differences among them, you will begin to realize that "There's nothing particularly interesting about any of these brains . . . or unusual," Prof. Finlay says. "That was kind of the point."

Still, Prof. Finlay asserts that their presence is significant. "This is a very important first step in understanding ourselves as material beings and our minds as material," she says.

Did she lose you? Still hoping to find that bloated "murderer lobe" behind Rulloff's cerebral cortex?

Try to work past it. The idea is to use *your* brain to ponder the physical brains before you. Is this the tangible, physical place where thinking and reasoning occur?

Prof. Finlay asks: "Is it the case that these things [brains] do the thinking and not some disembodied spirit or soul?"

And that, right there, is the power of eight brains in jars.

The Wilder Brain Collection is on display on the second floor of Uris Hall at Cornell University.

Is That Car Wearing a Tutu?

Ithaca

Artists mingle with farmers. Monks mix with belly dancers. And here comes a man on stilts—riding a bike!

A family brandishes window screens, slathers them with soap, and waves them around to make a breeze of bubbles.

The ladies from the Red Hat Society sit on bales of hay on the back of a red pickup truck as the He-Man Chainsaw Marching Band revs up a tune and the Geek Squad performs its rendition of *Stomp!* using computer keyboards.

Honk! Honk! Hey, buddy, it's the Volvo ballet! Wearing giant tutus, the cars accelerate in and out of formation, while men in leotards and tutus sashay through for the big finale—a dramatic pose across the hood! It's like *Swan Lake* meets "Greased Lightning." *Oh wella, wella, wella, well . . . Tell me more! Tell me more!*

This isn't your average small-town parade, with high-school marching bands and the local legion; this is how they do a parade in Ithaca.

Ithaca?

You wouldn't know it to look at this college/industrial city of 30,000, surrounded by farmland, gorges, and waterfalls, but Ithaca is brimming with artistic, cultural, and intellectual diversity. The city, just south of Cayuga Lake, has repeatedly earned itself a spot on nationwide lists, from "Most Enlightened City" to "Great Places You've Never Heard About."

The parade is part of a four-day artistic extravaganza, called the Ithaca Festival, which, it should be noted, defies its plain vanilla name. Everyone gets involved, from babies to seniors—even the neighborhood dogs!

★ ★

The festival includes music, arts and crafts, a food court to show off some of Ithaca's finest cuisine (did you know that Ithaca has more restaurants per capita than New York City?), and a Sustainability Fair, aimed at increasing green awareness, from solar-powered popcorn to vegetable-oil-fueled parade floats.

The Ithaca Festival is held every year on the first weekend after Memorial Day. For more information, visit www.ithacafestival.org.

Then strap on your stilts, pop out the window screens, and grab the dog's hybrid unicycle because we're having a parade—Ithaca style!

Coupe, jete, turn, and . . . drive!

★ ★

Hey, Buddy, Can You Spare an Hour?
Ithaca

While you're in Ithaca, you might notice a little funny money changing hands.

No, it's not Monopoly money, it's Ithaca Hours! Haven't you heard of it?

Ever the socially progressive city, Ithaca was one of the first US cities (in modern times) to develop its own currency. Called Ithaca Hours, the local currency is aimed at helping out small businesses and keeping money in the local economy. One Ithaca Hour is worth ten dollars. A tenth of an hour is worth one dollar. There's also one-eighth, one-quarter, one-half, and two-hour increments, but I'll let you do the math on those!

Here's how it works: Local businesses pay ten dollars a year for membership in the Ithaca Hours network. In return, they get their business listed in a directory of businesses that accept Ithaca Hours as well as two Ithaca Hours, the equivalent of twenty dollars, to spend at each other's businesses.

There are hundreds of businesses in the network. You can whittle away the Hours on everything from a cup of coffee to dance lessons. And, when you consider that all those businesses get two Hours per year, this initiative alone is pumping $12,000 into the local economy every single year—and keeping it there!

"We're taking the barter system a step further," says Stephen Burke, president of Ithaca Hours, the organization that runs the currency system. "Some people think they're like coupons. They're not. It's exactly like cash. It *is* cash."

Why is it called an Hour? It's meant to remind you that the currency represents someone's labor. It's also a political statement on the minimum wage. "No matter what kind of work you do, you should be making at least ten dollars an hour," Burke says.

One of the most amazing aspects of the currency system is that Ithaca Hours offers business loans—in Hours, of course—with zero

Don't wait until the eleventh hour to spend your
tenth of an hour (one dollar) in Ithaca!

percent interest! "We're here to help small businesses," Burke
explains. Plus, say a business takes out a loan worth $2,000. Because
it's in Hours, that money is guaranteed to stay in the local economy.
"It's putting it into circulation faster," Burke says.

Hours are also offered as grants to community projects and nonprofit organizations. Some employers even offer their employees par-
tial wages paid in Hours.

If you're just passing through and want to get a few Hours in, you
can trade your US dollars for Ithaca Hours at the Autumn Leaves Book-
store on the Commons, or at Small World Music, owned by Burke, on
West State Street.

Honestly, do you know how many Hours I spent on that?!

To read more about Ithaca Hours and find out which businesses
accept the currency, visit www.ithacahours.org.

Putting Your Feet to the Fire

Ithaca

If you take a workshop with Tony Simons, you can bet he is going to put your feet to the fire—literally!

Simons, who is an associate professor at Cornell University and author of the book *Integrity Dividend,* teaches workshops in firewalking.

He says he first got turned on to firewalking after taking a BHAG (big, hairy, audacious goal) class at the Wright Institute in Chicago. No one mentioned the words "fire" or "walking," but when he arrived, one of the assistants said, "Wait until you hear what we've got planned for you tonight!"

That night, they walked on fire.

"The next day, our lives were profoundly changed, knowing that we could walk on fire!" Simons says. "That's sort of the whole message of firewalking—we're all more courageous and powerful than we realize."

Now, he shares that supercharged confidence booster through his workshops.

So how does it work exactly: Do you show up, go through a few maneuvers, safety precautions, sign a waiver, and *poof!* you're walking on fire?

Not exactly.

Each workshop is about three and a half hours long, and there are several exercises leading up to the firewalk. First, everyone gathers around the long pile of wood and helps light it, stating their intentions. What does the fire signify for them? What do they want to get out of the evening? What are they trying to overcome?

The fire needs to burn down for a few hours before you can walk on it, so then everyone heads inside.

In the first exercise, everyone is handed a one-by-one-foot board. On that board, they write their barrier, their challenge, their habit— whatever it is they want to break through. Then, the board is set up on cinder blocks. Simons coaches the student to aim past the board—past their challenge, not at it—and crack! they break through, to their own amazement.

Next, they do a trust exercise, where each person stands on a table, clasps their hands in front of their chest, and falls backward, to be caught by the group.

Third—and here's where the challenges start to get really intense—is an exercise aimed at learning to fight through fear and self-doubt, where each person stands with an arrow between them and the wall with the point of the arrow aimed squarely at their throat. If they push hard enough, the arrow will snap. But they have to fight through the fear that it will puncture their throat.

"When they're ready, they step forward into the arrow and the arrow breaks," Simons says. "But before it breaks, it feels really uncomfortable."

"My heart was racing the whole entire time!" one young man said after the arrow exercise. "I don't know if it was the fear of being hurt or that mine might be the only one that doesn't break—I don't know," he said. "But I wasn't going to let it stop me. I was just going to tackle it."

And finally, everyone heads outside for the big finish—the firewalk.

"There is a technique," Simons says. "It comes down to relaxing into your fear. If you are tense, you'll concentrate your weight on a few points on your feet—that's how people get hurt," he explains.

Likewise, if you hop along like a cartoon yelling "HOT! HOT! HOT! HOT!" that will also hurt.

"You have to relax and put each foot down evenly and smoothly. Walk just as you would walk down the street," he says.

Simons finds the outcome is universally that people feel charged up, they feel empowered. "It's worth easily half a dozen therapy sessions!" he quips.

Testimonials on the website are peppered with phrases like "powerful" and "life-changing."

Walking on fire: It's you vs. your confidence. Who will prevail?!
COURTESY OF INTEGRITY DIVIDEND

"Challenging my physical limits is something I do quite often, but this made me realize that I can get my work done and get over my insecurities just as I can jump across buildings or walk across fire," one college student said.

Another man said, "Next time I hear either myself or somebody else say, 'Are you sure you can do that?' or 'I don't think you can do that,'" he responds: "Dude, I walked on fire!"

Dude, the next time I'm in Ithaca, I am totally walking on fire.

For more information, visit www.ithacafirewalks.com or call (607) 342-1091.

The Rutabaga Curling World Championship
Ithaca

Ithaca has one of the highest ratios of PhDs per capita in the United States. But it's not all brains. No, Ithaca is home to a number of elite athletes as well. This is the home of the Rutabaga Curling World Championship.

Well, kids, pull up your favorite root vegetable, and I'll tell you the story.

It all started more than ten years ago at the Ithaca Farmers Market (www.ithacamarket.com). The farmers' market runs longer here than in most other cities—it goes into December. If you know anything about central New York, you know that it gets pretty cold in the winter and they get a lotta snow. So, you might imagine that at the final farmers' market of the year, in December just before the holidays, they have to work hard to stay warm—and amused.

So Steve Sierigk, the owner of ecofriendly stationery shop Acorn Designs (www.acorndesigns.org) and a vendor at the market, decided to play a little practical joke. The day before the last farmers' market of the year, he set up a court right there in the middle of things. And on the day of the market, right there between the fruit and vegetable stands, sprung up the very first Rutabaga Curling World Championship!

That one looks like a winner right there!
PHOTO BY JERRY FEIST

He meant it as a prank, but it was such a hit, that it caught on and has been going for more than ten years.

Why a rutabaga? Well, when they were first kicking around the idea, one vendor had tossed a frozen chicken. "But that really felt sacrilegious," Sierigk says. "Turnips are too small, and potatoes are too irregular. Rutabagas are just right. Plus, the word 'rutabaga' is just a funny word!" he says.

It not only succeeded in keeping the vendors warm and amused, it also succeeded in attracting a lot more customers to the final market of the year!

The event opens with the carrying of the torch, which is handed off to a "Rutabaga Goddess," followed by a parade of athletes (just like the Olympics). There are two competitions—the adults compete in rutabaga "curling," though they really just toss them, and the kids compete in turnip tossing. They have at least one hundred contestants in the rutabaga competition, so they break it up into three rounds. Then, they take the five best from each round and have the fifteen finalists compete against each other. And of course, there's a medal ceremony!

A common thing you hear from the winners is, "This is one of the greatest moments of my life!" Sierigk says.

They try to have a celebrity toss out the first rutabaga—just like in baseball. One year, Sierigk recalls, the celebrity was Cornell astronomy professor Steve Squyres, who was the principal investigator on the Mars Rover mission. He said his colleague on the Rover project got to throw out the first pitch at a San Francisco Giants game—but getting to do the first toss of the Rutabaga Curling World Championship was way better!

And the crowd went wild!

For more information, visit www.rutabagacurl.com. And if you still doubt it's an official sport, well, "like" it or not, it's even got an official Facebook page—www.facebook.com/rutabagacurl.

Wine, Beer, and Spirits in the Dungeon
Little Falls

From the outside, it looks like the "Cousin It" of castles, covered in a dense mane of trumpet vines.

Inside, it's an elegant dining room with superb food. Eat, laugh, enjoy. Head down to the dungeon for a drink or a game of pool. But check your photos carefully when you get home; you never know what unexpected foggy swirl of a guest might jump in there!

(Cue Vincent Price laugh track.)

This is Beardslee Castle, a nineteenth-century estate-turned-restaurant. Yes, it's a castle, but it's not one of those froufrou castles that make you afraid to move for fear you'll break something. It's the kind of castle you want to explore, from first nook to last cranny, hoping that something gives you a reason to stop in your tracks!

The castle was built by Augustus Beardslee in 1860. Beardslee's son, Guy, ran the estate for a while. A subsequent owner, Anton "Pop"

Cause this is din-ner! Din-ner tonight. You're fighting your appetite inside of dinner, dinner . . . to-night!

Christensen, turned the property into a restaurant in the 1940s. After grappling with a terminal illness, Pop hung himself in what is now the side entrance foyer.

Psychics say the place has a lot of "restless energy," and the restaurant has a collection of stunning photos, taken by employees or patrons, that show ghostly figures. Some say the castle is haunted by Native Americans (this is Mohawk country, after all); some say it's the ghost of Pop. Some say they've seen Mr. Beardslee carrying a lantern out back looking for a lost child. Some say it's a woman in a white nightgown.

The current owner, Randall Brown, says, "I don't believe in clanking chains or anything like that," but adds that he gets about five to six really good photos a year from patrons or employees that have inexplicable humanlike images in them. "That's enough to make me wonder."

If you're thinking of coming to the castle with your Ouija board or séance circle, don't bother. Brown doesn't permit ghost rustling on the premises. His theory is: "If something's there, don't go poking on it!"

In jest, he says, when local kids are bad, sometimes their parents will threaten to "bring them to Old Man Beardslee's place!"

After all, isn't that what a castle's for? To scare small children into behaving? Well, that and the amazing food. Have I mentioned the food? Let's just say, Beardslee Castle, you had me at hello, oregano and rosemary rolls with olive tapenade!

Beardslee Castle is six miles east of Little Falls at 123 Old State Road. For more information visit www.beardsleecastle.com or call (315) 823-3000.

Uphill, Both Ways
Middlesex

The next time your parents or grandparents haul out one of those "In my day, we used to walk to school uphill . . . both ways!" stories, try this one on them.

There's a place in the town of Middlesex, on the east side of Canandaigua Lake, that the locals call Spook Hill. Heading north on Newell Road, if you drive to the dip between a slight hill and the steeper Spook Hill and put your car in neutral, it will appear that your car is being pulled backward . . . uphill.

It works both ways. If you're driving south on Newell, just as you descend Spook Hill, it will appear that your car is being pulled forward, up the hill.

This isn't one of those feelings you get on a stationary train when a moving train passes and you just feel like you're moving. Your car will *actually* be moving.

Is it an optical illusion, or the work of something sinister?

It depends on whom you ask.

The eerie occurrences on Spook Hill—optical illusions or something more sinister? Put your car in neutral and decide for yourself!

Legend has it that an Indian chief killed in battle was once buried on the hill and his spirit still lingers there, causing the freaky occurrence. Another local tale tells of a man named Silas Pratt, who lived nearby and was said to practice black magic. One day, he vanished. He liked to walk his dog on that road, and some say, more than one hundred years later, his ghost still does.

The more pragmatic explanation is that it's an optical illusion. The two hills are merely bumps on a larger hill. So, gravity is pulling your car down the large hill, appearing to go upward when it hits the smaller bump on the hill.

Still, kids try it on their bikes, young men take their dates there to impress them, and for some local teens, it's a rite of passage as soon as they get their driver's license. Scientists are drawn to the site, out to prove, through detailed measurements, that it's merely an illusion.

Whatever you choose to believe, it works. And it's bizarre.

To try it for yourself, take Route 364 and turn west on South Vine Valley Road. (Not North Vine Valley Road.) The third left is Newell Road. The dip is between Woods Road and Spike Road. If you're iffy on the directions, call the Yates County Chamber of Commerce at (800) 868-9283.

These are local roads, and the traffic is light, but while your mouth is hanging open in amazement, please don't forget two very important things: 1) Steer. 2) Keep an eye on the rearview mirror for approaching traffic.

Boo!

The Start of Something Grape!
Naples

The village of Naples, four miles south of Canandaigua Lake, is among the smallest communities in New York State, but that hasn't stopped it from doing grape things: It's known as the "Grape Pie Capital of the World."

I know what you're thinking. Grape pie? Why have I never heard of this? Grapes aren't a rare ingredient like, say, the hair of a unicorn, so why isn't the grape pie right up there with apple, blueberry, and pumpkin?

The reason is because grape pies are labor intensive. You have to peel and de-seed each grape before you can make the filling. And really, who has time for that? Apparently, the people of Naples.

It all started in the early 1960s, when Al Hodges, owner of the Red-wood Restaurant in Naples, wanted to come up with something new to draw more customers into his eatery. When he came across a recipe for grape pies from a local German woman, he realized it was the perfect thing, given the abundance of grapes in the area. But, Hodges and his chefs didn't have the time. Meanwhile, Irene Bouchard, who lives across the street from the restaurant, had just quit her job at Widmer Wine Cellars and opened a bakery in her home. So, Hodges recruited her to churn out the grape pies, which were selling like hotcakes. (Well, hot pies.) That first year, she made fifty pies during the fall grape season. By the 1980s, she was making thousands of pies.

Bouchard, known as "The Grape Pie Queen," inspired other local bakers to grape-ness, and today, it's estimated that 70,000 grape pies are sold in Naples each year. Most bakers only make the pies during the fall grape-harvest season, but some, such as Monica's Pies, freeze the grapes so they can sell the pies year-round and even online (www .monicaspies.com).

A good time to visit is for the Naples Grape Festival (www.naples grapefest.org) in September, which features all kinds of grape things, including grape pies, tarts, cookies, jellies, and ice cream, and a pie contest to crown the "World Champion Grape Pie Baker."

Isn't that grape?

Small on Space, Big on God
Oneida

There are at least a dozen tiny churches from New York to California, but the World's Smallest Church just may be in Oneida.

The Cross Island Chapel is four by seven feet and seats two. It's built on a man-made island in the middle of a pond, so you'll need a boat to get there.

For weddings, the chapel can fit the happy couple, two witnesses, and a minister if they're standing, but if you're inviting more than two people, you might want to bring a few extra seats. (Might I suggest canoes?) Better yet, just have everybody else watch from shore.

★ ★

The chapel, which is nondenominational, was built by Chandler Mason and his daughter Beth in 1989. Chandler, a Baptist, had already built another tiny island on the pond and pitched a small, wooden cross on it as a symbol of God. His wife, Kay, recalls that, when neighbors saw the cross, they said to Chandler, "You need a church to go with it!" Taking the dare, Chandler looked up "smallest church" in the *Guinness Book of World Records* and made sure his was even smaller.

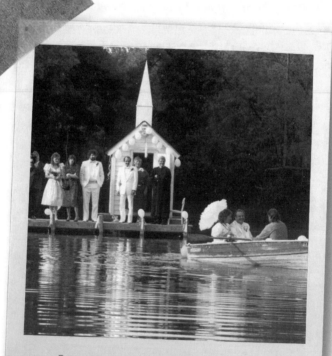

Row, row, row your bride gently to the chapel!
PHOTO BY CHANDLER MASON

The interior has two chairs and a pulpit. There are two stained-glass windows to let the light in, but, amazingly, there's also electricity inside. There's one overhead light and an outlet so you can plug in your boom box to play the wedding march. Of course, the walk down the aisle would probably be more like an aerobics-style march in place, but hey, you're getting married in the World's Smallest Church! And, five-six-seven-eight . . .

A handpainted sign on the shore says the chapel was "Dedicated as a witness to God," which, Kay says, was intended just as the cross was, to "remind people of God." And, in case you haven't put it together yet, the Cross Island Chapel got its name from that island with a cross on it that Chandler had built a few years earlier.

The church may be small, but getting it out to the middle of the pond was no small feat. Kay says it was done in the winter, when the pond was covered in a thick sheet of ice. About twenty of the neighborhood guys brought their snowmobiles to help Chandler drag it out across the ice!

The pond is on the Masons' property, off of Sconondoa Road in Oneida (three miles from the New York State Thruway), but visitors are welcome.

Free Love and Flatware
Oneida

Once you hear this next story, you'll never look at a spoon the same way again.

John Humphrey Noyes founded the religion known as Perfectionism in 1848. He was raised in a deeply religious household, and the idea for this "perfect" community sprang from his refusal to feel guilty for his sins.

Focusing on the community over the self, one of Perfectionism's core doctrines was that every member of the community was married to every other member of the opposite sex. And so, Noyes and his

300 followers lived in a 93,000-square-foot mansion as one big happy family.

OK, people, let's make some Noyes!

To be clear, Noyes believed that he was doing God's work. Once you converted to the religion, you were absolved of your sins and could focus on personal and social perfection.

The community disbanded in 1879 amid a failed leadership transition and persecution from the outside. Many members married quickly but, after more than thirty years, some had a hard time integrating into traditional society. So, the community reorganized in what was called a "joint-stock company," which later became Oneida Ltd.

One good thing about striving for perfection was that it created a strong work ethic in the community, which proved useful when they formed the company that went on to become one of the most recognized names in silverware.

Of course, the company doesn't like to talk about its free-love past. The only reference on its website (www.oneida.com) is: "The company originated in a utopian community established in the mid-nineteenth century, and has had a strong reputation for quality since that time." Knowing the real story, I think we will all view their slogan, "Bring Life to the Table," in a whole new light!

Today, you can take a tour of the Oneida Community Mansion (www.oneidacommunity.org), which is run separately from the company, to learn more about the history of this utopian community-turned-silverware maker.

Did you ever think your tableware had such a provocative past?

Fork, you sexy thing!

A Shot of Caffeine for the Old Factory

Oneida

The old Oneida silverware factory in Sherrill got a shot of caffeine in the past few years: A couple of twenty-something engineers from New Jersey who invented a product called Coffee Joulies recently revved up part of the facility to meet exploding demand for their product.

Joulies are stainless-steel beans the size of an egg that instantly cool down your coffee and then keep it hot for up to five hours. The inventors, Dave Petrillo and Dave Jackson, launched their idea on Kickstarter.com, a grassroots fund-raising site, with the goal of raising $9,000. They raised $300,000, enough to take their product from a mold and a few prototypes to the factory to meet demand—they had preorders for 8,000 sets of Joulies before they even went to the factory!

After Oneida and other American manufacturers were hammered by cheaper competition from overseas, the company filed for bankruptcy protection, and a few former employees bought the factory in 2005. They now rent out parts of it to more than a dozen smaller companies like the Coffee Joulies guys.

The Daves hired some of the same employees that used to make silverware to help them perfect and mass-produce Joulies with the same quality and craftsmanship as Oneida silverware.

One of the factory's owners, Matt Roberts, told the Utica *Observer-Dispatch* that the boys have given the factory a breath of fresh air with their youthful exuberance and knowledge of viral marketing.

"They've created a buzz," Roberts said to the paper, adding that he hopes they can help generate some buzz for the factory. "We want to sell directly to customers. And I want to ask these guys for their help to go viral with it," he explained.

For more information on Coffee Joulies, visit www.joulies.com.

★ ★

Oh, One More Thing before I R.I.P.—
Owego

Have you ever pondered your own epitaph? Are you happy with one of those stock engravings such as "In Memory of" or "Rest in Peace"? Or, do you feel it needs to say a little more?

Well, at Evergreen Cemetery in Owego, a couple of bombastic bards got a little carried away. They wrote one of the longest epitaphs in the US, clocking in at 135 words!

Here it is:

> *Well, we have got what was coming to us, and here in this burial plot we lie:—*
>
> *We fourteen skeletons of Gibsons, Tinkhams, Drakes, Pixleys, and Curtises, that once were clothed with flesh and lived and loved and laughed and danced and sang and suffered just like you till the God-created life-transmitting spark that had been passed down to us from its beginning died.*
>
> *But we were not animals, or insects, or plants, which likewise have their life-transmitting sparks, but beings into whom at our birth had been breathed a soul-entity that came directly from God.*
>
> *And to him our soul-entities have gone to be dealt with by Him as our treatment of others whom He had created deserves.*
>
> *What think you of these beliefs?*
> *—Erected in 1935 by E. T. G.*

Thanks for asking, you guys. Well, first, you probably didn't need to tell me you were once clothed with flesh. I got it. And you definitely didn't need to tell me what you were not—animals, insects, etc. Got that, too, thanks.

Second, you could've left it at lived and loved and laughed. By the time you tacked on dance and sang, it seemed a little desperate, like maybe God was paying you by the word or something.

WELL, WE HAVE GOT WHAT WAS
COMING TO US, AND HERE IN THIS
BURIAL PLOT WE LIE:—
WE FOURTEEN SKELETONS OF
GIBSONS, TINKHAMS, DRAKES, PIX-
LEYS AND CURTISES, THAT ONCE
WERE CLOTHED WITH FLESH AND
LIVED AND LOVED AND LAUGHED
AND DANCED AND SANG AND SUF-
FERED JUST LIKE YOU TILL THE
GOD-CREATED LIFE-TRANSMITTING
SPARK THAT HAD BEEN PASSED
DOWN TO US FROM ITS BEGINNING
DIED.
BUT WE WERE NOT ANIMALS, OR
INSECTS, OR PLANTS, WHICH LIKE-
WISE HAVE THEIR LIFE-TRANSMIT-
TING SPARKS, BUT BEINGS INTO
WHOM AT OUR BIRTH HAD BEEN
BREATHED A SOUL-ENTITY THAT
CAME DIRECTLY FROM GOD.
AND TO HIM OUR SOUL-ENTITIES
HAVE GONE TO BE DEALT WITH
BY HIM AS OUR TREATMENT OF
OTHERS WHOM HE HAD CREATED
DESERVES.
WHAT THINK YOU OF THESE BE-
LIEFS?
ERECTED IN 1935 BY L.T.G.

In loving memory of the English language.

And, finally, it was just shameless to repeat—not to mention dilute—a powerful phrase such as "life-transmitting spark" twice!

To be fair, you made some excellent points. I liked the stuff about living life to the fullest and treating others fairly. But, all the sparks and repetition made it feel more like a cigarette that you couldn't quite get lit.

With all that literary flicking, I'm not so sure your neighbors will be able to rest in peace.

Lord knows it's going to keep me up tonight.

The Ghost Stays in the Picture

Palmyra

Not only does this small town have four churches on four corners, it also has four museums.

There's the Alling Coverlet Museum, which has the largest collection of handwoven coverlets in the country. It makes me feel a little guilty now that I just throw my quilt carelessly on the bed!

There's also the Print Shop Museum, which features a collection of 19th-century printing presses made in Palmyra; and the Palmyra Historical Museum, a former boardinghouse hotel that houses a variety of historical artifacts. There's an entire room devoted to religion, featuring everything from history on the four churches to the adorable "Catholic Corner."

Perhaps the most intriguing is the William Phelps General Store. It's a three-story building, with a store on the bottom floor and a house on the upper floors where the Phelps family lived. Everything is left intact from 1905—from dirt on the front door to the eggs in the cooler!

Apparently, Julius Phelps, who inherited the store that year, was a bit of a slacker. He made not one change to the place after his father died, not even electricity. When World War I broke out, he didn't want to deal with ration coupons. So, one day, he walked out, locked the front door, and never came back. Just left everything inside.

You'd never suspect that it would be the slacker son to make the biggest contribution to history, would you?

Adding to its intrigue, the place is haunted by at least five ghosts, according to Bonnie Hays, executive director of Historic Palmyra. One of the ghosts, Julius's daughter Sibyl, had run off to New York City to become an actress. When she ran out of money, her father made her come back home.

Well, Sibyl may have been a little resentful about that dream deferred, because she used to be a pretty ornery ghost. "Chairs would rock. Things would fly from one spot to the other," Hays says. "We lost some visitors one day because they just got too scared. Oh well!" she says, laughing.

Sibyl was a Spiritualist, so recently, they started bringing in mediums on her birthday to do readings. They even put on a little show for bus tours, where Hays plays the Sibyl character. That seems to have settled her down.

"I think she has really come to enjoy her fame now," Hays says of Sibyl. "I call her the star of her own show!"

★ ★

Jesus Goes Hollywood

Palmyra

When you think of Mormonism, you probably think of Utah. Well, thank your latter-day saints you bought this book. I'm here to tell you what you *should* be thinking: Palmyra.

I'll give you three reasons: 1) Mormonism was founded in Palmyra. 2) Only 14 percent of the world's Mormons live in Utah. 3) In Palmyra, you can watch Jesus *fly*.

The divine aerial display is part of the annual Hill Cumorah Pageant, a dazzling Hollywood-like production that tells the Mormon story. It's put on by the Church of Jesus Christ of Latter-Day Saints in Palmyra every summer.

Hollywood on the Hill known as Cumorah.

The *Rochester City Newspaper* described it this way: "If Heaven isn't as spectacular as this [show], some of us will be very disappointed."

If you don't believe that Hollywood can come to a town of about 8,000, let me give it to you by the numbers:

There are more than 600 cast members, from all over the country, in the epic show. The outdoor stage is the size of half a football field, spread over ten levels. There are more than 2,000 costumes and 400 wigs. There's free seating for 9,000 people at each of seven shows held each year. The pageant has been performed for more than seventy years.

Impressed yet? Wait. There's more.

You also get techno-tacular Hollywood effects, including waterfalls, an earthquake, and a ship caught in a storm of thunder, lightning, and rain. Plus, pillars of fire and the flight of Jesus Christ as he descends thirty feet to Earth.

Man, his career has really taken off since he went Hollywood!

You don't have to be a Mormon to attend, but you do have to be a Mormon to be in the show. So, if you have dreams of being Jesus Christ, skip the Shakespeare and brush up on your Joseph Smith. (You know, the guy who wrote the *Book of Mormon*. Seriously, you're going to have to know this stuff if you want to be Jesus.)

For more information visit www.hillcumorah.org.

All Steepled Together

Palmyra

At the intersection of Main, Church, and Canandaigua streets in Palmyra, there's a church on every corner, all built in the 1800s! Hey, Ripley, can you believe it?

The "Four Corners" churches represent four branches of Christianity: the Western Presbyterian Church (built in 1832), the First United Methodist Church (1867), the First Baptist Church (1870), and the Zion Episcopal Church (1873).

★ ★

Why are they all at the same intersection? Wasn't land wide open in the 1800s?

Maybe it was one of those Ingalls-Olsen rivalries like in *Little House on the Prairie,* and they were all jockeying for positioning and parishioners. Hey, everybody, come to my church!

"I know you'd like to think that, that there was some sort of competition," says Bonnie Hays, executive director of Historic Palmyra. "But I don't think it was any kind of plan. I think what happened was simply that those were the lots available."

Remember, this was just after the wave of religious fervor spread across western and central New York. At the same time, Palmyra was becoming a hub, with the installation of major north-south and east-west roads, plus the Erie Canal and the railroad. "All the denominations were trying to get a foothold out here in the new western lands," says Wayne County Historian Peter Evans.

At the time, the Presbyterians were meeting in East Palmyra, but as Palmyra got hip, they thought it was silly to keep schlepping out to East Palmyra, and so, set up shop—er, steeple—in downtown Palmyra as the Western Presbyterians.

There wasn't much parishioner-stealing going on among the churches, Hays says, but she notes that several Presbyterians opted to change teams to Episcopalian after their preacher began pushing temperance and abolition.

Hays says that today all the congregations remain friendly and even attend holiday events or early masses at each other's churches. "Sometimes they'll have a joint mass, like for Easter. One church will have it, and everybody comes. They work very well together." The churches have also combined their annual fund-raising bazaars so that people can hop from one to the next.

That's all fine and good, but what about the parking?

"Parking is probably one of the biggest foes that history has!" Hays declares unexpectedly. "We need more parking, let's tear down another building!"

Alas, that is the casualty of a church on every corner. Two of the churches tore down nearby homes to build parking lots. The others use street parking or municipal lots. You might even on occasion catch a parishioner parked in another church's lot. "Just don't tell the pastor!" Hays jokes.

Two of the church bells still work, and yes, they ring at the same time! They toll at mass times, as well as at noon and dinnertime. Isn't that a bit of a cacophony?

"No, it's cool!" Hays says. "It's more like a round, like 'Row, row, row your boat.' It's kind of melodic."

If you'd like a tour of the churches, go to www.visitpalmyrany.com and click on "tours" or call (315) 597-6981.

Look Out Below!
Phelps

The village of Phelps, in the Finger Lakes region, has a unique historical bragging right: It has a two-story outhouse.

(I'll give you a minute to let that sink in.)

There are, if you can imagine, other two-story outhouses in the US, though more than a few of them are gags. The two-story outhouse in Phelps is no joke. It was functional—both upstairs and downstairs—for about thirty years until running water came along. It is thought to be the only two-story *brick* outhouse in the United States. (Yes, it's a brick you-know-what house. I'm not going to make any vulgar jokes. You go on ahead without me.)

It's really the minivan of outhouses, with a-commode-ations for three upstairs and three downstairs. The seats are spaced a few inches apart. Who, you ask, would want to take care of their business so close to another person? Well, if you look closely, you'll see that the holes are three different sizes: One for papa, one for mama, and one for baby! (Goldilocks would've loved it.)

The outhouse is actually attached to the main house, which was built in 1869 for Dr. John Quincy Howe. However, you can't access

This isn't bathroom humor; it's a real two-story outhouse!

the outhouse from inside the house for . . . um . . . aromatic reasons. You have to go outside. In the case of the upstairs outhouse, you have to walk across the kitchen roof. (Imagine that in the middle of a cold winter night!)

And now, the part you've been waiting for: How does the two-story part work?

"The people downstairs just had to lean forward!" Don Tiffany, of the Phelps Community Historical Society, likes to joke with visitors.

Then he demonstrates, with arms outstretched wall-to-wall, that the downstairs is a few feet narrower than the "penthouse privy," as he likes to call it. All of the . . . ahem . . . deposits are going to the same place, but they're being dropped a few feet apart. So, while it's great fun to imagine all of the "Look out below!" scenarios, there was never any risk to the people downstairs.

Just to be on the safe side—I call top!

You can take a tour of the Howe House, now owned by the historical society, and if you ask nicely, they just might show you the outhouse. But please, don't leave anything behind.

The Howe House is located at 66 Main Street in Phelps. For more information visit www.phelpsny.com and click on "historical society" or call (315) 548-4940.

Try the Kraut Cake
Phelps

The village of Phelps is famous for something besides its two-story outhouse: It was once known as the Sauerkraut Capital of the World.

Phelps used to be one of the major processing centers for sauerkraut, and that's because Ontario County is the biggest cabbage-farming area in the world.

So, you've got all that cabbage, then all that sauerkraut—what do you do? Of course, you hold an annual Sauerkraut Festival! All the sauerkraut factories have long left the village of Phelps, but the festival has kept going for more than forty years, earning it the added distinction of being one of the oldest festivals in the state.

The four-day festival includes a parade, with catchy slogans such as "Sauerkraut and More in 2004!" and "We're forty-one and still having fun!" There's also a cook-off, a decorate-your-own-cabbage-head contest, and a Phelps Sauerkraut 20K race.

And, of course, there are the food vendors, who've managed to tuck kraut into every food imaginable, from salsa to fudge. Most people opt for the traditional kraut and hot dogs, but a festival specialty is the chocolate sauerkraut cake. It might sound gross at first, but I'm told that you don't even notice the kraut—it just makes the cake moist.

There are so many possibilities for sauerkraut that the festival organizers sell a book called *Cookin' with Kraut,* featuring sixty kraut-infused recipes. It's got everything from spicy sauerkraut pizza to key lime cheesecake (with a cup of kraut) and my personal favorite, Phelps Phajitas (with one and a half pounds of kraut).

The mayor once described Phelps as a "quaint, historic village" that will soon be "its own version of Mayberry." But I'm telling you, these people know how to kick it with kraut. If you're going to make a fajita, that's phajita with a "ph"!

Stop by the gift shop at the Howe House (of two-story outhouse fame) and pick up a copy of *Cookin' with Kraut* for five dollars. For more information on the festival, visit www.phelpssauerkrautfestival .com.

A Town Gets Its Wings
Seneca Falls

Fans of the film *It's a Wonderful Life* have often speculated whether or not the town of Bedford Falls, where the Frank Capra holiday classic takes place, really exists.

Well, the town of Seneca Falls, tucked between two Finger Lakes— Seneca and Cayuga—claims that it is, in fact, the real Bedford Falls.

Just a minute. Just a minute. Now, hold on, Mr. Potter. First Oz in central New York, now Bedford Falls?!

That's right. Consider this: Both places, the fictitious Bedford Falls and the real Seneca Falls, were mill towns with a canal, steel-truss bridge, Victorian homes, and large Italian populations. Why, even the Main Streets, with their grassy medians and globe street lamps, look identical! Capra's even been to Seneca Falls; a local barber will testify to having cut the director's hair on numerous occasions. There was even a real-life character in Seneca Falls who sounds an awful lot like Mr. Potter!

So, every year, Seneca Falls hosts an *It's a Wonderful Life* weekend in early December. Of course, there's a screening of the film. There's also a parade, a tree lighting, pictures with Santa, and the town is decked out in replicas of the Christmas lights from Bedford Falls!

Karolyn Grimes, who played George Bailey's (Jimmy Stewart's) youngest daughter, Zuzu, attends the festival every year. On her website, www.zuzu.net, she describes her first visit to Seneca Falls. "While I stood there, I watched the halo of air that came from my mouth . . . and then I saw it—the bridge. It was lit with beautiful, white lights and provided a path over a canal to the other side of town," Grimes writes. "Was I in Bedford Falls or was I in a New York town called Seneca Falls? I felt like I was in both! . . . In a sense, I was 'home.'"

Clarence! Clarence! Get me back to Seneca Falls!

For more information visit www.therealbedfordfalls.com.

Excuse You, Lake!
Seneca Lake

It is said that the Finger Lakes are shaped like fingers because the Great Hand of the Father touched the land, making it fertile for growing crops.

The lakes even appear at times as if divine power is at work. Seneca Lake, the deepest of the Finger Lakes at more than 600 feet, can go from glassy calm to a mighty storm in five minutes.

But sometimes, a funny noise comes out of the lake.

"It sounds like a big gawump!" says Bill Whitwell, a graphic artist who's lived on Seneca Lake his entire life.

★ ★

The locals now refer to the noises, which sound like a cannon or sonic boom, as "Seneca drums," a term that references the area's Native American heritage. The Seneca Indians used to say that this was the sound of the drums of their ancestors, perhaps an indication of evil spirits, or maybe a grumble from the God of Thunder.

But in the past, the noises have been called everything from "Seneca guns" to the more illustrative "lake farts."

One scientific explanation is that the drums/guns/farts are caused by natural gas being released from the cracks in the bottom of the lake. No one has actually seen a lake bubble to support this theory—they've only heard the sounds—but it's still pretty plausible, since the area is rich in natural gas.

That explanation would lend itself most fittingly to the term lake fart, but let's face it, that's not good for tourism or real-estate prices. Imagine the classified ad: "Five-bedroom, two-bath restored Victorian home, big porch, breathtaking views of Seneca Lake. Hear the wind rustle through the trees, the birds chirp, and the lake fart!"

The booms are usually pretty benign; most Seneca-area residents barely notice them anymore, though some believe that the noises are loudest just before a natural disaster.

This phenomenon isn't entirely unique to Seneca Lake; it can also be heard coming from nearby Cayuga Lake and bodies of water in Connecticut, North Carolina, and other parts of the world. The Dutch call them *mistpoeffers,* the Italians refer to them as *brontidi,* and the Japanese say *uminari.* But only in America, land of liberty and justice for all, will you hear the term "lake fart."

God bless America. This land is your land. From sea to shining, farting sea.

★ ★

Chewie the Dancing Camel

Spencer

Some people have dogs as pets. Others have cats. Some have horses.

Gail Fulkerson has a pet camel.

She named him Chewie because he looks like Chewbacca from the movie *Star Wars* and "he makes all the Chewbacca noises!" Fulkerson says. "Whoever wrote that part *had* to be around camels."

Chewie is a Bactrian camel, which means he's got two humps. Well, he's got two, but one is flat and floppy. That usually means that a camel has been without food for a long period of time and had to cash in the fat (not water, that's a myth) stored in one hump to survive. However, it could also be genetic.

Fulkerson, who runs the Heaven Llama Farm, has a soft spot for animals that nobody wants. When she saw Chewie and that adorable flat hump, she knew she had to have him.

Now that he's in Heaven, Chewie appears to be smiling all the time. "He loves snow!" Fulkerson says, as she prepares to feed Chewie a carrot from her mouth. One thing that's not on Chewie's schedule, however, is parades. "He gets too hyped up with the music, and then he has to dance!" Fulkerson explains. "He does the happy camel dance."

He makes Chewbacca noises *and* he dances? Oh my goodness. I'm in love!

Fulkerson clarifies why the farm is called Heaven: "When there's an animal no one wants, we say, no problem! We'll send him to Heaven." Last I checked, Heaven had nineteen llamas, seven alpacas, and two guanacos, which are cousins of the llama.

That's a lotta llamas.

No wonder: "Llamas are like potato chips," Fulkerson says, "you can't have just one!"

She takes some of the animals to visit the elderly, disabled, and kids in juvenile detention centers. The animals "have to walk through the security gate and everything!" Fulkerson says.

★ ★

When she's not dancing with Chewie or sending a llama through a security check, you'll find Fulkerson in her art studio, where she makes and sells pottery. One of her most popular creations is the "Mommy Pot," a small pot no taller than your thumb, for dandelions and other short-stemmed flowers that your kids bring home.

"That's what pays for my animal habit!" Fulkerson says.

If you'd like to visit Chewie and the gang, or buy a Mommy Pot, call Fulkerson at (607) 589-4886 or send an e-mail to pots@lightlink.com.

It's true. I've been known to bust a move every now and again.

Where Leprechauns Go for a Beer

Syracuse

Coleman's Irish Pub is a true Irish pub, with rich wood paneling, a long bar, a fireplace, and Celtic stained-glass windows. It was founded in 1933 as a workingman's saloon in Syracuse's Tipperary Hill, a neighborhood with a strong Irish population—many of whom came over to help build the Erie Canal.

**Of course, you need a leprechaun door.
How else would they reach the handle?!**
PHOTO BY WAINWRIGHT PHOTOGRAPHY

The front door is a heavy wood number with an oval leaded-glass window—just the sort of substantial door you'd expect at an Irish pub. But as you approach, you notice something odd: Right next to it, there's a tiny door that's an exact replica of the big one.

Of course, it's for leprechauns!

Well how else would they get in? They can't reach the doorknobs!

Peter J. Coleman, who took over the bar from his dad in the 1960s and did a renovation in the early 1970s, says the door was actually his sister Mary Jo's idea.

"She was really creative," Coleman says. She was also, incidentally, a nun for more than twenty years!

He thought it was a great idea and had a local cabinetmaker, Dan Kerstetter, make the door for him.

But Coleman didn't just stop there. He had one of those signature red phone booths from the UK out front—and he had Kersetter make him a small replica . . . for leprechauns!

And upstairs by the fireplace in the banquet room, he has a tiny table and chairs—yep, for leprechauns!

In addition to being a pub, it's also a family restaurant. So when kids come in, Coleman likes to tell them that if they're good, the leprechauns might leave them something upstairs on the leprechaun table.

Poof! Candy and other little goodies magically appear there.

You can see the twinkle in the kids' eyes, Coleman says, when they realize that, like Santa Claus, the leprechauns here at Coleman's, along with the magic and candy they sprinkle around them, are real!

For more information, visit www.colemansirishpub.com or call (315) 476-1933.

Giving 'Em the Green Light

Syracuse

A lot of the Irish immigrants who came to Syracuse's Tipperary Hill neighborhood to build the Erie Canal stayed on after the job was done because there were many factories in the area which provided good jobs.

Look kids, the red is on the bottom!
PHOTO BY WAINWRIGHT PHOTOGRAPHY

When the city of Syracuse started putting up traffic signal lights in the 1920s, they put one at the corner of Tompkins Street and Milton Avenue in Tipperary Hill.

Some local Irish youths started throwing rocks at the red light, breaking it repeatedly—they were outraged that the city would put the "British red" above the "Irish green!"

And, while such a feat might get you arrested in a lot of cities, for reasons that are unclear in historical accounts, the city eventually gave in and flipped the light upside down so the green light was on top and the red light was on the bottom!

Today, it's the only known traffic light in the United States that's upside down. It's so famous, when the prime minister of Ireland came to visit in 2005, he had his picture taken at that light!

"What they were up to in those days was kept for the future," he said. "I'm not sure how legal it was . . . but anyway . . . ha ha ha!"

In 1994, some local businesspeople, including Peter Coleman of Coleman's Irish Pub and his good friend, Jerry Wilson, owner of the local jewelry store, got the city to demolish an old building and build a small park in Tipperary Hill, called "Stone Thrower's Park." They also raised money for a statue: a family of four pointing at the light. The son has a slingshot in his back pocket—a wink to the light's stone-throwing history.

After Wilson's death, incidentally, Coleman also had a bronze sculpture of his friend sitting on a park bench made, which now sits right outside Coleman's.

I'll drink to that!

Hey, Who Lives Up There?!
Syracuse

The Penfield Manufacturing building on North Salina Street looks like a typical old factory building until you look on the roof. There's a little Victorian-style house up there!

The house has been part of local lore for a long time. One story goes that perhaps when the land was purchased by the Moyer family, the house was "grandfathered" in and could not be removed, so they moved it to the roof! Elizabeth Leader, who recently visited Syracuse and photographed the building as a "stunning example" of urban decay, says one of the stories she heard was that maybe the factory owner's wife, Mrs. Moyer, refused to move to Syracuse when her husband bought the factory, so he moved the family to the roof where they lived happily ever after! Another story goes that it was the home of the mistress of the former owner. (Because if you're trying to sneak around, and odd house on top of a factory would be the most discreet location possible!)

Well, that's one way to ensure your house has a good view. Say, where's the doorbell on this thing?!
PHOTO BY ELIZABETH LEADER

The truth, according to Syracuse's visitors' bureau, is that the house was actually built as an advertising gimmick for the factory, which used to make mattresses but closed in 2005.

Well, I guess it worked—we're still talking about it!

If you want to get a better look, the building is at 1710 North Salina Street.

Gr8 Pl8z

Waverly

No matter where you live, Don Merrill's got your number.

That's because he's got one of the largest collections of license plates in the world. He keeps them neat and organized on 180

★ ★

floor-to-ceiling panels that flip like a book. If you spent five minutes looking at each board, that would take you fifteen hours!

There are license plates from US presidents, including a 1937 Georgia plate that says simply, "FDR." There are plates from celebrities, including Jackie Gleason, and rare plates such as the first one ever issued in the state of Virginia. It is—you guessed it—numbered "1."

**Don Merrill just can't stop collecting—
even in the commode!**

A former car dealer, Merrill is somewhat of a legend in the license plate–collecting biz. They call him "Uncle Don." He is revered as the first and only person to amass a collection of plates from every state for every year, a collection he later sold to a museum in Vermont.

When he was inducted into the Automobile License Plate Collectors Association Hall of Fame (oh, snap!), the tribute described Merrill's collection this way: "In the plate-collecting fraternity, a visit to Waverly was—and remains—a visit to Mecca."

Merrill is a serious collector but maintains a sense of humor. The bathroom near the plate collection is covered from floor to ceiling in license plates. Even the TP dispenser and overhead light fixture are made of license plates. "My Tiffany lamp!" Merrill calls it.

And Merrill's eclectic collecting doesn't stop at the bumper. He's got dozens of other collections—everything from vintage automobiles to oil cans (in an original display case); even vintage bubble gum!

He built two buildings behind his family home to house the collections, which are punctuated by some rare one-off items such as a full-bodied, taxidermied moose and a booth from the local soda fountain with about 200 pieces of chewing gum stuck under the table. "We cleaned the benches and left the gum intact as a part of history," Merrill explains.

Oh, so that's the vintage gum? Nope! "That's modern gum," Merrill explained. "But over here, I just bought this original gum from a gum collector in Czechoslovakia!"

His wife even caught the collecting bug; she's started a collection of toy sewing machines.

"I think she started collecting in self-defense!" Merrill said.

Is there anything this guy won't collect?

"I threatened to collect blondes once, but my wife didn't go for it!" Merrill joked.

The Merrill Collection is a private museum, but Merrill gives tours by appointment.

North Country & the Adirondacks

3

North Country & the Adirondacks

Where Pirates Roam and Raccoons Eat Cracker Jacks

Welcome to the *Thousand Islands—all 1,864 of them! (What's a few islands among friends?!) While you're here, be sure to take a tour of two of New York's most fascinating castles—Boldt and Singer. One is a fairy-tale castle, and the other is straight out of a mystery novel— whatever you do, don't lean against the bookcases. And, if you time your visit to the Thousand Islands right, you just might meet some pirates!*

The Adirondacks may not have the highest peaks in the land, but Adirondack Park is so large, it's the size of five other national parks combined, including the Grand Canyon!

Feeling strong? Head to Thendara, where you can test your Super-man skills and race . . . a train! Oh, and great news, I found out that you've still got a shot at winning a gold medal in Lake Placid—no athletic ability required.

If you've ever wondered what Santa does the other 364 days of the year, stop by North Pole, New York, and ask him yourself.

Don't forget to pack your binoculars because legend has it that the Loch Ness Monster's American cousin lives in Lake Champlain!

It Eats the Grand Canyon for Breakfast

Adirondack Park

Adirondack Park may just be a dark green blotch on the map to you, but did you know it's the same size as Vermont? Maybe this will help put it in perspective: It's bigger than Yellowstone, the Grand Canyon, Yosemite, the Everglades, and Great Smoky Mountains national parks . . . combined!

Here are some more facts for you to chew on:

There are over one hundred villages and towns inside the massive park, but guess what? No cities!

Now, stop right there. Hamilton County, in the heart of the Adirondacks, is the third-largest county in the state, but please drive carefully: There are no stoplights!

Lewis County, the westernmost county in the Adirondacks, has twice as many cows (53,000) as people. Why all the cows? This area has the largest concentration of milk producers in the state (New York *is* the third-largest dairy-producing state), and they contribute to the world's largest cream-cheese factory, located in Lowville.

Not far from Inlet and Old Forge, on the southeast shore of the Stillwater Reservoir, there's a small hamlet called Beaver River. There used to be a road that went there, but it got washed out when they flooded the reservoir. The train stopped running in the late 1950s. The only way to get there now is by snowmobile in the winter and boat in the summer. A few families still live there year-round.

Beaver River is home to the Norridgewock Lodge (www.beaverriver .com), a resort that capitalizes on its remote location, saying, "Getting here is half the fun!"

Of course, the lodge would like a new road put in to broaden its appeal to include those who want to get there, *then* have fun. But, you'll never believe it: Some of the residents are fighting it! They don't want a road. They like the solitude—and those low real-estate prices.

"There's a real self-reliant spirit of people here," says Mitch Lee, a tourism official for the town of Inlet and a great Adirondack storyteller.

★ ★

The rest of us like to act like we're accustomed to the wilderness when we visit in the summer, but you really have to have a hearty spirit to live in the Adirondacks year-round.

In the winter, "I commute with a chainsaw in my Jeep in case there's a stray tree in the road," Lee relates matter-of-factly. "You can't wait for National Grid to show up two hours later. You just cut the tree and move on."

Check out www.visitadirondacks.com.

Yar, It's an Invasion!
Alexandria Bay

Ahoy, maties! Me lookout up in the crow's nest just spotted a boat-load of pirates and those scurvy dogs are headed fer Alexandria Bay!

Every August, pirates invade the village of Alex Bay for the horn-swagglin' good time that is Bill Johnston's Pirate Days. Bill Johnston, also known as the "Pirate of the Thousand Islands," earned his pirate stripes by plundering and setting afire a British steamer during the Canadian Rebellion in 1838.

The ten-day festival kicks off with the arrival of a few pirates, scouting the location. They are confronted by soldiers in the street. Some hilarious one-liners are exchanged, and then it's a cacophony of clanging swords as the village attempts to defend itself from these ne'er-do-wells.

Round one goes to the village—hooray! The pirates are rounded up—even the kids in the crowd dressed as pirates—and marched down to a military encampment on the shore.

Down on the waterfront, the swordplay continues. There are chants of "Let the boy go!" for a young pirate, clad in chains, as the pirates toss gold coins into the crowd to win them over.

Then, all of a sudden, a soldier yells, "Fire in the hole!" and the crowd goes silent as everyone sees it at the same time—a spectacu-lar multi-sailed pirate ship is approaching. Why, it's Bill Johnston, the famous pirate of the Thousand Islands! Cannon and musket fire fill

Well, shiver me timbers, it's a pirate ship!

the air, and the tension builds. If the pirates win, they'll take over the town!

The crowd, always up for a good invasion, begins chanting: "Take the bay! Take the bay!" A woman shouts, "Treasure, here, Cap'n!" As more gold coins are flung into the crowd, a boy yells out, "Pirates rule!"

And, of course, they do! The pirates win and a Mardi Gras–like celebration ensues, with pirates dangling from every level of the ship, tossing beads and coins.

The festival includes a weeklong treasure hunt in town, as well as a pirate magic show, pirate juggling, a children's pirate parade, daily "fight a pirate" events where kids can help battle pirates, and a Little Pirate Putt minigolf tournament. There's also live music every night and other events for the adults.

For more information visit www.alexbay.org or call (800) 541-2110.

Fueling Up and Taking Flight

Amsterdam

A trip to the gas station and convenience store is usually pretty uneventful. Gas pumps out front, rows of chips and beef jerky lit with fluorescent lights on the inside.

But a trip to Tower Shops is a real trip! From the minute you drive up, you know this isn't your average pit stop: The building is shaped like a control tower for an airport and inside you'll find all kinds of aviation memorabilia, including about a dozen model planes, old charts, and maps.

It's the brainchild of Mark Murphy, a real-estate developer in the Adirondacks who's had a lifelong passion for aviation.

It's a bird! It's a plane! It's a trip to the gas station in Amsterdam, New York!
PHOTO BY MARK MURPHY

Murphy, who also has another convenience store, though that one is designed like an Adirondack log cabin, says he thinks that his unique shops have helped him weather the tough economy.

"If I had built a standard plain Jane convenience store, I don't think I could've competed with the big guys," Murphy says. "If all things were equal, why would you come over here?"

But all things are not equal here at Tower Shops: As you enter through the control tower, you'll find a twelve-foot-long model of a Waco biplane, a common plane during the thirties and forties, hanging overhead in the tower. There's also a mural of the old Perth airport that used to be here. There's a compass drawn on the floor, and you're greeted by a life-size statue of a World War II pilot.

In the back of the store, the walk-in cooler where they keep the beer is actually called the "Officer's Club." The handle is a 15mm bullet, and inside there's a four-foot-tall bomb! (Don't worry, it was just a practice bomb in World War II—it's not live.)

"Even if you're not an aviation fan, people walk in, stop, look around, and say, 'Oh my goodness this is the coolest place!'" Murphy says.

It's even cooler when you're the pilot in command: Murphy and his wife, Diane, have their offices up at the top of the control tower, with windows all the way around. And they put a wind sock on top of the control tower, so when they're flying one of their private planes out, they know which way the wind is blowing!

For more information, visit www.towershops.com.

Outhouse Archaeology
Ballston Spa

The last time you bought a bottle of water or soda, I'll bet you tossed it in the recycling bin or (*gasp!*) trash, without giving it a second thought, didn't you?

Bottles have been disposable for so many years, we've forgotten they are historical artifacts—even the ones that come from former outhouse pits!

"Old outhouses are actually a main source of obtaining bottles for collectors," says Jan Rutland, the former director of the National Bottle Museum in Ballston Spa.

The museum has an exhibit called "The Privy Pit," which is a backlit illustration of all the different layers, from two feet (bottles from 1910 to 1915) to nine feet (early 1860s).

Think about it: Before recycling and modern trash disposal, they used to burn garbage. But glass won't burn, Rutland says, and you wouldn't want to leave it above ground for someone to cut a foot on. "You already know where there's a hole dug!" Rutland explains, so you tossed medicine, whiskey, or poison bottles in the outhouse pit.

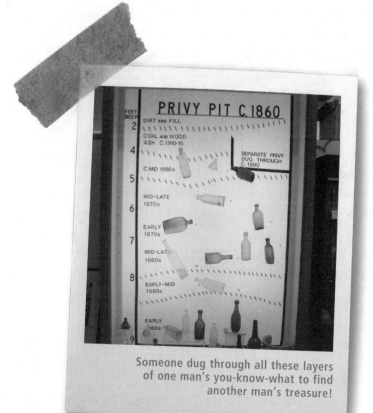

Someone dug through all these layers of one man's you-know-what to find another man's treasure!

Bottles used to be handmade, which makes some of them extremely valuable. That might explain why someone would want to go digging through prehistoric poop to find them! (Apparently, it's no longer technically excrement after one hundred years—it's composted dirt—but still!)

The museum has a video of a Travel Channel *Cash and Treasures* episode in which host Becky Worley goes on an outhouse dig. She starts out skeptical but gets hooked after a few hours. "This toilet is a gold mine!" she exclaims.

Of course, in the biz, they don't call it prehistoric poop digging, but rather, "outhouse archaeology." (I trust you will find a way to work this newfound knowledge into the conversation at your next cocktail party.)

Beyond the novelty of the privy pit, the National Bottle Museum has an extraordinary collection of glass bottles. I highly recommend the poison bottles. (To view, not ingest.) They're cobalt blue, which was intended to warn people, but it actually had the opposite effect and attracted children (whoops!). So, bottle makers started putting skulls, coffins, and spikes on them to convey the danger. There are also some cool liquor bottles shaped like violins, and candy bottles in the shape of phones, ducks, and even guns.

I promise, you'll never look at a bottle—or outhouse—the same way again!

For more information visit www.nationalbottlemuseum.org or call (518) 885-7589.

Please, No Jumping on the Bandwagon

Copenhagen

How often do you hear the expression "jump on the bandwagon?" Well, in Copenhagen, they actually have one!

The Copenhagen bandwagon resides in a small, white-sided building with four square windows, so you can see it from the road. There's black lettering on top that says COPENHAGEN BANDWAGON.

The bandwagon was built around 1875 for the Copenhagen band and used for about twenty-five years. It spent some time on loan to a museum in Cooperstown, before being returned to Copenhagen in 1969 for the village's centennial. In the 1980s, a local legislator and a team of volunteers jumped on the bandwagon, so to speak, giving it a much-needed overhaul and a permanent home.

At sixteen feet long, the bandwagon is a wooden carnival-sleigh-like vehicle on wagon wheels. The undercarriage and wheels actually came from a circus. There are white swans painted on the front, and it is inscribed for J. H. Raymond's Cornet band, so named for the band's second leader, John Raymond. It was used in the late 1800s for parades and political rallies, with the band all decked out in brass-trimmed uniforms and black chapeaus with a red ostrich feather!

Just because other people jump on the bandwagon, doesn't mean you have to, too.
PHOTO BY HELEN JONES

★ ★

The band has long stopped playing, but the bandwagon, which seats about ten people, is still sometimes used for parades at Memorial Day and Christmas.

Kate Fazio and Gertrude Horning were among the volunteers who helped with the restoration. Kate pulls out a photo of people in nineteenth-century costumes riding on the bandwagon during the 1969 centennial parade.

I inquire about who would've been riding in the bandwagon for its Copenhagen homecoming, to which Gert quickly replies: "Well, there's the mayor, and the rest are wealthy or influential people. Basically, people who are impressed with themselves," she says, sitting up straight in her chair. "You know, they're from Pucker Street!" she adds, pursing her lips like a haughty socialite.

Oh, and contrary to the popular expression, "jumping on the bandwagon" isn't as easy as it sounds. "It's hard to get into because it's pretty high up there," says Gert, who got to ride in it once as Mrs. Claus. Plus, there are no cushy seats, which can be a little rough on the posterior when you're bumping along on wooden wheels.

So, kids, let that be a lesson to you. Be yourselves. Don't go jumping on the bandwagon. It's not that comfortable anyway. But, if you want to see one, head over to Copenhagen. Look for the little white building across from the family medical-care practice on Route 12.

Bake to the Future
Crown Point

Talking to Yannig Tanguy, you don't really get the sense that he's a Renaissance man so much as you feel like he's *actually from* the Renaissance period and stuck here because his time machine broke down.

Tanguy, a young entrepreneur who owns the Crown Point Bread Company, makes his own bread using local ingredients and flour he mills himself. But it doesn't stop there. He also builds his own clay ovens! Some of them are at historic sites, and Tanguy actually uses them to bake bread for the troops during reenactments.

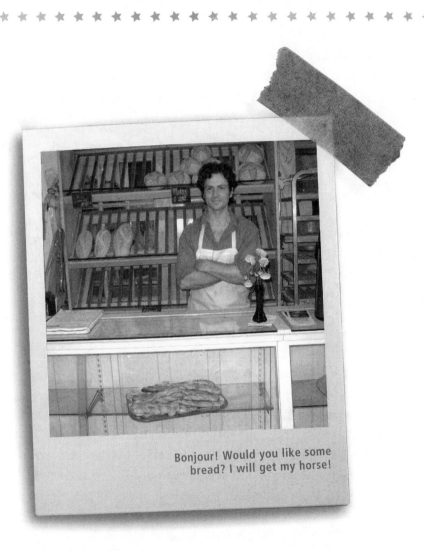

Bonjour! Would you like some bread? I will get my horse!

Tanguy's father is from Brittany, in western France, and there's one thing that stands out from his visits there as a child. "I loved bread and butter," Tanguy says. "French bread was a real treat."

But isn't it hard doing everything by hand?

"It's a challenge doing everything the old-fashioned way," Tanguy admits. But, "it's about being a really good artisan," he says.

When he's not baking bread using 300-year-old recipes, or tending the counter of his cafe, which makes you feel as if you've been

★ ★

transported to the French countryside, you'll find him traveling through town with a horse and cart, selling his bread the old-fashioned way.

"Right now, there's no faster way to do delivery than with a horse and wagon," Tanguy says. (Notice he's vague about the time period in which he's speaking.)

Tanguy has tried selling his artisanal bread at farmers' markets, but there are a few downsides: You have to be there consistently to do well, the transaction cost for one sale is high, and you're beholden to the weather.

So, he's expanding his horse and cart business to other nearby cities like Saratoga Springs, a very horse-friendly town as it's home to the Saratoga Race Course, a thoroughbred horse racing track. (Not to mention, very tourist-friendly!)

"It's going to allow me to go anywhere," Tanguy says of the cart.

Not to mention, more quality time with his horse.

The cart-delivery business is "largely due to my passion for horses. I've had horses since I was a kid," Tanguy explains. "This is a way for me to be able to give my horse enough attention."

If the bread, oven-making, and horses aren't enough to convince you he's a true Renaissance man—he also plays the fiddle!

In a 2003 article, *Adirondack Life* magazine savored the artisanal quality of his bread: "A slice of his Swabien rye, a dense, grainy bread seasoned with fennel, anise, coriander and cumin, topped by a hunk of organic farmer's cheese . . . is a hearty meal in itself."

"Food is magic," Tanguy says. "Cooking is magic."

And so is that time machine you flew in on, buddy. More bread, please!

For more information visit www.crownpointbread.com or call (518) 217-8549.

The Truth Is Out There

Great Sacandaga Lake

Rumor has it that an Adirondack Atlantis sits at the bottom of the Great Sacandaga Lake.

One guy in Albany told me that he heard you can actually see the city below you when you're boating on the lake! Some say divers swim in and out of the houses. Others say there's a locomotive sitting at the bottom of that lake, as well as a Native American burial ground.

The tales are so prolific, they even spawned an *X-Files* episode!

Well, I did some digging and . . . the truth is out there.

In the mid-nineteenth century, the Sacandaga River Valley was positioning itself as the "Coney Island of the North," with a large hotel, rustic theater, roller coaster, midway, boxing matches, baseball, and more. But every spring, the valley would flood, as would the upper Hudson River area around Albany and Troy. So, in 1930, they made it permanent by flooding the valley, including twelve communities, to create a reservoir today known as Great Sacandaga Lake.

The flooding displaced more than 1,000 residents, and nearly 4,000 graves from more than a dozen cemeteries had to be moved. But, I'm sorry to report, no Atlantis. Most of the buildings were moved, dismantled, or burned.

However, when the water level is low, usually in the fall, you might see a few "islands" (hills from the former valley), including Sport Island, where the baseball diamond was, and foundations from former buildings.

So, how did all the rumors start?

"It flooded much faster than they had anticipated," says Bill Loveday, a former Fulton County historian, "which cut short removing some of the things."

As for the train rumor, Loveday recalled a picture of a locomotive sitting in four or five inches of water. People assumed it was left to be flooded, but Loveday says it was actually removed. There are, however, still some train tracks on the bottom of the lake.

Group Dynamics in the Graveyard

Hadley

There is a cemetery on Bruno LaVerdiere's property that wasn't there when he moved in.

What is—*gulp*—going on over there? Have there been any reports of disappearances in the past ten years?

No, no. Nothing like that. LaVerdiere is an artist. (Ah, should've seen that coming!)

"I get my inspiration from historic sites—shrines, graveyards, monuments," LaVerdiere says. He recalls that, when he first moved to the Adirondacks, one of the first things he noticed was all the old, charming cemeteries of thirty to fifty headstones, or stumbling upon a small family cemetery in the woods.

He started building these little monument-like sculptures. "I didn't really think of them as gravestones," LaVerdiere said.

One day, he decided to take a couple dozen of them out to the road leading up to his house and bury—I mean, display—them on the side of the road. Suddenly, it was a graveyard. "There's a different energy when you put all the pieces together," LaVerdiere says.

Looking at it, it's hard to remember that no one is buried there. It reminds me of family vacations as a kid. Whenever we'd drive past a cemetery, my dad would say, "Hey, do you know how many people are buried there?" No, Dad. How many? "All of 'em!" he'd reply, with that smug I-got-your-nose! look.

So, Dad, do you know how many people are buried in this cemetery? None of 'em!

"A lot of people think it's real," LaVerdiere said. "That was never my intention."

Perhaps some of LaVerdiere's reverence comes from the fact that he spent fifteen years in a monastery training to be a monk. Not surprisingly, he was the guy who cut all the gravestones for the monks.

Turns out, that wasn't his calling.

However, that sound you hear is him calling. Back on the porch, LaVerdiere, now in his seventies, runs over to a giant clay horn suspended from the ceiling and begins, well, tooting his own horn—another sculpture he's made.

"Blow in it, and they'll hear you across the river!" he says. "Dogs bark back!"

The minute LaVerdiere's lips purse, his brother Rome pops out of his seat on the porch and dashes to an even bigger horn set up in the yard like a swing set.

Aw, isn't that sweet. Two brothers having a horn-to-horn conversation!

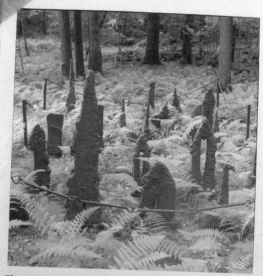

The newest little old cemetery in the Adirondacks.

★ ★

One strange-but-true tale is that, with all of the farmland in the valley, the stuff that made the crops grow washed into the lake during the flooding and the fish ate it.

"It created an atmosphere for the fish that made them huge!" Loveday says. Just a few years after the flooding, the reservoir/lake snagged the world record for the largest northern pike!

To learn more about the flooding of the Sacandaga River valley, visit the Fulton County Museum, open May through October, at 237 Kingsboro Avenue in Gloversville. Check it out online at www.fulton countymuseum.org.

Ping-Pong Independence Day
Inlet

If you spend your Fourth of July in the town of Inlet, you'll have a ball!

A couple thousand of them, actually.

Every Fourth of July, children gather in Fern Park, wearing little red bows in their hair, white-starred tops, red-hooded sweatshirts, navy shorts, and Uncle Sam hats. They run around for a while before it's time to line up behind the rope, their legs dancing in anticipation.

Then, a father yells, "Here it comes!" Suddenly, a small plane emerges from behind the tree line. Thousands of Ping-Pong balls, in all different colors, rain on the field. The children dart out to scoop them up. Then, just as fast as they got out there, they're already on their way back, eager to cash in their Ping-Pong balls for prizes.

There are three drops, for different age groups, and each child can collect three balls. Prizes are awarded according to the color of the Ping-Pong ball. There are commemorative water bottles, glow sticks, temporary tattoos, and kaleidoscopes, as well as coupons for doughnuts, dinner, and other items from local businesses. Out of the roughly 9,000 balls dropped, there are nine golden balls (Daddy, I want a golden ticket!) that yield grand prizes such as a family cruise on nearby Raquette Lake.

Ready! Aim! Fire the pillowcases!

★ ★

Oh, and in case you're wondering how they do the drop, it's a bunch of guys leaning out of a seaplane with pillowcases full of Ping-Pong balls!

I think it's wonderful that somebody finally decided to give the Ping-Pong ball a proper Independence Day, liberating it from a mundane existence of being thwacked by a paddle a couple thousand times, only to be lost in a dusty hairball in the corner of the basement or garage.

> And the Ping-Pongs' red glare!
> The blues, greens, and yellows in air
> Gave proof on this day
> That our Ping-Pongs, we do care
> Oh say does that star-spangled child yet wave,
> Three Ping-Pong balls with glee—
> And the prize she will have!

For more information on Inlet's Fourth of July Ping-Pong Ball Drop, call (688) GO-INLET or visit www.inletny.com.

We'll Be Recyclin' Down the Mountain When We Come . . .
Inlet

What is it about cardboard boxes? There's something magical about them that makes cats want to jump in them and little kids want to turn them into a secret fort.

Well, in Inlet, they hop in and race 'em down the hill!

The Cardboard Sled Race occurs the last Saturday in February, and the rules are pretty simple: Design and build a person-powered sled, capable of withstanding the descent of the sledding hill at Fern Park, using nothing but cardboard, tape, and glue. That means no motors and nothing sharp like nails or staples.

People really get into the creative designs. In the past, there have been sleds shaped like penguins, dragons, submarines, and fighter jets. Some have racing stripes, some have smiley faces.

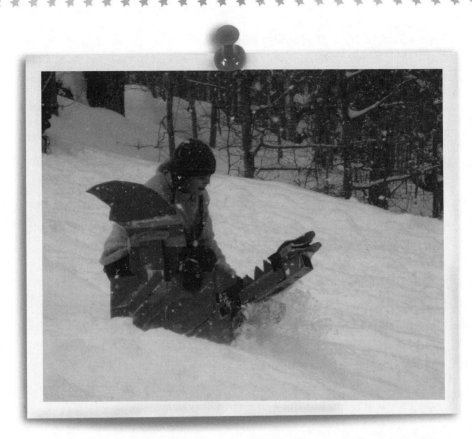

It's a bird! It's a plane! It's a . . . cardboard dragon!
COURTESY OF INLET INFORMATION OFFICE

"There's lots of duct tape, paint, and markers!" says Adele Burnett, the Inlet tourism director.

They give awards out for "Best in Show," "Great Spirit," and, of course, the fastest.

And, while it doesn't specifically say it's just for kids, pretty much all the sleds are piloted by kids.

The race is part of the annual Frozen Fire and Lights Festival, which includes all kinds of events for kids, plus a bonfire with free hot dogs, doughnuts, and hot chocolate and a fireworks display.

For more information, visit www.inletny.com.

One Square Mile of Floating Hope
Inlet

Inlet sits by a lake, the fourth in a string of eight lakes that is aptly called Fourth Lake, so they love to get out on the water here.

Somewhere along the way, they decided to vie for the *Guinness Book of World Records* title for the "World's Largest Floating Raft." It doesn't have to be one continuous raft, so the record-holder is composed of around 2,000 kayaks, canoes, and other single-occupant boats.

But also somewhere along the way the much-larger city of Pittsburgh decided it wanted the title, too.

And a rivalry was born.

"When the little town of Inlet decides to win, we do it in a big way!" exclaims Connie Perry, organizer of the project, called One Square Mile of Hope. The event raises money for the Susan G. Komen breast cancer foundation.

Inlet is small, with a population of less than 400, but scrappy—they managed to get nearly 2,000 boats out on that lake in 2011, clinching the title for a second time.

That's a lotta hope!

For more information, visit www.onesquaremileofhope.org.

Where Raccoons Eat Cracker Jacks
Keene

Man, is this place wild!

Deer, moose, antelope, and buffalo jut out of the walls. A couple of animals appear to be burrowing back *into* the walls. An otter leans over a branch to look for dinner in the pond below. One of the raccoons is having Cracker Jacks for dinner. (I guess he didn't feel like cooking tonight.) A couple of his friends are paddling in a tiny canoe as a fox lurks behind. A bear roams the floor as the king of the jungle shows his teeth. Overhead, mountain lions strut on a beam and a white peacock perches on a branch.

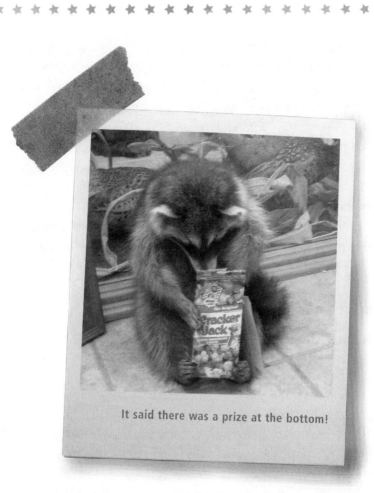

It said there was a prize at the bottom!

This is North Country Taxidermy and Adirondack Reflections, a virtual department store and fine-art gallery for taxidermy. It's all pre-shot and pre-stuffed, so you don't need a gun to collect one of these trophies—your weapon of choice will be a credit card.

I'm not a fan of stuffed dead animals, but this is a must-see for anyone visiting the North Country. Surrounded by some of the highest peaks in New York State, this shop has something for everyone. There's traditional taxidermy—deer mounts and full-size bears for the hunting purists—and plenty of birds and antler candelabras for those looking to add a little hunting-lodge chic to their home.

Some of the whimsical poses show that taxidermy doesn't just have to be about a trophy, it can also be fine art—and hilarious! Who knew?

There are hundreds of taxidermied animals on display—everything from mice to moose. (Seriously, they have taxidermied rodents!)

Prices range from $50 for a mouse to $1,200 for those paddling raccoons and more than $5,000 for a full-size bear.

If you've already got taxidermy but it's, um, on the geriatric side and in need of a replacement or two, the shop also offers feet and replacement parts.

For the man who has everything, might I suggest a deer rump?!

For more information visit www.northcountrytaxidermy.com or call (518) 576-4318.

Champ the Lake Monster
Lake Champlain

You've heard about the famous Loch Ness Monster in Scotland, but did you know he had an American cousin?

Legend has it that a similar, serpent-like creature lives in Lake Champlain. The locals call him "Champ."

Dee Carroll, who runs a restaurant and ship store at Westport Marina with her husband, Bob, swears she's seen it. When they were driving once, Dee was looking out the window at the lake. "I turned to Bob and said, 'What's that post-like thing?' I looked back and all that was there were two concentric circles." Dee says. "Posts don't do that."

Bob, however, is a little more skeptical. A local group has been tracking head sightings versus body sightings for some time, Bob says. Body sightings can be more questionable, since it could easily be the way the light is hitting the waves. Well, that, and, Bob points out, "Most of the body sightings have been close to shore, between 4:00 and 6:00 p.m.—the cocktail hour!"

Still, he muses, "There's something out there that people are seeing."

There was a wedding party of thirty to forty people on a boat, the Carrolls recall, and all of them came back convinced they'd seen it. The

Carrolls' son was on a boat with his wife and thought he saw a giant log. "Then, the log started swimming!" Dee says.

I asked Dee if she was afraid to go out on the water. She said no. "If Champ were gonna be vicious, he would've done it by now!"

Lake Champlain, like Loch Ness, lends itself to tales of a creature living there, as it's a freshwater lake that doesn't freeze over in the winter because it's so deep.

But there are a few problems with the lake-monster story. Early Native Americans claimed they saw a "horned serpent," and European settlers first reported seeing the creature in 1609. Four hundred years is a long time. So, is there a Mrs. Champ, baby champs, and grand-champs? Or, is it the same monster with a really long life span?

The locals have embraced all the Champ lore—there's even a park named after him, Champ Beach Park, where you can go swimming, play basketball, or just look for Champ—and even camp overnight. For more information, visit www.porthenrymoriah.com and click on "Campgrounds."

If you want to swap theories, head to Port Henry's Bulwagga Bay on the first Saturday of August for the town's annual Champ Day. For more information visit www.porthenrymoriah.com and click on "visit," "attractions," and then "Annual Champ Day."

The Secret Map of Lake George

Lake George

I've come across a mystery, and I think you should check it out.

Go to Beach Road, on the southwest corner of Lake George. Here, you'll find a row of shops and restaurants.

For darn's sake, put the GPS away! This is one of the busiest tourist spots in the northeast, and I'm pretty sure you couldn't get lost even if I blindfolded you. Now, pay attention.

On Beach Road, there's a restaurant called Adirondack Sandwich Works, formerly Big Bob's Burgers & More.

Did you find it?

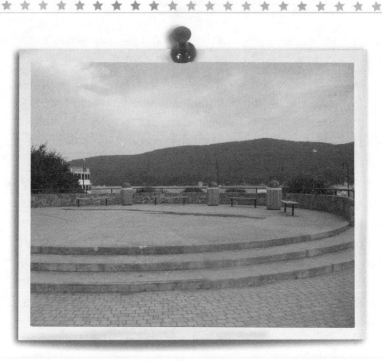

Step right up. Do you have something to say? (say . . . say . . .)

Good.

Now, across the street . . .

Hey! Focus. Do *not* get distracted by the doughy, warm smell of panini. The first rule of mystery club is always eat *before* mystery club. Do you want to check out this mystery, or not?

OK, across the street are three wide, round steps. At the top, a map of the lake and a compass circle are etched in the sidewalk. I want you to stand exactly in the middle of the circle.

Now say something.

If you do it right, you'll hear an echo of your own voice as if you're standing in some sort of invisible chamber! No one else around you will be able to hear it; they'll hear your normal voice.

Some people, when they get to the middle of the circle, speak timidly, then get a funny look on their face as if they've just seen a ghost. Others sing.

"We just kept saying 'hello' over and over, and then started calling our son's name," says Laura Zamrok, who visited the spot with her husband, Brian, and infant son Christian. "It sounded as if we were standing on top of a hollow, metal tube!"

Once you get the hang of it, you might try: "I'm the king of the world!" or "Activate the cone of silence!" It's so fun and empowering to hear the boom of your own voice, you just might surprise yourself and announce a run for the presidency!

May I have . . . your attention . . . PLEASE! (please . . . please . . .)

Well, in any case, you'll have your own attention!

Do It for Your Country!
Lake Placid

The winter Olympics were held in Lake Placid more than twenty years ago, but did you know that you still have a shot at winning a gold medal?

It's part of an environmentally conscious program called "Gold for Green." If you drive a hybrid car to Lake Placid, they'll give you a gold medal!

"We've always thought that we have a responsibility, living in the Adirondacks, to the environment," says James McKenna, president of the Lake Placid Visitors Bureau.

The tourism bureau bought hybrid cars for the office, but decided to take it a step further with visitors. "We wanted to identify these people as leaders," McKenna says of hybrid drivers.

Richard Austermann, of Southwick, Massachusetts, drove his family to Lake Placid in a Prius and came home with the gold. "It's cool," Austermann says. "You go on your vacation, you come back with a little perk . . . a gold medal!" Ever a humble medalist, Austermann adds, "It's still hanging on our rearview mirror. We figured the car earned it, not us!"

Regardless, you will always have that medal and go down in history as a champion in the sport of fuel efficiency!

And the gold medal goes to . . .
YOU! Congratulations!

Imagine how much fun it will be at the next gathering of family or friends to say, "Hey, did I ever tell you about that time I won a gold medal in Lake Placid?"

To claim your "Gold for Green" medal, drive your hybrid car to the visitors bureau in Lake Placid's Olympic Center at 2610 Main Street (800-447-5224). For more information, visit www.lakeplacid.com.

Good luck!

Brewin' with the Big Dog

Lake Placid

When Chris Ericson got into the beer-brewing business, he needed a name for his beer. As it turns out, the first beer he made was pretty big as beers go, clocking in at 7 percent alcohol. (Most beers average 4 to 5 percent alcohol, 3 percent for baseball games to keep the crowd from getting too rowdy.)

★ ★

So, he named the beer after one of the pub's most loyal regulars: a dog named Ubu!

"Ubu was a 125-pound chocolate lab with a head the size of a basketball," says Ericson, brewmaster and owner of Lake Placid Pub & Brewery. "We named the big beer after the big dog!"

Ubu was legendary in Lake Placid. His owner used to stop in for a drink every night after work. Ubu knew the routine, so he'd bum around town all day, doing his big-dog thing, then head to the pub to wait for his owner. "Everyone in town knew Ubu," Ericson says.

Ubu Ale is a smooth, malty, garnet-red colored English Strong Ale. And, at 7 percent alcohol, it packs a punch. Don't act surprised if it takes you down like a chew toy. (Hey, we said Ubu Ale, not Chihuahua ale!)

The beer is so popular that it has a cult-like following in the Adirondacks and has won several national awards. Former President Bill Clinton liked the beer so much after a 2000 visit to Lake Placid, he had some Ubu Ale shipped to 1600 Pennsylvania Avenue!

Good brew, Ubu, good brew!

For more information visit www.ubuale .com or call (518) 523-3813.

Ubrew. Brew! brew! brew! brew! (That's Labrador for "We hope you enjoy our beer.")
PHOTO COURTESY OF LAKE PLACID PUB & BREWERY

Love Those Loons

Aside from the Adirondack chair, the loon is probably the most popular icon of the Adirondacks.

So, what makes some people so crazy for loons?

"Loons are an enigma," says Mike Prescott, who runs a guide service called Paddling Through Time and is—this is no judgment on his sanity here—known as "The Loon Man."

Loons look like ducks decked out in contemporary formal dress, with black and white feathers and a red-eye accent. But they're not ducks. Ducks can actually walk on land; loons can't. Loons have prehistoric-like legs that make even getting into the air a chore. "They need at least 100 yards" of runway (runwater?) space in order to take off," Prescott explains. Once airborne, they can go up to seventy miles an hour!

Loons are perhaps best known for their diving abilities and poetic cry. "When loons are alarmed, they don't fly like most birds, they dive," Prescott says.

Meanwhile, that cry may sound like an expression of loneliness, but, in fact, the loon is trying to tell you that you are too close to his family, so back it up, OK?!

That part cracks me up. You watch people get really close to them, then the wailing starts. The person is probably thinking or saying, "Wow! What a beautiful sound. How nice that he's singing for me!" Meanwhile, the loon is like—"What part of BACK IT UP don't you understand?!"

If you ever see a loon walking on water with its wings tucked tight (and I hope you only see it on the Discovery Channel), that's known as the "penguin dance," and it means, "You have completely invaded my personal space and I am TOTALLY FREAKED OUT!"

One step closer and I swear, I'll scream.

Once you know the ground rules, you can paddle to your heart's content, watching them as Prescott does. "I'm sort of like the CIA of the bird world!" he says proudly. But the loons haven't done anything wrong or worthy of a covert investigation. Just the opposite: Prescott finds they're an important indicator of environmental health and water quality.

If you ever notice a loon waggling her back foot, Prescott explains, that's to help her cool off, "like when you're too hot in bed and need to stick your foot out of the covers!"

While we're on the pillow talk, loons are pretty territorial when it comes to their families, so the cruisin' loons go elsewhere. "We have a couple of lakes that we call singles bars," Prescott says, "because the loons haven't hooked up yet!"

Imagine the lines you'd hear in that place: "Hey, hot foot. What are you drinking?"

Sportsmanship with a Blowtorch

Lake Placid

In the 1980 Lake Placid Winter Olympics, the men's 15K cross-country skiing event was an intense, hair-splitting race between Thomas Wassberg of Sweden and Juha Mieto of Finland.

So close, in fact, that Wassberg edged out Mieto for the gold by one one-hundredth of a second! After the race, Wassberg, knowing how much Mieto wanted the gold medal, said to him: "We must split this medal in half as one one-hundredth of a second is nothing in a fifteen-kilometer race!"

Even the International Ski Federation agreed that it was a ridiculous margin and, from that point on, began rounding all of their times to the nearest one-tenth of a second.

It would've been easy enough to say, "Sure, give me half your gold medal!" But demonstrating what an honest, respectable athlete he was, Mieto replied: "A gold medal should not be split in half."

The story has become somewhat of an urban legend. (Can you have an "urban" legend in the Adirondacks, where there are no cities?) Some say Wassberg had his medal cut in half anyway and that the medals were re-welded as half gold, half silver. One man, on a visit to the Olympic Center, even claimed to have seen one of the half-and-half medals.

The truth is, the medals were never split. "At one point, Thomas Wassberg said he thought it should be split, but it never was," says Nat Brown, a former Olympic coach in cross-country skiing and a friend of Wassberg's. "I doubt if Mieto would have accepted it," Brown adds. "He was—and is—far too proud a man."

Thomas, meanwhile, "was never very proud of that medal," Brown says. In fact, he had trouble finding it after the ceremony, according to Brown, because it was "scrunched up in his pocket!"

Still, it was a true exchange of sportsmanship—even if it didn't *actually* involve a blowtorch—and the Olympic spirit among two competitors who genuinely earned the title Olympian.

I've Got a Handful of Cream Cheese. Catch!

Lowville

Welcome to Lowville, home of the world's largest cream cheese factory!

What do you do with all that cream cheese?

Well, let's see. You can make the world's largest cheesecake. You can have a bagel-and-cream-cheese–eating contest. Heck, you can even get crazy and have a cream cheese–tossing contest!

These are just some of the fun events at the annual Cream Cheese Festival (www.creamcheesefestival.com) in Lowville (rhymes with "How-ville").

There's also a cream cheese recipe contest, cream cheese bingo, and a feed-your-partner-cheesecake contest. Try your waitressing skills in the milk-tray relay, carrying a tray filled with glasses of milk. Put the pedal to the metal in the tractor race or leave it to lady luck in the tractor raffle.

If you're wondering why all this creamy, cheesy goodness is here in Lowville instead of Philadelphia, it's because this is where the world's largest cream cheese plant is. Also, remember that I told you New York is the third-largest dairy-producing state and here, in the western foothills of the Adirondacks, there are twice as many cows as people!

While you're in Lowville, be sure to try the cheese curd and Croghan bologna, which is similar to kielbasa but sliced like pepperoni, according to Michelle Castor of nearby Copenhagen. It's such a popular combination, Castor says, "it's like peanut butter and jelly" here!

For the uninitiated on the divine gift that is cheese curd, here's a little tip: "You know it's fresh because it squeaks!" says Gert Horning (of Copenhagen bandwagon fame). "If you refrigerate it, it takes the squeak out!"

For that perfect I-went-to-dairy-country photo op, head to the Lowville Producers Cheese Store on Route 12 and get your picture taken with Lady LeWinDa Milkzalot, billed as "the largest dairy cow in New York State." (Don't forget to say "cheese!") Her measurements

Welcome to cow country.
My name is Lady LeWinDa Milkzalot!

are ten feet six inches high, fifteen feet long, and five feet wide. Her name, the product of a local contest, is a nod to the area's dairy farming and giant windmill farm.

During the off-season, you can order your cheese curd, Croghan bologna, and other New York treats at www.gotgoodcheese.com.

Trivia

Spreading the Truth

Where was cream cheese invented?

You said Philadelphia, right?

Wrong!

Hand me that butter knife. I've got some truth to spread!

Cream cheese was invented in 1872 by a dairyman in Chester, New York, which is about 250 miles south of Lowville and 150 miles north of Philadelphia.

So, how did Philadelphia wind up getting all the credit?

When A. L. Reynolds started distributing the cheese in tinfoil wrappers in 1880, according to Kraft, he called it "Philadelphia Brand" cream cheese because, at that time, a lot of high-quality foods were being produced in Philadelphia. The city's name became synonymous with quality. You would say that something was "Philadelphia quality."

Because it was referring to a standard and not a city, in some cases, the packaging would have the word "Philadelphia" in quotes.

So, the next time you say, "We need to buy Philadelphia cream cheese," be sure to add some air quotes with your fingers on the word "Philadelphia" for added amusement and historical accuracy!

★ ★

Dude, You're the Man!
Mayfield

For thirty years, the twenty-four-foot-tall Leather Guy stood outside Alvord's House of Leather on Route 30, greeting customers and welcoming visitors to the Adirondacks.

He wore a tan, fringed jacket, jeans, and matching knee-high boots. He had a brown comb-over haircut with sideburns, a moustache, and oddly shaped beard. He wore thick black glasses. He was known at times as The Leather Guy, The Hippie Dude, or The Big Man.

He was the kind of guy that whenever you arrived in the Adirondacks, you wanted to pat him on the back (well, the back of the ankle, anyway) and be like, "Dude, what's up?!"

So, when Steve Alvord took him down, it raised concern among the locals as well as longtime tourists.

Oh no. Did someone . . . uh . . . stick it to The Man?

Nope! He's just moved up the road but still on Route 30. He found a new job as the spokesdude for Adirondack Traditions, a company that builds Daniel Boone Log Homes.

Originally designed to look like Alvord, the big guy got a makeover to pull his look out of the seventies. So, sorry, ladies, love 'em or leave 'em, the sideburns are gone, as are the goofy glasses.

"He's the perfect Daniel Boone guy," says Marty Greco, owner of Adirondack Traditions, who bought and restored the big guy and helped him with his transition into the twenty-first century. "Steve had the statue made to look like him. It was actually called Big Steve. I want to call him Daniel Boone."

The Big Guy is a great calling card for a business, Greco says, but he's also a gateway to the Adirondacks. As a kid, you knew you were getting close to camp when you saw him. "He was a mile marker," Greco recalls. "You knew you were there."

"If I didn't have a business," Greco adds, "I would've bought him anyway and dedicated him to every father that ever took his kid to camp in the Adirondacks."

So, the next time you're headed to the Adirondacks via Route 30 and someone from the backseat yells, "Are we there yet?" you can say, "Not yet. We're waiting for The Big Guy!"

The Big Guy is located on Route 30 between Riceville and Mayfield. If you're driving north, he's just before the Tags Upholstery (www.tags upholstery.com) shop. You can also friend the Big Guy on Facebook—search for "Alvord Leatherman."

The Big Guy gets a little help with his makeover.

Faster than a Locomotive!

North Creek

If you secretly believe you have Superman tendencies, now is your
chance. Put yourself to the "Faster than a speeding bullet! More powerful than a locomotive! Able to leap tall buildings in a single bound!"
test and actually race a train.

Race the Train is a scenic 8.4-mile race on the Saratoga & North
Creek Railway (www.sncrr.com) from Riparius to North Creek station.
The proceeds go to Dollars for Scholars, an organization that raises
money for local college-bound students.

Spectators can buy a ticket to ride the train with the runners. The
runners get dropped off in Riparius, where they literally race the train
back to North Creek. The spectators get to stay and cheer on their
superpeople from the train.

The race starts on a bridge, with whitewater rushing below. As they
exit the bridge, the dirt road curves uphill, and one by one, they taper
the cacophony and vanish around the corner to run alongside the train
and the Hudson River.

So, does anyone ever beat the train?

Among the more than 200 runners that compete, "there are a
certain number of racers each year who do beat the train," says Ann
Arsenault, co-director of the race and president of the local Dollars for
Scholars chapter.

This would probably be a good time to tell you that they don't
actually run the trains at "full speed ahead." The trains are set to eight
miles an hour, or an eight-mile minute as they say in runner lingo. The
trip takes one hour, seven minutes for the train. One of the past winners pulled it off in just over forty-five minutes, which put him at a
5.23-minute mile!

"I'll tell ya, he was the real locomotive!" Arsenault remarks.

After the race, there's a second event called a Family Fun Run. This
is a simple one-mile race, Arsenault says, designed to encourage kids
who aren't ready for the big race but are still excited about it.

One fun historical tidbit for you: The North Creek train station was where, in 1901, then–Vice President Theodore Roosevelt found out that McKinley had died and that he would be the next president of the United States. It's preserved exactly as it was at that time period as a museum in addition to a train station.

The race is held the first Saturday of August. For more information go to www.adirondackrunners.org.

The Adirondack Timbuctoo
North Elba

How many times have you said something like, "Oh, that place? It's way out there in Timbuctoo!"?

Today, Timbuctoo has become some far-flung funny-named place, but once upon a time, it was a very real, very unfunny place right here in New York State.

In 1846, abolitionist Gerrit Smith decided to give forty acres of land in Essex, Franklin, and Hamilton Counties to newly freed slaves. It wasn't the best land. Some farms were very hilly; others were under-water. But as landowners, these former slaves could now vote.

The area, just south of Lake Placid in the northern Adirondacks, was unofficially dubbed Timbuctoo, after a city of the same name in central Africa that was desirable but hard to reach.

In May 1849, a white man named John Brown moved his family to the Adirondack Timbuctoo to help the community.

"Most of the newly freed slaves were city slickers—from Schenectady, Albany, and New York City—and didn't know much about farming," says Brendan Mills, historic site assistant at the John Brown Farm. Brown shared everything he knew about farming and frontier living with the community to help them make a go of it. They grew what they could on the land: mostly potatoes, but also hay, rye, corn, peas, and turnips.

Timbuctoo ultimately became more of a stepping-stone to a free life. Some of the former city dwellers never adjusted to farm life, while

★ ★

others found the land too tough to tend. Most of the families left within ten years.

Today, John Brown's farm is all that remains of Timbuctoo. You can visit the farm, restored to a typical nineteenth-century Adirondack farmhouse. There, next to a large rock Brown used to call his "thinking rock," the body of John Brown is interred.

So, the next time you hear someone say "out there in Timbuctoo," you'll know exactly where that is and what it means.

John Brown's Farm is at 115 John Brown Road in Lake Placid, New York. For more information, call (518) 523-3900.

Way out there in Timbuctoo, John Brown's farm.

★ ☀ ★ ☀ ★ ☀ ★ ☀ ★ ☀ ★ ☀ ★ ☀ ★ ☀ ★ ☀ ★ ☀ ★ ☀ ★ ☀ ★ ☀ ★

Christmas in July

North Pole

You might've thought that Santa was toiling away up there at the northern tip of the Earth's axis, but if you paid attention in geography class, you'd know that the North Pole is actually in the middle of the Arctic Ocean!

Don't worry, though, I found him! All this time, his workshop was right here in North Pole, New York!

Opened in 1949, this North Pole was the very first theme park—predating even Disney. (In fact, Walt Disney studied the North Pole

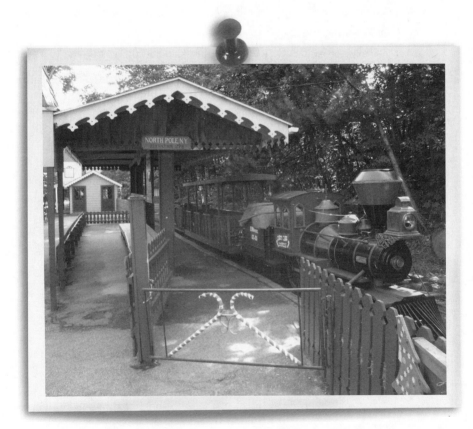

All aboard! Next stop—Santa's house!

before he built Disneyland in 1955.) The North Pole was created by Julian Reiss, a Lake Placid businessman, who wanted to make his daughter's dream of visiting Santa's workshop come true. Adirondack artist Art Monaco brought that dream to life.

The park, on the slopes of Whiteface Mountain near Lake Placid, features all sorts of specialty shops, amusement rides, Santa's house, a reindeer stable, and live musical shows. There's even a Talking Tannenbaum and a real, solid ice North Pole that stays frozen—even in July!

Walking through Santa's candyscape village is magical, even for adults, as elves show you how they make the toys and the candy, and fairy-tale characters such as Red Riding Hood and Little Bo Peep pass by. You can visit with Santa's live reindeer in the barn and watch them fly with Santa during the show!

It's a hot July day, and a bunch of giggling kids run up and press their hands on the frozen North Pole. "Feel my hand!" one boy yells.

"You see the magic every day and it's so real to the kids," says Matt Stanley, a park operation manager. "If they're on the verge of not believing, after visiting here, they do!"

In fact, when kids walk out of Santa's house, you'll hear them say, "I think that's really him!"

On my visit, I heard a child crying around 4:00 p.m.—and realized that, up to that moment, I hadn't heard a kid cry all day. Why 4:00 p.m.?

"That's because they have to leave!" Stanley explains.

Aw, man! Is it time to leave already?

For more information visit www.northpoleny.com or call (800) 806-0215. And, if you're wondering how many days until Christmas, just check the website—they've got the counter!

✴ ✴

The Jumping Frogs of Herkimer County

Old Forge

If you're a bett'n man, I reckon you're gonna like this next story.

Every Father's Day in Old Forge, people run out and git themselves the most edercated frog they can find, then they bring 'em to town for a frog-jumpin' contest.

You're not allowed to touch the little fellers—that means no punchin' 'em, Smiley—but you can blow on 'em with a straw or cup your hands around 'em to see if that'll get 'em jumpin'.

The winn'n frog is measured by the total distance of one . . . two . . . three! . . . jumps. If you miscalcerlated and got yerself a walkin' frog instead of a jumpin' frog, well, that's gonna cost you. Every step counts as a jump.

There are awards for the fastest frog, fastest business frog (not an MBA-edercated frog, but rather, a frog sponsored by one a them local businesses), heaviest frog, lightest frog, longest jump, and furthest-traveled frog. They also give an award to the dad with the ugliest tie. You reckon yours is uglier'n all the other ties in Herkimer County?

A few tips: Catch 'em the night before. (The frogs, not the ties.) Change the water in the morning, 'cause it gets mighty cold at night and there's nothin' makes a frog more ornery than a cold bum. Don't hold 'em in yer hands too long, neither, because there ain't no award for best baked frog.

You'd best keep 'em in a separate can from them other frogs. Once, there were these two brothers brought their frogs tergether, and when they opened the can, well, let's just say, there was only one frog ther!

Maybe you've had experience with frogs and maybe you're only an amateur. The only requirement is that you can't be a squeamish feller. Dealin' with frogs, now, you're gonna get wet and slimy.

I ain't got no frog, but iff'n I did, I'd bet you that's a dern good way to spend Father's Day!

For more information on the Father's Day Frog Jump, visit www .oldforgeny.com.

★ ★

Synchronized Snowplows
Old Forge

St. Patrick's Day parades tend to have your usual fare: Lots of people dressed in green, politicians, local Irish celebrities, the rotary club, cars advertising local businesses, a marching band, and maybe even some bagpipes.

But in Old Forge, they've got something you don't see every day—synchronized snowplows! It's kind of like synchronized swimming, only—you guessed it—with snowplows!

"Creativity is always the main theme of this parade," says Daniel Roberts, the ringleader of the group. "Along with the usual participants, many groups are secretly making costumes and floats that will be a surprise for this year's parade—they're always trying to outdo themselves from the previous year!"

They get about six to ten snowplows each year and, while you might think that would be complicated to coordinate—it's really not, says Roberts, who does maintenance at the Enchanted Forest Water Safari and admits he's a bit of a MacGyver—he can fix just about anything.

"We get as many trucks in line as we can," Roberts explains. "It's not rocket science. . . . You see the lead plow drop, you drop. We drop the plow at the same time. Rise it at the same time. Angle 'em to the right or angle 'em to the left."

They don't have music. They don't have radios to chat with one another—just follow the leader. "My wife stuck her arm out the window and was giving hand signals—that worked one year," Roberts says.

They don't practice either. A couple of days before the parade Roberts makes a few phone calls to get some guys together.

And the crowd goes wild.

The competition has gotten pretty tough—other acts have started to get more hoots and hollers than the Roberts team has.

✶ ✶

"I'm gonna try to get them to get me in early so we can zip around and go through twice!" Roberts says.

For more information, visit www.oldforgeny.com and click on "events." Though this really is the kind of thing you have to see in person—or on YouTube. Search "synchronized snowplows Old Forge."

And up, down, left, right . . . up, down, left, right . . .
PHOTO BY LISA ROBERTS

★ ★

Dance of the Shopping Carts

Old Forge

Not to be outdone by the snowplows, Old Forge's St. Patty's Day parade also has a team of "Precision Shopping Carts!"

If the plows are like the big dog, moving along slow and steady, the Precision Shopping Cart team is like the little dog, bolting out the front door and running all around.

Dressed in green with Irish flags on their carts, about six to ten cart pushers take off running, hooting and hollering, then form their way into a circle. Then, they form a straight line and pop a wheelie one at a time.

"We go back and forth doing weaves and that kind of stuff," describes Chip Keifer, owner of Souvenir Village in Old Forge and one of the cocreators of the shopping-cart team. "It's a pretty good workout!"

And, while Keifer owns a store—the carts aren't from his store (they don't have them at Souvenir Village), and this isn't about advertising his business.

"Everyone knows where we are," Keifer says of the store. "It's cold in March, so this is about letting loose and having fun!"

And Keifer admits that while their name is Precision Shopping Carts, there isn't a whole lot of precision. Like the snowplows, they don't rehearse. They pick up their shopping carts a few days ahead of time and decorate them. Then just show up and run around.

"It's really just us making a lot of noise!"

And yet, they look so coordinated—and they really do rev up the crowd with all that running and hollering.

The snowplows and shopping carts aren't the only wacky groups out there.

"Every year there are zany groups in the parade," Keifer says. There are the Redheads of Old Forge, where anyone with red hair can march and the Brides of March where—yep, you guessed it—a bunch of ladies dress up like brides. And, one year, the Grand Marshalls were

★ ★

On your mark . . . get set . . . shop!
PHOTO BY MIKE FARMER

The Kellys of Old Forge—basically anyone named Kelly, first or last name.

There's a healthy rivalry for Best in Show, though there aren't any prizes. There's just one traveling trophy with an Irish Santa Claus on top. (Of course there is!) And, the judging is a little unconventional with extra points for how much you suck up to the judges and how decked out in green you are (green clothing, green hair, etc.).

For more information, visit www.oldforgeny.com and click on "events." Or, head to YouTube and search "precision shopping carts Old Forge."

Gentlemen, rev your shopping carts!

The Olympic Prison

Ray Brook

If you've ever been to Lake Placid, looked around and said, "Gee, where did they put everyone during the Olympics?" here's your answer: prison.

That's right, they threw them in prison! Welcome to America! As a gesture of goodwill and peace, we've got your cell right here!

No, no. It wasn't like that. Here's what happened:

Hosting the Olympics is expensive. So much so, that the Lake Placid Club, which is the reason the Olympics ever came to Lake Placid in the first place, was forced to shut down under a mound of debt following the 1980 games.

So, that year, Lake Placid got a little help from the federal government. But, there was one teensy-tiny stipulation: As soon as the Olympics were over, the Olympic Village dormitories that housed the athletes were to be converted into a prison.

The Olympic Village was built seven miles from Lake Placid in Ray Brook, halfway between the host city and Saranac Lake, as a security precaution after eleven Israeli athletes and coaches were killed at the 1972 Olympics in Munich. One small mountain road went in and out, there were twelve-foot high chain-link fences, and the dormitories had narrow windows.

In other words, with apologies to the athletes who had to stay there, it was a perfect prison!

Today, the Adirondack Correctional Facility at Ray Brook is a medium-security facility that houses seven hundred inmates.

Aside from Olympic athletes, this place has had some other famous guests, including John Gotti Jr., who spent five years here after winning the gold in racketeering.

You Name It, He's Got It

Rensselaer Falls

Everything in Kyle "Fireball" Hartman's world is an opportunity. But it's not about finding one door that opens; it's about finding 1,000 of them!

Literally, Hartman has a collection of 1,700 doors—and counting—and authentic period hardware. He's also got 1,500 windows, 1,000 shutters, and 80 classic cars. (He got his nickname, "Fireball," for his love of restoring and racing old cars.)

Hartman has a collection of just about everything imaginable, from mannequins and manual washing machines to church pews and antique taxidermy—even a collection of coffins!

River House Wares and Restoration (www.riverhousewares.com) is the name of the architectural salvage business, but the Hartmans call it "Kyle's World."

Kyle's World is housed in three buildings: the main house they call River House; a former Purina Chow Mill–turned–art gallery (run by his wife, Sally); and a replica of an old railroad station that Hartman constructed in 1985 to house the thousands of salvaged items he has for sale.

The main house has a second-story open porch that displays some of Hartman's taxidermy, which he calls his "Dead Head" collection. Hartman strolls the porch like it's a museum you can walk through with a beer, then stops to tell the story of the 150-year-old taxidermic puma. "I took him drinking one night!" Hartman said mischievously. I'm still not exactly sure what happened, but all I know is, there was some sort of scuffle and the puma came home with only one eye!

Out front, there's a '57 Ford Cabover truck body up in a tree house that Hartman built for his son, David.

"Growing up, I didn't have a swing set," David Hartman says, unapologetically. Nope, he had a truck in a tree! Not to mention, a whole front yard full of cars, including a Volkswagen his mom painted to look like "Herbie, the Love Bug."

Ding! Ding! Ding! Now entering Kyle's World station!

They say if you're looking for an odd-shaped window or other hard-to-find item, Hartman probably has two. (Seriously—he buys one to sell and one to keep for himself.)

Kyle's World runs from 208 to 317 Front Street in downtown Rensselaer Falls, which Hartman calls "The Honeymoon Capital of the North Country." Stop by to purchase that hard-to-find restoration item, add to your own collections, or just browse through it as a museum. If you can't find Hartman right away, look for the big kid zipping down Front Street in a golf cart.

Kyle's World is "open by chance or appointment." Call (315) 344-8882 or 344-7247. You can also send him a postcard from anywhere in the world. Mail it to: Kyle 13860 USA.

They'll know *exactly* who you're talking about!

Shall We Vacate?

The Adirondack region is a great vacation destination, but did you know that the word "vacation" originated in the Adirondacks?

By the early 1900s city people had begun to realize that the summer months were prime time for deadly diseases. So, they started "vacating" their homes in the city and heading for the fresh mountain air of the Adirondacks.

This time period was loaded with misconceptions and hoaxes (hello, Cardiff Giant), but if you've been paying attention, you know that there is definitely some truth to feeling better in mountain air. Remember the negative ions of Niagara Falls? Well, there is also a concentration of negative ions around mountains and forests. And guess what? The Adirondack region has both!

So, if you've ever wondered why Americans take a "vacation" instead of a "holiday," like the British, that's why—it came from the need to vacate cities and avoid disease!

Now, who's up for a vacation in New York City?

Living in a Cold War Missile Silo
Saranac

There are unique homes, and there's this house.

During the Cold War, the government built a massive underground missile silo, complete with a launch command center that could withstand a nuclear attack. In the event of an attack, a hatch would open and out of the ground would emerge a gigantic missile, ready to be targeted at the enemy.

When the Cold War ended, that site was decommissioned. And in 1991, it was purchased by Gregory Gibbons, who saw house potential in the 15,000-square-foot underground space. He called in his cousin, builder Bruce Francisco, to transform it into a livable space.

Francisco built an 1,800-square-foot log cabin–style home above ground (it would've been a shame to waste those Adirondack views!) and adapted 2,300 square feet of livable space underground. The underground "home" was built in the launch command center. The area where the missile was stored, the size of a seven-story skyscraper, is still raw space. You wouldn't even know it's there—you open a door

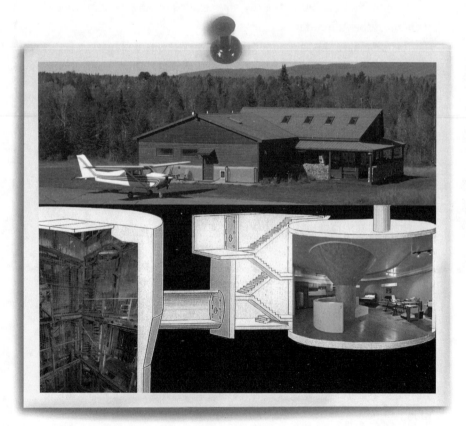

Now that's what I call a man cave!
PHOTO BY BRUCE FRANCISCO

that could easily be a closet, and it goes into a fifty-foot tunnel that leads to the missile silo.

If running around there doesn't bring out the kid in you, I don't know what will!

Francisco also developed a private airport there, so you can get in and out either by road or flying your private plane.

Gibbons lived there for ten years, mostly in the aboveground house, using the underground as his man cave—a man cave that still makes grown men drool!

Now, with a wife and kids, he's ready to give up the ultimate man cave: They're looking to sell it. Francisco said the possibilities are endless. Beyond a man cave, it could be used as a resort, a bed-and-breakfast, a movie set, a recording studio, a corporate meeting center, a data-storage facility, or even a unique dance hall.

In all, the pair own 240 acres of land, which includes the private airport, subdivisions up for sale, and a log cabin 2,000 feet away from the silo home, which they rent out to honeymooners, skiers, or those just looking for a quiet getaway (www.adirondackloghomeforrent.com).

Who knows, maybe the ultimate man cave will become the ultimate man cave resort or a super hot club. Welcome to the Silo . . . *boom ts, boom ts, boom ts . . . .*

For more pictures, videos, and information, visit www.silohome.com.

No Spitting, Please

Saranac Lake

Not only did people vacation in the Adirondacks to avoid deadly diseases, they used to go there to be cured!

Saranac Lake became known as a cure community for tuberculosis after Edward L. Trudeau, infected with TB, went there in 1873, planning to spend his remaining days in a serene mountain setting, only to make a full recovery!

Not one to take his cure and run, Dr. Trudeau set up a facility for other TB patients called the Adirondack Cottage Sanitarium (later

★ ★

renamed the Trudeau Sanatorium), which helped many other patients recover as well. The sanitarium was so popular that it was overflowing, prompting locals to convert their homes into "cure cottages." (This was before they discovered that TB was contagious.) In old photographs, you'll often see the porches of these cure cottages lined with beds so patients could take in the "curative" mountain air.

A Prisoner's Palace

Saranac Lake

What do you get when you mix kindhearted royalty, prison labor, and a famous comic-strip artist?

The Saranac Lake Winter Carnival!

In order to break up the long Adirondack winter, every February, Saranac Lake hosts a ten-day winter carnival, featuring a coronation ceremony of the king, queen, and court, selected for their contributions to the community. There are theatrical performances, sporting events, woodsmen's events, an ice-sculpture contest, an Arctic Bar-B-Que, and funny competitions such as the Ladies' Frying Pan Toss. There are also two parades and two sets of fireworks, set high above the carnival's famous Ice Palace.

It's like Disney World in the Adirondacks! (Only, it eventually melts.)

The Ice Palace is a fifty-foot-high castle built of hundreds of ice blocks chipped out of a nearby lake. Sounds like pretty hard labor, right? Well, you can volunteer if you want to, but, for more than twenty years, they've had a little help from inmates at the nearby Camp Gabriels state prison! (Don't worry, though, it's a

* *

Of course, the air wasn't some magic cure, but it did give a boost to the patients' immune systems. Antibiotics hadn't been invented yet, and the immune system was a patient's only defense against TB.

The patients were encouraged to rest but weren't bedridden. "There were no restricted activities," says architectural historian Mary Hotaling. "So, they went horseback riding—it was like a vacation!" Performers

Sure beats making license plates.

minimum-security facility and the labor is securely monitored.)

Another fun bit of trivia about the festival is that the illustration for the carnival commemorative button is designed by Doonesbury creator Gary Trudeau. Trudeau, the great-grandson of TB-cure community founder Edward Trudeau, spent part of his childhood here and continues to give back to the community by doing the illustration every year for the winter festival.

For more information visit www.saranaclakewintercarnival.com. If you can't make it to the festival, you can pick up a button year-round at the Town Hall on the corner of River and Main Streets in Saranac Lake.

were brought in by the William Morris Agency to entertain patients and raise money; as a result, there are still weekly concerts and theater events in Saranac Lake today.

The Trudeau Institute, now a broader medical research facility, isn't open to the public, but if you're in Saranac Lake, you can see the statue of Dr. Trudeau out front, created by the same artist who designed Mount Rushmore! His former lab, the Saranac Laboratory on Church Street, is being converted into a museum. As you walk around this picturesque mountain town, try to pick out the "cure cottages" by their long porches. Saranac Lake also has a thriving art community and variety of wellness programs.

So head on over to Saranac Lake and take a nice deep breath of that fresh mountain air. Oh! I should warn you: Whatever you do, don't spit! A holdover from the area's TB past, there's still a village "expectoration" law on the books that says you'll be fined up to $250 if you're caught, well, expectorating.

But, seriously. I shouldn't have had to tell you that. You should know better!

For more information visit www.saranaclake.com and www .trudeauinstitute.org.

Getting a Leg Up

Saratoga Battlefield

The map says that stop number seven on the Saratoga Battlefield tour is Breymann Redoubt, commemorating a key win for the American side during the American Revolution.

What they don't play up too much is that there is a monument to Benedict Arnold's leg here!

I guess they *can't* play it up too much, given that whole traitor thing. The inscription on the back of the monument doesn't even mention him by name. Instead, it says, "In Memory of the most brilliant soldier of the Continental Army, who was desperately wounded on this spot . . . 7th October 1777 . . . winning for his countrymen the

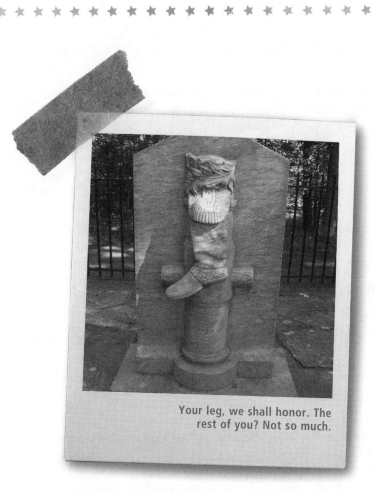

Your leg, we shall honor. The rest of you? Not so much.

Decisive Battle of the American Revolution and for himself the rank of Major General."

You have to remember this was P.T. (pre-treachery) and Arnold was one of the best generals we had. He was crucial in winning the Battle of Saratoga, the turning point of the Revolution. He was severely wounded in the leg during this battle, the same leg that had been injured previously in Quebec.

Purportedly, the monument refers to the response Arnold got from an American soldier he'd taken captive while working for the British army A.T. (after his famous traitorous act). He'd asked the soldier what the Americans would do if they captured him. The soldier replied: "We would cut your leg off and bury it with full military honors for your work at Quebec and Saratoga. The rest of you we would hang."

For the record, it never came to that. After he got busted for trying to surrender West Point to the British and narrowly escaped via the Hudson River, Arnold commanded troops for the British army for a few years and then retired to London, where he died in 1801.

The real leg, incidentally, is buried at St. Mary's Church, Battersea in London, along with the rest of him.

To figure out how to get to that leg monument, visit www.nps.gov/sara or call (518) 664-9821, extension 224.

This Here's a Robbery!
Thendara

Shortly after the train chugged out of Thendara station, a woman came through the aisle in a mighty purdy yellow dress.

"My name is Miss Lill," she said. "I'm handin' out government money just in case somethin' happens. . . . It won't. Naw, we won't need it. But iff'n we do . . ."

We were chattin' it up real nice with Miss Lill when all of a sudden . . . four men appear outside the train window, some on horseback, some firin' guns!

"Dougy, we're going to get robbed!" shouted Sandy Hastings, a fellow passenger across the aisle. Chrissy, in a raspberry derby, giggled excitedly as she looked out the window.

Next thing we know, a few a them bandits boarded the train, bickering. Annie Oakley was hot on their heels, attempting to fight them off, along with the help of some growls and cheers from the kids on the train. But it was no use: We had to hand over that "government money" Miss Lill gave us.

"It's been a pleasure robbin' you today!" one a them bandits shouted, just before we entered Carter station.

**Wait just a dern minute. I thought we wuz
the ones doin' the robbin'?**

On the way back to Thendara, we met some other characters, including a mail-order bride, Miss Prudence, and a man who introduced himself as Sam Wayne. They call him One-Shot Wayne, Quick-Draw Wayne, or Frilly-Knickers Wayne, but don't ask about that!

Outside, the scene unfolds again, and, while the bandits were ultimately defeated in a dramatic shoot-out, we never did get that government money back.

Oh well.

Being from New York City, it seemed odd to pay money to get "robbed" on a train, but here in the Adirondacks, where a friend once said it's so safe you could leave a bag of money in your unlocked car and no one would take it, that's just a fun way to spend the afternoon!

The "Loomis Gang Train Robberies," based on a famous nineteenth-century family of thieves, are held every Wednesday in July and August on the Adirondack Scenic Railroad. Most of the actors come from the Mystery Company theater troupe from Rochester.

You never knew it could be so much fun to get robbed! Hastings makes it a regular part of her summer.

"Chrissy goes every year and Doug has been 'robbed' at least once since then," says Hastings, who's also brought her grandsons Taylor, Andrew, and Cody to be robbed.

The plots and characters are always changing, so you never know who's gonna rob you. Just take my advice and have your government money ready!

For more information visit www.adirondackrr.com or www.mystery company.net.

A Tale of Two Castles
Thousand Islands

There are not one but two castles in the Thousand Islands. They were both built at the turn of the twentieth century, but their stories are quite different. One is a romantic fairy-tale castle, the other is a peculiar mystery-novel castle!

Boldt Castle (www.boldtcastle.com) is better known because it has been open to the public longer. It's called a "Monument to Love" because it was built by George C. Boldt, millionaire proprietor of the Waldorf-Astoria Hotel in New York City, as a Valentine's Day present for his wife, Louise. It's located on Heart Island, and the heart-shaped motif infiltrates every last nook and cranny, from the stained-glass ceiling to the garden—even the island's seawall is in the shape of a heart! Alas, this love story has a tragic ending: Louise died suddenly before the castle was completed. Heartbroken, Boldt immediately ordered all 300 workers to cease construction. He walked away and never returned.

Boldt Castle remained abandoned and unfinished for an astounding seventy-three years, exposed to wind, rain, snow, and vandals. The Thousand Islands Bridge Authority assumed ownership of the castle in

Boldt Castle, the ultimate Valentine's present!

1977 and began the long process of restoration. It remains unfinished today, but you can still take a fascinating self-guided tour.

If Boldt Castle is the princess of castles, then Singer Castle is her black-nail-polish-wearing Goth sister!

Singer Castle (www.singercastle.com), located on the appropriately named "Dark Island," was a private residence for about one hundred years before being opened for public tours in 2003. It was built as a summer home for Frederic Bourne, director of the Singer Sewing Machine Company.

The architect modeled Singer Castle after a castle he read about in Sir Walter Scott's novel, *Woodstock*. There are hidden passageways,

★ ★

accessed through trick bookcases and other clever disguises, and secret lookout spots through ventilation grates and even—how cool, how cliché—through a painting! It was really a child's (i.e., my) fantasy come to life, but the practical application was that the servants would always be able to monitor when someone needed a refill of their drink without ever having to pass through and disrupt the conversation. (Well, excuse me!) There's also a fully equipped dungeon (though never used as one), an underground labyrinth, and lots of odd gadgets, high-tech for their time, including an "electric light-bath cabinet." (There's a reason you've never heard of it!)

Oh, and in case you're wondering, the two millionaire castle owners did indeed know each other. They used to race their speedboats between the two castles.

That is *totally* what I would do if I owned a castle on an island!

You can take a boat to both castles with Uncle Sam Boat Tours in Alexandria Bay (www.unclesamboattours.com).

Are There Really a Thousand?

Thousand Islands

Why do they call them the Thousand Islands? Are there really 1,000 islands in the St. Lawrence River?

In fact, there are actually *more* than 1,000. I guess "One Thousand, Eight Hundred Sixty-Four Islands" was too much of a tongue twister for the French explorers who named the area! The number is technically closer to 2,000, but you can't say Two Thousand Islands because 1) that's just weird, and 2) it's not true!

So, we'll leave it at a cool 1,000 then. Isn't that grand? (Har har.)

(Look, I know this whole thing was decided in French, but my jokes are in English, okay?)

In order to qualify as one of the Thousand Islands, an island has to be at least one foot in diameter, host one tree or shrub, and be above water 365 days a year.

★ ★

The smallest island is Tom Thumb, a three-square-foot hunk of rock with a tree sticking out. Another island is called Just Room Enough because it has just enough room for one house. (How cute is that?) The largest is Wolfe Island, part of Canada, at forty-nine square miles. (The US-Canada border zigzags between the islands.)

Sisters Island is famous because there's a lighthouse going straight through the middle of the island's only house, but the residents carry on about their business like no one notices the big elephant—er, lighthouse—in the middle of the room. Deer Island is owned by a member of the clandestine Skull and Bones society, and the local chapter has held retreats there.

Another fun bit of Thousand Islands trivia is the fact that there are more than one hundred shipwrecks in this channel. (Hey, it's not easy navigating 1,864 islands, cut them some slack!)

And, to answer your other burning question, yes, Thousand Islands salad dressing was invented here!

As the story goes, around the turn of the twentieth century, Sophie LaLonde of Clayton created it and served it to dinner guests. Its public debut was at the Thousand Islands Inn, but it really caught on after George Boldt, hotel magnate and lover extraordinaire, found out about it and started serving it at the Waldorf.

The rest is, as they say, dressing on the salad!

Before you go adding "visit all 1,864" Thousand Islands to your bucket list, you should know that you can't set foot on all of them because most are private. You can visit the islands of Wellesley, Wolfe, Howe, and Simcoe, as well as the St. Lawrence Islands National Park, which is a group of twenty-one islands along the Thousand Islands Parkway in Ontario that are open to the public. So that's twenty-five that are public—that should keep you busy with your bucket list for a while!

For more information, visit www.visit1000islands.com. For a tour check out www.unclesamboattours.com.

Trash Talking on Your Own Island

Thousand Islands

Do you think that you or I could just buy one of the Thousand (1,864) Islands? I mean, if there are so many of them, why not?

The quick answer is: Yes! Anyone can buy an island, since most of them are private property. But it's not as easy as you think, being your own island.

First, winters are cold, so most of the private islands are vacation properties. (Yeah, my second home is an island.) Second, you're going to pay at least half a million for your own island, probably more like a couple million. (OK, I fold. But I'll continue telling the rest of the story in case you're still interested.)

Then, there's the little matter of electricity. Most islands have electricity through underwater cables, as with telephones, says Gary DeYoung, director of the 1000 Islands Tourism Council. Some islands still don't have electricity; they use generators or gas-powered appliances. If you want to have underwater cables installed, here's a reality check: It costs about $150 per foot!

"Internet is a challenge, outside of dial-up," DeYoung said, adding that some islands now use wireless Internet. (Yeah, my island has Wi-Fi.)

Now, it's time to do a little trash talking. There is no curbside pickup on an island, and you can't just throw it overboard—I mean, over porch! Taking out the trash means putting it in your boat and hauling it to the nearest mainland landfill. Each town has a transfer station, DeYoung says.

"It's like when you go grocery shopping," explains Melanie Curley of Thousand Islands Realty. "You put it in your boat and drive it to your island."

OK, whose turn is it to take out the trash?!

You may not even need a car once you get to shore. "The super-market in Alexandria Bay has a dock in its parking lot," DeYoung says, adding that "municipal parking" often includes boat docks.

The key to private-island living, Curley says, is planning ahead. You have to check the weather, so you're not boating to your island in a massive thunderstorm. Plus, she adds: "When you run out of toilet paper, you have to get back in your boat and go back to the mainland!"

Oh, and there are no street numbers on a river. So, in case of an emergency, DeYoung warns to have your GPS coordinates handy!

Grab the Ax, Chainsaw, and This Here Greased Pole!

Tupper Lake

Is your closest lumberjack connection using Brawny paper towels? Wearing a flannel shirt in winter?

Well, put down the paper towels, Nancy, cuz we're headed to the Adirondacks for some good, ol' fashioned lumberjackin' and we're gonna get dirty! (Cue the banjo: Dug, dugga dig a dug dug, doog doo doo . . . digga digga dooga dug doo . . .)

If you want to really experience the mountain life in the Adiron-dacks, head to Tupper Lake in July for the annual Woodsmen's Days

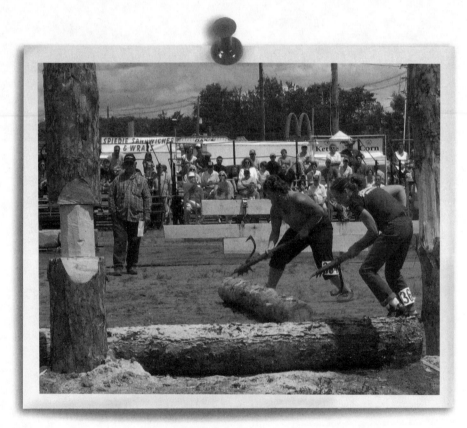

How do you roll a log? You need a really big stick!

(www.woodsmendays.com). The festival features Lumberjack and Lumberjill contests, where men and women compete in log rolling (it's much harder than you think!), ax throwing, tree-felling, and other events. There's also a chainsaw-carving contest; a horse-pull competition; and the pièce de résistance, the Saturday night main event—the greased-pole climb! (It's a team sport, so it's sort of like a mountain-man totem pole with Crisco added.)

It's great entertainment and an excellent opportunity to buy the little missus a chainsaw-carved bear for the porch!

There are at least half a dozen other lumberjack festivals in New York State. They're held throughout the summer, so you can find the one that fits best with your schedule, or spend the whole summer hoppin' from one log roll to the next, like the lumberjack groupie that you are!

The New York State Lumberjack Association website (www.eteamz .com/nylumberjacks/) lists the whole lot of them: Bath (May), Deposit (July), Boonville (August), Stony Creek (August), Clarkson (August), and Macedon (September).

You can do a lumberjack crawl across the state or just friend the lumberjack association on Facebook by searching for "New York State Lumberjack Association."

You never knew there was so much elbow grease in New York State, did you?

Directions to the Funny Farm
Warrensburg

When people used to drive by the late Forrest Lanfair's house on East Schroon River Road in Warrensburg, they slowed down. Some got out of the car. Others walked right up on the lawn to see what the heck was going on there!

Lanfair, a former postmaster and self-taught artist, had created dozens of life-size comical sculptures on his lawn: a farmer and his horse,

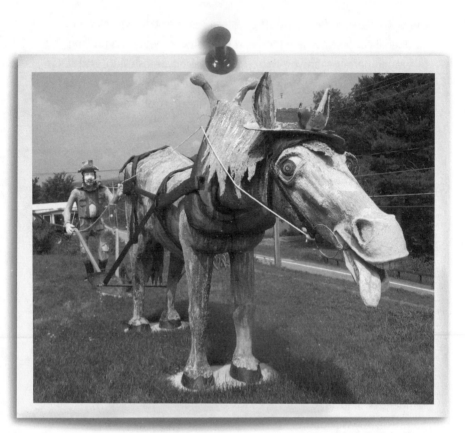

Looking for the funny farm? You found it, buddy!

the farmer's wife chasing a goat with a broom, a cave family, a tree family, a couple of town drunks, an elf—even an Adirondack skeeter!

He called it "Fun & Farm," which he told the *Glens Falls Post Star* was a play on "funny farm."

When Lanfair passed away in 2003, his daughter inherited the house and lawn museum, but she died a few years later after a brief illness. Lanfair was a private man, and his wish was that, when he died, someone would dig a hole and bury the sculptures. But his daughter's family was left with big medical bills, and they decided to sell or auction most of the collection, much to the delight of longtime fans such as Bill Dow and Susie West.

Dow, who owns the Boardwalk Restaurant and Lake George Steamboat Company (www.lakegeorgesteamboat.com) in Old Forge, bought a dozen of the sculptures, including the town drunks (er, let's call them lamppost people) and an elf, which is perched on the restaurant's wooden railing, as well as the skeeter, a pig, a cow, a lady being butted by a goat, and a couple of Revolutionary War heroes.

A few others were sold to Magic Forest, a small theme park in Lake George, according to an article in *Adirondack Life* magazine.

Perhaps the most popular, the farmer, with his belly poking out of his worn-out shirt, and his tired old horse, with its tongue lolling out, were bought at auction by West, Lanfair's first cousin once removed (Lanfair's mother and West's grandfather were siblings).

The farmer and horse were, like many of the concrete and mesh sculptures, in pretty bad shape. The horse had two broken legs and needed a lot of repairs. West recalls, "My husband said, 'Can you believe my wife bought a dead horse?!'"

How does that expression go—if you can't beat a dead horse, join him?!

The Wests repaired the sculptures, added cement bases, and today proudly display them on their front lawn on Route 418, across from Schroon River.

So, if you think you're about ready for the funny farm, drive around Old Forge and Warrensburg and you'll find it!

Southeast, the Catskills & Hudson Valley

4

Southeast, the Catskills & Hudson Valley

Fender Rockets and Sleeping Beer

The southeastern part *of New York has long been a getaway for weary city folk, with plenty of restful spots nestled in the Catskill Mountains and in the picturesque Hudson Valley.*

As you're driving to your little chalet—well, here they call them motels—you'll soon realize the area's got a knack for kitsch— everything from an oversize fork at, appropriately, a fork in the road, to the world's largest garden gnome.

It was on the way to the world's largest kaleidoscope (of course) that a friend and I discovered one of the best curiosities—rockets made from 1950s car parts shooting out of the ground at Steve Heller's Fabulous Furniture on Route 28. And, if you've ever said, "Oh, I'd love to have my own castle—if only I were rich," then you need to go to Millbrook to meet Peter Wing, a man who built his own castle out of found objects.

Speaking of castles, little known fact: They're great for storage of explosives or other items you might have lying around, as you'll learn at Bannerman Castle on Pollepel Island in the Hudson River.

A few words of advice before you go: If you're touring Howe Caverns, shhhhhhhhhhh! Be quiet or you'll wake the beer. And, if you're in Canajoharie, always stay to the right of the Dummy Light.

A Little Nippy Up There

Albany

On the outskirts of Albany, a four-ton dog sits on top of the Arnoff building, with his head cocked like maybe he just heard the word "treats."

If he looks familiar, that's because this building used to house an RCA distributor, and he's Nipper, the famous dog from the RCA ads. This fiberglass-and-steel-mesh Nipper was erected in 1954. Many RCA buildings used to have Nippers like this one; only this one and another in Baltimore remain.

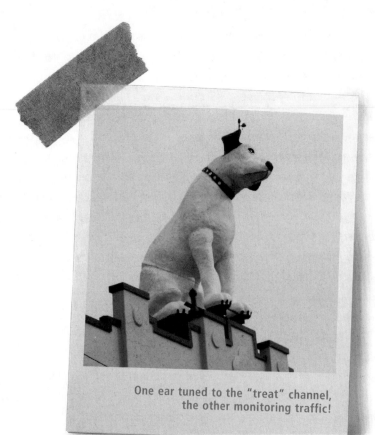

One ear tuned to the "treat" channel, the other monitoring traffic!

He's an old dog, that's for sure: The real Nipper, whom the statue was based on, was a bull terrier/fox terrier mix born in 1884 in Bristol, England. He got his name because he liked to nip at the back of people's ankles.

After Nipper died in 1895, his owner, a struggling artist named Francis Barraud, painted a famous picture of Nipper looking into the bell of a phonograph. Nipper was, apparently, puzzled by where the voices were coming from when the phonograph was on. The title, *His Master's Voice,* suggests that maybe he was listening to the voice of his former owner, Francis's deceased brother Mark. (Or maybe it suggests the painter was having a hard time selling the painting.)

The painting was ultimately bought by the Gramophone Company in 1899. Nipper became a trademark for HMV Records and RCA. "His Master's Voice" also became the name of a record label. RCA updated the Nipper ads in 1991 with a little Nipper-snapper named Chipper; actor dogs continue to play both dogs today.

The Nipper-topped building in Albany is now home to Arnoff Moving and Storage Company, but these guys just can't bear to let an old dog down.

The real Nipper is buried under some magnolia trees in a London park. The original painting resides at EMI Music's Gloucester Place headquarters, also in London. And the big dog, well, he sits on the Arnoff building at Broadway and Tivoli Streets, listening to the sound of the cars whizzing by.

Panda, the Seeing-Eye Horse
Bethlehem

Some blind people use a cane to navigate. Others use a guide dog.

Ann Edie uses a guide horse!

Edie has been guided by Panda, a two-and-a-half-foot-tall black-and-white miniature pony, since 2003. Panda is one of three or four Seeing Eye horses in the United States.

"I go a lot of different places with my job," says Edie, a

special-education teacher. The main reason to have a guide animal is that it "allows me to travel more smoothly and faster than with a cane."

But isn't it hard getting around with a horse?

Nope. Edie says she takes Panda everywhere—grocery stores, hotels, train stations—even bookstores.

What about restaurants? Surely they turn away a woman with a horse.

What's a girl have to do to get a carrot around here?

Nope! "We always get the best service when I take Panda," Edie explains. "All the waiters fight over who gets to wait on the table with the horse!"

"The only place I've had a problem is with airlines," Edie goes on. "The FAA has some concerns about her size. Unlike a dog, she doesn't fit under the seat!"

That's true. So, why a horse instead of a dog?

It costs less to feed a horse than a dog, Edie says. Plus, dogs are more easily distracted by small animals. Horses are more deliberate in their footing and can identify overhead obstacles like tree branches that dogs can't reach. Perhaps most importantly, horses live up to thirty years longer than dogs.

Panda taps her foot to let Edie know when to step up, and puts her nose up to doorknobs to guide Edie's hand. If Panda needs to go out to her shed in the backyard to see a man about a—never mind—she rings a jingle bell on a doorknob with her nose. She might even nibble on some grass while she's out there.

Inside—yes, she's allowed inside—Panda enjoys playing Frisbee and other retrieval games. And, when Edie's chopping vegetables in the kitchen, you'll find her glued to Edie's side, hoping for a handout.

You truly haven't lived until you've heard the clip-clip of a horse's hoofs on the kitchen linoleum!

For more information about horses as guide animals, visit www.the clickercenter.com.

Fabulous Fender Rockets

Boiceville

Steve Heller makes beautiful—sorry, *fabulous*—organic-shaped wooden furniture out of odd or misshapen trees that he and his team retrieve themselves.

But the first thing you notice when you drive by Steve Heller's Fabulous Furniture on Route 28 in the Catskills is that there are rockets shooting out of the front lawn!

★ ★

These lawn rockets are just a hint of what's
inside at Steve Heller's Fabulous Furniture.

Wait a minute, is that a fender?!

Heller's been looking for old trees to carve since his paper-route
days, and he started tinkering with recycled metal from his father's
scrap collection. But Heller says his real passion is cars.

He takes the fins off of 1950s cars—his favorite make is Cadillac—
and seamlessly welds them together to create these amazing rockets
and spaceships.

"I'm just putting them back together the way they should've
been!" Heller says.

He also turns vintage car parts into furniture; those big Caddy trunks, if you stand them upright, make a great bookshelf. And the taillights? Of course, a floor lamp!

"My father took me to the Museum of Modern Art when I was a kid," Heller says. "I saw Picasso's *Baboon and Young.* The head of the baboon was two toy cars put together. It freaked me out! I knew from then that this is what I needed to do."

An old cement mixer becomes a spaceship. An unwanted box of wrenches becomes a flame-shooting, soapbox-derby-winning wrenchosaurus!

His masterpiece is a brand-new Mercury Marquis that he stripped and restored with 1950s car parts from ten different cars. So, it's vintage on the outside, brand-new on the inside! It seems implausible, but Heller pops open the trunk and you can see where the old trunk ends and the new one begins. Or, wait, is it the other way around?

On this sleepy stretch of Route 28, Steve Heller's Fabulous Furniture is a magical glitch in the matrix, where things go in broken down and come out transformed into something amazing.

The only thing that's bugging me is the "fabulous" part. Heller is a cool, laid-back biker-type dude, the kind of guy you want to grab a beer with after you buy something from him. He just doesn't strike me as the kind of guy who would use the word "fabulous."

Well, unless it was #*@%-ing fabulous.

Which it is.

Check him out at www.fabulousfurnitureon28.com or call (845) 750-3035.

Wait. You know what? Don't do that. Just go. Trust me.

The Dummy Light
Canajoharie

Five roads converge on the small town of Canajoharie, making it necessary in the days before cars to have a policeman directing traffic.

There was also a monument, with built-in bowls for the horses to drink water, right in the middle of the five-way intersection!

★ ★

When the automobile came along, it became a lot more dangerous. In 1926 they moved the monument to a nearby park and installed one of those newfangled pedestals, or "dummy" lights, to direct traffic with lights that turned red, yellow, and green.

It was all very confusing. No one knew what any of those lights meant. So, the *Canajoharie Courier* printed lengthy instructions, including: "Go ahead on GREEN and stop on RED." It advised caution when making a left turn and set the conditions for turning right on red. "Cut out this summary and paste in your hat," it said.

Please, get it right.

You can imagine the scene that followed: When approaching the intersection, people were taking their hats off, left and right, to consult the directions!

When the new wave of technology brought hanging traffic lights, the state wanted to replace the dummy light, but the people of Canajoharie protested and the state backed down. Today, there are two traffic lights in Canajoharie, and, you guessed it, the dummy light is one of them! It's one of only a few dummy lights left in the United States.

There's a sign on the pedestal that says keep right so, even if you're making a left turn, you stay to the right of the light to avoid an accident. Not everyone gets that, and, let's just say, people notice.

"People just abuse it," says Barbara Spraker, the unofficial town historian, wearing an "I Have Seen the Light!" dummy light T-shirt. "They disrespect it."

They may not know how to use it, but they've all seen the light.

"Anyone who's been here knows that light," says Phyllis Lapi, owner of the Picture Perfect Art Gallery in downtown Canajoharie. "My husband was stationed in Guam. We met people and they asked where in the US we were from. When we told them Canajoharie, they said, 'Oh, that town with the light!'"

Now, if only everyone who drives past it would learn how to use it!

Someone Had to Do It

Canajoharie

H-h-hey, are you throwing out that paper bag? Before you do, let me tell you something about that bag.

It was during the Civil War, and cotton was scarce. Canajoharie businessman James Arkell started tinkering with some paper and what do you know? He invented the paper bag!

It was a much bigger deal than creating a vehicle for your five-patty burger and supersize jumbolicious fries. It freed up cotton supplies, making more available for bandages for the Union troops.

★ ★

"Imagine the ingenuity to take paper, lay it out, put folds in it and put it through a machine to glue it together," remarks Barbara Spraker, the unofficial town historian of Canajoharie. "You don't just put the paper in there and it comes out a paper bag!"

Arkell and Smith, as the company was known, had struck gold—well, paper—and the business expanded rapidly. They made paper bags for just about anything you can think of—sugar, salt, dog food, fertilizer, cement, you name it.

Everyone in Canajoharie has either worked at the Arkell factory or knows someone who did. "When you were a new employee," recalls local resident Sue Beaver, "they'd send you out to look for the bag stretcher!" (There wasn't one.)

Arkell's son, Bartlett, inherited his father's nose for business and went on to found the Beech-Nut Packing Company with a few other business partners. It's Arkell money, says Spraker, that has kept the town going. So, if you're driving through and think to yourself, "Wow! That's a really nice museum for a small town," you know it was made possible by ham, ketchup, peanut butter, gum, baby food—and paper bags!

There's a mural of James Arkell and his great invention, with nurses applying bandages to Union troops in the background, at the Canajoharie Post Office on Main Street.

For more on Arkell and Beech-Nut, visit www.arkellmuseum.org.

Seng It from the Mountaintops
Catskill

Mark Twain's dad was into it. So was Daniel Boone. Ditto for John Jacob Astor, one of the richest men in US history. Heck, Bob Beyfuss has a shoulder-to-elbow tattoo of it!

I am, of course, referring to ginseng, a root known for its energy-enhancing and youth-preserving abilities. Some say it can alleviate fatigue in cancer patients and that it has other . . . um . . . uplifting effects.

★ ★

The United States has been exporting the coveted herb for nearly 300 years, and New York, particularly the Catskill region, is known to have some of the best soil in the world for growing ginseng. "One guy—he was from Ohio or Virginia—called New York ginseng, 'ginseng on steroids'!" recalls Dr. Beyfuss, former agriculture and natural resources educator with the Cornell Cooperative Extension in Greene County who has studied ginseng for more than thirty years.

The most potent is wild ginseng, grown in the woods. The older and more gnarly the root, the better. The theory is that, when a plant lives a long time, it accumulates a strong chi (pronounced "chee"), or life force, that is transferred to you when you consume it raw, in tea, or as an elixir. You can tell how old a root is because it has scars for each year, like rings on a tree stump.

If you're wondering what rock you've been under that you've never heard of New York ginseng, that's because it's a pretty secretive business. (Think *The Orchid Thief* meets fountain of youth.) Growers won't even tell you where their ginseng farms are for fear of poachers. They protect their crops with cameras, motion detectors, dogs—even guns.

Sure, you can buy a bottle of ginseng tablets at a health-food store for sixteen dollars, but it's not the same. When Beyfuss was at Cornell (he has since retired) he organized an annual Catskill Ginseng Festival. There, it wasn't uncommon to find Ziploc bags of wild ginseng root marked $500 and $1,000 per pound! A really old root can run into the thousands—*plural.*

Beyfuss says he's had people offer to pay him $1,000 just to show them where the ginseng is!

Now, don't go getting all starry-eyed that you're going to get rich quick on ginseng; it takes a minimum of eight to ten years to mature. And no Meryl Streep/Chris Cooper–type adventures looking for the secret ginseng farms, OK? Next thing you know, you get shot, someone gets arrested, and I'm hauled in for questioning.

But maybe, the next time you're driving through the sleepy Catskills, you'll look at those forest-covered mountains just a little bit differently.

⭐ ⭐

Bob Beyfuss may just be the only man in the world with a ginseng tattoo.

Today, Beyfuss does consultations for city people who buy property in the Catskills—helping them identify all the plants on their land and how to care for them. He also sells about twenty pounds of ginseng seeds each fall and about five to ten pounds of wild or wild-simulated ginseng root.

Beyfuss's tattoo, incidentally, shows a ginseng plant with everything from leaves to roots.

"I got it back in 2000 after my second wife left," Beyfuss says. "I figured I was due for a midlife crisis and the tattoo was cheaper than a sports car—and it will last longer!"

If you're curious how one finds himself with a ginseng tattoo, here's how the story goes: Beyfuss met a botanical illustrator who was putting together some woodland illustrations but was unable to find a ginseng plant to draw. Beyfuss let her sketch one of his and even pulled it up so she could see the roots. She gave him a portrait of the sketch as a thank-you. Beyfuss took one look at it and immediately thought: tattoo! He met a tattoo artist who offered to charge him a much lower rate—just to have the tattoo in his portfolio.

"It has served me remarkably well in these past twelve years!" Beyfuss says.

Wait, does that mean it gives him street cred in the ginseng world or helps him pick up chicks?!

Could be both—but Beyfuss only admits to the former. He says he's famous in the ginseng world because of it. It's also the reason that he gets people in the heart of Appalachia to agree to talk to a Yankee!

"It has opened doors and led me to places I never would have been able to access without it," Beyfuss explains.

For more information about Beyfuss and purchasing his ginseng, visit https://sites.google.com/site/drbobsginseng/.

Sign Here for the Chili

Cherry Valley

Few things say Americana like a four-story (fifty-five-foot) tepee.

As you drive by it, you can't help but wonder why someone would go to all the trouble. . . . Your inner monologue brakes only after a hair-raising shout of "CAN WE STOP?!" from the backseat.

You know it's inevitable. Oh yeah. You're stopping at the tepee.

The TePee (that's literally what it's called), on Route 20 in Cherry Valley, was built in 1950 and has all the makings of a typical tourist trap, but the current owners, sisters Donna and Dale Latella, have a great eye. It's a really well-done gift shop.

Native Americans in this area never actually lived in tepees (they lived in longhouses), but the native gifts at the TePee—such as

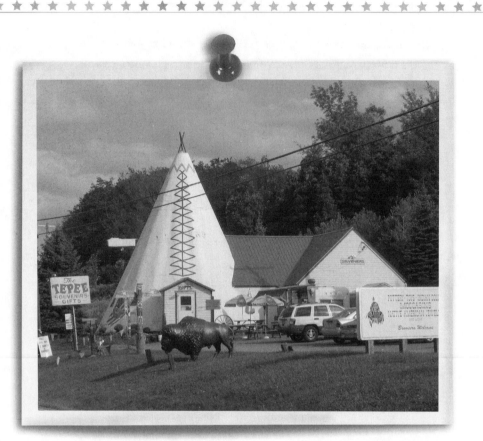

We come in peace, prepared to sign the Great Chili
Treaty of Cherry Valley.

deerskin moccasins and dream catchers—are authentically native-made. The shop also has a beautiful selection of jewelry, pottery, pewter, wood carvings, and more. The TePee-branded items are also surprisingly tasteful, like the tiny tepee in a snow globe and the TePee Taffy!

Next door is TePee Pete's Chow Wagon, operated by Donna and Dale's brother, Pete. Sure, he serves your average roadside fare of hamburgers and hots, but he's also got a few items you didn't see coming, including hot apple salsa, red tart cherry salsa, buffalo burgers, and Pete's special Seven-Pepper Chili, the only chili for which you'll ever have to sign a release form! (Seriously, you can't eat it if you don't sign it!)

Picnic tables between the TePee and Chow Wagon make for one of the most pleasant roadside stops in the entire state. Just try to be discreet if you order a buffalo burger; don't brandish it in front of Buffy the Buffalo, the fiberglass beauty who's been keeping watch on Route 20 for the past twenty-five years!

Pete is humble. "I am just a guy with a pot of chili and a dream," he says. But, the reviews on www.tripadvisor.com speak for themselves—he's the #1 restaurant in Cherry Valley, and he's just a wagon next to a giant tepee!

This one time is worth giving in to the backseat contingency.

The TePee and TePee Pete's Chow Wagon are located at 7632 US Highway 20. For more information visit www.thetepee.biz or call (607) 264-3987.

Get Your Knickers Straight

Cherry Valley

When moviemakers need an army of tweed knickers, where do they go?

Do they scour vintage stores until they find the fifty pairs of pants they need? Do they buy imitation tweed and ask the costume designers to just fake it?

No, they call Rabbit Goody, who runs Thistle Hill Weavers, a textiles manufacturer that reproduces seventeenth-, eighteenth-, and nineteenth-century fabrics for vintage clothing as well as historic homes (curtains, bedspreads, rugs) and vintage automobiles.

As we're sitting in her office, in walks the FedEx guy with a letter and swatch of fabric from a movie producer. Goody inspects the gray herringbone wool with her magnifying glass. "What's neat about this is that it has a colored yarn in it. You see? It has a purple thread in it!"

Her clients usually send a swatch of fabric, but sometimes they include a whole article of clothing. "We'll have a brief overnight visit

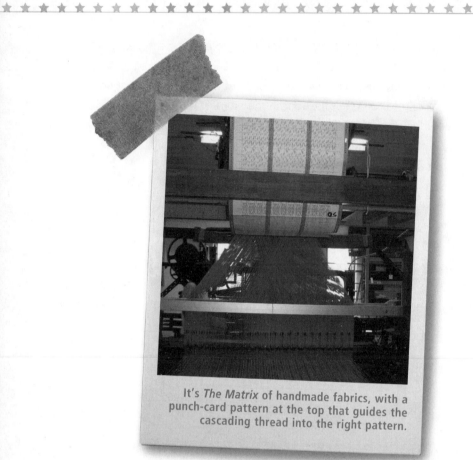

It's *The Matrix* of handmade fabrics, with a punch-card pattern at the top that guides the cascading thread into the right pattern.

from the pants if necessary," Goody says matter-of-factly, as if the pants were in-laws.

Thistle Hill made the fabric for the children's World War II–era clothing in *The Chronicles of Narnia: The Lion, the Witch, and the Wardrobe,* the striped prison fabric in *O Brother, Where Art Thou?,* and the fabric for Tom Hanks's suit in *Road to Perdition,* among other films. They've also done fabric for *Lincoln,* directed by Stephen Spielberg, and TV miniseries "John Adams."

What makes the shop unique, Goody says, is that it can make smaller-quantity orders than big commercial mills. Thistle Hill has a twenty-yard minimum; most mills won't run a fabric order for less than 5,000 yards.

"Companies in China can't do custom," Goody says. "That's our niche."

Most of the equipment was purchased secondhand from mills going out of business. Only one loom is computerized; the rest are old hand-run looms, guided by a pattern punched in paper.

Doing things by hand has been a lifelong philosophy for Goody, who has a degree in anthropology and lived without electricity for fifteen years. "I didn't need a generator," Goody says. "I wanted to use systems that were in place 200 years ago."

So, the next time you need a pair of 200-year-old pants, you know whom to call.

For more information visit www.thistlehillweavers.com or call (518) 284-2729. To find out their latest movie and other projects, friend them on Facebook. Just search "Thistle Hill Weavers."

The Odd Cave Couple
Cobleskill

Much like the Thousand Islands has its tale of two castles, so Cobleskill has a dark tale of two very different caves. (Literally, it's dark down there!)

Howe Caverns is like the Disney World of caves, with its preppy-jacketed guides and brick path. Secret Caverns, by contrast, is like the Grateful Dead's underground den, with goateed guides and uneven stairs.

You know something is different about Secret Caverns by the psychedelic billboards you encounter on your way to the cave. There are graphics of cavemen, dinosaurs, and bats, with cheeky slogans such as "Like a Limestone Cowboy: Secret Caverns" and "Four out of Five Dentists Prefer Our Cavity." One billboard was upside down and said something like, "You'll Flip for Secret Caverns!" (I nearly wrecked the rental car on that one!)

Howe's slogans, meanwhile, would be what they call tongue-in-cheek. (Try to suck your cheeks in a little when you say that.) "It's the 'Coolest' Place Around!" Howe's marketing department jests, adding, "Let Us Show You Howe!"

You descend to Howe Caverns via an elevator with two buttons: "L" for Lodge and "C" for Cave. (I actually did laugh at that one!) At Secret Caverns, you take the stairs, buddy.

At Howe Caverns, they'll tell you what a "cave kiss" is: drips of water from calcite. At Secret Caverns, you'll learn what "cow snot" is—flowstone.

Howe Caverns has "Titan's Temple," a sixty-five-foot-high room with great acoustics, and a "Bridal Altar," with a six-inch piece of semitransparent heart-shaped calcite set in the brick floor and lit from below. Secret Caverns has cave formations it calls "The Cavern Monster" and "Alligator."

Howe Caverns will encourage you to come caroling in the cave at Christmas, or to have your wedding at the bridal altar. Steve, our guide at Secret Caverns, stresses: "Being cold, wet, and miserable is crucial to the cave experience!" (It wasn't, but it's the thought that counts!)

The pièce de résistance at Howe is an underground boat ride on the Lake of Venus, while the big guitar-slammin' finish at Secret Caverns is a 100-foot waterfall.

I would take my mom to Howe Caverns and my teenage son (if I had one) to Secret Caverns, but personally, I think everyone should go to both!

For more information visit www.secretcaverns.com and www.howe caverns.com.

★ ★

No, I Declared Before You Declared

Coxsackie

When in the course of human events it becomes necessary to hit the panic button, let us hold these truths to be self-evident, maintain our God-given right to live . . . oh, and I call shotgun!

Concerned by the violence they were seeing as the American Revolution began, more than 200 Coxsackie residents got together in 1775, a year before the US Declaration of Independence, and whipped up their own declaration!

Known as the Coxsackie Declaration of Independence, the document was signed at the Bronck House, now a museum, and later found in an Albany attic by the former president of the Albany Institute of History & Art, where it remains today.

The signers were "convinced of the necessity of preventing the anarchy and confusion" that come with a revolution. They declared that they were "never to become slaves" and agreed to associate based on religion, honor, and love of their country. (Mm hmm. Mm hmm. I'm with you . . .)

They opposed the execution of "several arbitrary and oppressive acts of the British Parliament." (Yeah! Darn, right!) But here's where it gets weird. The rest of that sentence reads: "until a reconciliation between Great Britain and America or constitutional principles . . . can be obtained."

"If you read it, it wasn't a declaration of independence at all!" the late Ray Beecher, a former Greene County historian, said in an interview before his death in 2008. "What it did was reaffirm allegiance to the king of Great Britain!"

Oops. Maybe that's why someone buried it in the attic. Thank goodness for that *other* declaration!

The Cradle of the Cave

Cobleskill

Howe Caverns may be the Disney World of caves but there's something unexpected lurking under that tarp around the corner. No, it's not Gollum hiding out until the *Lord of the Rings* reunion special. It's beer and cheese!

Fly Creek Cidermill has a couple hundred pounds of McCadam's (what else) New York cheddar aging in the cave and Cooperstown's Ommegang Brewery has a couple hundred cases of Belgian-style beer down there.

The cave provides perfect conditions: At 156 feet below ground, the temperature remains at fifty-two degrees Fahrenheit year-round.

Cave aging isn't a new concept; it's how they used to age beer and wine before refrigeration, and it's still used in the Champagne region of France today.

"We set out to replicate as closely as possible the conditions that produce extraordinary champagnes," says former Ommegang brewmaster Randy Thiel. "There is no doubt that these dark, silent, subterranean 'cathedrals' are the ideal surroundings for secondary fermentation and maturation of wines (and beers)."

For beer, keeping it between fifty and fifty-five degrees slows the maturation and leads to greater complexity, Thiel says.

As for the cheese, the cool temperature and humidity of the cave allow the cheese "to age and mellow far better than other methods," according to Fly Creek. "The result: a sharper yet smoother New York cheddar." You can buy some of the cave-aged cheddar at Howe's gift shop and decide for yourself.

In the fall, the cave hosts a "Waking the Beer" party, with hors d'oeuvres and beer tasting to properly welcome the beer into the drinking world.

Until then, shhhhhhhhhhhhhh! Keep your voice down or you'll wake the beer!

CAVERN MONSTER

Look out for cavern monsters and beer
when you're spelunking in Cobleskill!

Cradle of the Trotter
Goshen

Goshen, New York, has had a long, historic love affair with horses. As early as the 1750s, people were racing horses down Main Street. In 1838, a circular track was installed—and it's now the oldest horse-racing facility in use in the United States.

But after the arrival in 1801 of an English thoroughbred known as Messenger, who took up residence at the stable of Anthony Dobbin's Stagecoach Inn, it earned a new title—"Cradle of the Trotter."

Step right up. Have a seat. And hold on tight!
COURTESY OF ORANGE COUNTY TOURISM

Harness racing is a form of horse racing in which the horses pull a two-wheeled cart, which requires a specific gate or trot.

Messenger's offspring "showed an inclination toward a new gait, a long, slinging step at the walk which, when accelerated, produced the trotting gait," according to the Harness Racing Museum & Hall of Fame, which is now located here.

Today, Goshen and the surrounding area are known for their Standardbred farms that continue to produce champions.

The Harness Racing Museum & Hall of Fame was set up in 1951 in a building that was erected as a stable in 1913. Here, you'll find everything from historic bronze horse statutes and iconic examples of harness-racing advertising to drivers' uniforms and a 3-D simulator so you can *really* feel what it's like to be in the driver's seat. They have horse-themed games, interactive exhibits for the kids, and even a summer camp. Plus, lectures such as "How to Drive a Standardbred" and "How to Spot a Fake." Inspired by William H. Macy in *Seabiscuit?* They also have a workshop on how to be a race announcer and call a race.

And, if all that has you wanting to see the horses in action, the Goshen Historic Track is right behind the museum.

For more information, visit www.harnessmuseum.com and www .goshenhistorictrack.com.

The Kiltmaker's Apprentice
Highland

So, you're getting married and you want to wear a kilt to honor your Scottish heritage.

N-n-no, wait. I know. You and your buddies are going to a *Braveheart* reenactment and you're gonna need a kiltload of that special Mel Gibson tartan.

Have I got the place for you!

And guess what? It doesn't involve a trip to Scotland!

On the west bank of the Hudson River, in a hamlet appropriately named Highland, is the Kiltmaker's Apprentice, a shop devoted entirely

I SAID it's a sporran, not a purse!

to handmade kilts. They order all of their tartan fabrics from Scotland and will even special order your family tartan.

If you're not up for the commitment of owning your own kilt, you can rent one from them—even if you live in California! In fact, the owners, Doreen and Robert Browning, say they do most of their business over the Internet.

It's not just kilts: You can buy the whole Celt-lovin' getup, from the Prince Charlie jacket to a belt, hose, and shoes. Of course, you're gonna need a sporran, which is a man-purse-type thing, because kilts don't have pockets. "That was probably the original fanny pack!" Bob says.

They've really thought of everything, from a tartan bridal gown to a camouflage kilt for the soldiers in Iraq—even a bride and kilt-wearing groom cake topper!

They even do alterations on kilts—in case, um, yours shrunk in the closet. It's apparently a common request to have a kilt let out. That closet joke was on the home page of their website!

Doreen says the most common question they get is: What's worn beneath a kilt? Bob jumps in with the *correct* answer: "Nothing is worn beneath the kilt; it's all in working order!"

Visit the Kiltmaker's Apprentice at 54 Vineyard Avenue in Highland (800-859-KILT) or order online at www.highlandkiltshop.com.

The Octagon House

Irvington-on-Hudson

On West Clinton Avenue in Irvington, on a hill overlooking the Hudson River, there's a unique octagon-shaped house, done in an ornate Victorian style.

Whether you're taking a walk or a bike ride, it's sure to catch your eye. In shades of red, pink, blue, and gray, with a patterned dome resembling an Oriental rug, the house is mesmerizing. You half expect there to be magical things going on in there, like in the movie *Mr. Magorium's Wonder Emporium.*

"It looks like some eccentric astronomer lives there," says Frederick LaSenna, a local resident. Looking at the circular windows on top, you wonder, "Is there a telescope in there?" LaSenna goes on.

"You half expect the roof to sliver open, revealing this steampunk astronomer in goggles, gazing at the stars through his telescope!" LaSenna adds.

Wait, is that a telescope I see?
PHOTO BY FREDERICK LASENNA

Known as the Armour-Stiner House, or Carmer Octagon House, the place was built between 1859 and 1860 by financier Paul J. Armour. The dome was added during a renovation between 1872 and 1876 by tea importer Joseph Stiner. Octagon houses were actually quite a common style during this time period, but this is thought to be one of the most lavish—and one of the few with a domed roof.

Historian Carl Carmer lived there from 1946 to 1976 and maintained that the house was haunted. As the story goes, a young girl that once lived there fell in love with a neighbor, but the family of the boy disapproved. They set out to run away to New York, just twenty miles away, by steamboat, but the boiler of the ship burst and the entire ship caught fire. Both perished. When the girl's body was returned to the house in a pine box, an angry woman refused to accept it.

In the book, *Portrait of a Village: Wolfert's Roost, Irvington-on-Hudson,* Carmer explains that, on several occasions, his wife had woken at the end of a strange dream where she said she saw a girl walking up the driveway, surrounded in a mellow, golden light. An older woman darts out and blocks her path but the two later reconcile.

Fittingly, the house was the setting for the 1981 horror film *The Nesting,* about a Gothic mystery writer who moves into this eerie Victorian mansion that was once a brothel and is now haunted by the ghost of a madam.

The house, designated a National Historic Landmark in 1976, was sold to preservationist architect Joseph Pell Lombardi, who describes it as having the "domed colonnade shape of a classic Roman temple." It's also been described as looking like "an arrested carousel," Lombardi writes on his website.

The house, which remains a private residence today, is located at 45 West Clinton Avenue in Irvington.

Hello, My Gnome Is Chomsky
Kerhonkson

Gnomes have been gknown to nap in the garden. Guard treasures. Get you good deals on hotel rooms.

This one welcomes you to what may be the world's only edible minigolf course and—oh, how sweet, you shouldn't have—he's picked you a bouquet of wildflowers!

His name is Chomsky (Get it? Gnome Chomsky), and at thirteen feet, six inches tall, he is officially the world's largest garden gnome.

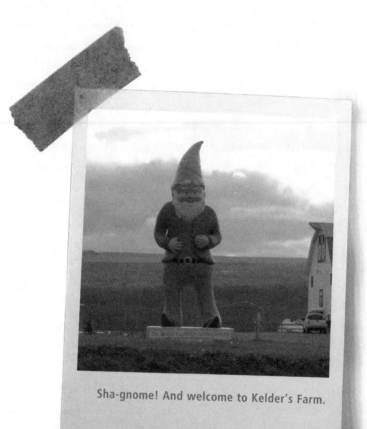

Sha-gnome! And welcome to Kelder's Farm.

He stands on Route 209 in front of Kelder's Farm and Homegrown Mini-Golf, a ten-hole course landscaped with real fruits, vegetables, herbs, and the occasional chicken!

In the summer Chomsky often holds a bouquet of wildflowers, since the farm features pick-your-own flowers as well as vegetables and fruits. After a flood in the area, they gave him a life jacket (I always say, make your gnome a prepared gnome), and the local 4-H made him a scarf to keep him warm in the winter. When the local high school football team, the Rondout Valley Ganders, plays, he holds a football. (Go Ganders!) And during the holiday season—you guessed it—he holds a Christmas tree.

Stealing garden gnomes has been a favorite American pastime, but I wouldn't mess with Chomsky. Have you read any of his work? You don't want to get on that guy's bad side. Plus, he may look like an innocent country bumpkgnome, but this guy grew up in New York City!

Well, that, and he's more than thirteen feet tall.

For more information visit www.kelderfarm.com or call (845) 626-7137.

More Fun than a Barrel of Grapes

Marlboro

So, you have a hankering to get closer to your food chain? Missing old-world Europe?

Well, take off your shoes and head up to the Benmarl Winery in the Hudson Valley because we are going to do some grape stomping!

Every fall, after the grape harvest, the winery holds a Harvest Grape Stomping Festival, featuring music and wine tasting, tours of the winery, and, yes, grape stomping.

There are two big tubs with spigots so you can compete with your friends to see who makes the most juice!

Before you get grossed out, you should know that it's just for novelty; they don't actually make wine from the grapes stomped by all

★ ★

Making Feet-o Noir at the Benmarl Winery.

those stinky feet! In fact, they use Concord grapes, which aren't used in wine.

To make it more interesting, they often toss the winemaker in one of the barrels, so you can ask him any questions about the winemaking process while you're pretending to be Italian. (You know, spin around and hum—Dit da dada. Dit da dada. Dit da dadada da. Hey!)

You'll learn the secret to one of the winery's signature wines, Baco Noir, an extraordinary cherry-vanilla flavored wine with a peppery finish.

"I like a lot of fruit," says winemaker Kristop Brown, with his pants rolled up to the knees and his feet dyed wine red up to the calves. "I taste the juice and think that's delicious. I don't want to lose it."

The name Benmarl comes from the Scottish Gaelic *ben,* meaning small hill, and *marl,* meaning slate, which is a major component of the soil where the grapes are grown.

"I believe it's the oily slate in the ground that makes our Baco so good," explains Benmarl owner Victor Spaccarelli Jr.

After you've finished your rousing rendition of *Stomp!* and had your feet hosed down, grab some wine and cheese and head to the round white tables behind the winery, to take advantage of the spectacular hilltop view of the Hudson River and valley.

For more information visit www.benmarl.com or call (845) 236-4265.

They also do grape stomping at nearby Brotherhood Winery, the Cobblestone Farm Winery in the Finger Lakes Region, and at Casa Larga Vineyards near Rochester.

I mean, you have to put your foot down sometime.

Excuse Me, Are You Using That Bridge?

Millbrook

Here's proof that your last name doesn't have to be Hearst to live in a castle.

Peter Wing didn't have a lot of money when he returned from Vietnam in 1969 and got married. So, he scrounged around and spent the next thirty years building his own castle out of found objects!

He salvaged a large quantity of stone from an old railroad bridge that had been blown up. You'll also see remnants of old barns, churches, or buildings, as well as household objects. The spires, for example, are made from toilet-bowl balls and upside-down wrought-iron plant stands! He even borrowed the books to study architecture!

The castle is a melting pot of styles—Spanish, German, Greek, Tibetan, and Japanese—with a healthy dose of organic liberty. You'll

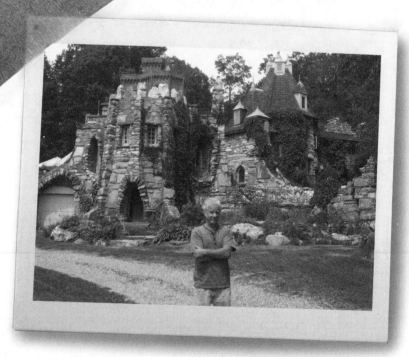

find unexpected stained-glass windows in the passageways, as well as human forms protruding from the stone. "I found a rock that looked like a torso," Wing says, as if he had no choice. There's even a Gaudí-inspired mosaic staircase of two dragons. "Walking between dragons is good luck," Wing explains.

The living room has a balcony that looks like the bow of a ship protruding from the second-floor landing. Surprisingly, in this land of recycled make-believe, it was never a ship, but created from an old

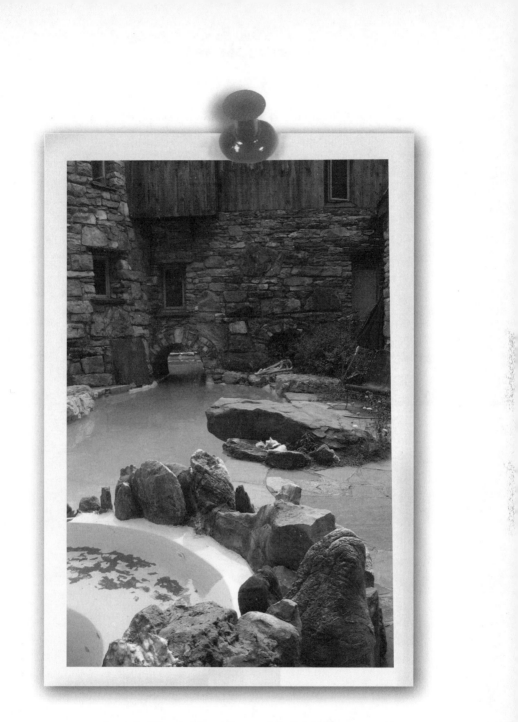

A man's home is his castle—and it should have a moat!

wooden porch arch and barn beams. A floor-to-ceiling fireplace on the opposite wall looks like a cathedral.

Wing and his castle give off an esoteric, macabre vibe, like you just walked onto the set of a Fellini film. Where most people put wreaths and eucalyptus sprays on the mantel face, Wing has a fan of knives. Overhead, a vintage velvet military coat looms, with the head from a suit of armor. Suspended from the ceiling are carousel horses that Wing says he "bought from a carny for two dollars each."

The bathroom is a clover-shaped, palatial oasis, complete with an antique bird feeder for a sink and a Victorian-era golden garden planter for a tub!

Of course, no castle would be complete without a moat: This one doubles as a swimming pool, with a hot tub on one end!

With all that weaponry, I wouldn't dare launch an assault on the castle. I might linger in the moat, though!

If you call (845) 677-9085, Wing or his wife Toni will give you a tour—and they might even let you spend the night, since they're starting a bed-and-breakfast at the castle. In the summer they host "Shakespeare at the Castle," part of a children's summer camp put on by the Annandale Shakespeare Troupe.

For more information, visit www.wingscastle.com and www .shakespeareatthecastle.com.

The Divine Brotherhood of Wine

Washingtonville

The Brotherhood Winery, started by French Huguenot immigrant John Jaques in 1839, is often referred to as the oldest continually operating winery in the United States.

The reason is that the winery was able to continue making wine through Prohibition in the 1920s.

How is that possible? Was it some sort of back alley operation like you might see on the HBO show *Boardwalk Empire*?

The answer is a little more, ahem, divine than that.

It's because the winery made sacramental wine for religious ceremonies. Wine used for medicinal and sacramental purposes was excepted to the Eighteenth Amendment, which prohibited the manufacture, sale, import, or export of intoxicating liquors.

The divine cellars of the Brotherhood Winery.
COURTESY OF ORANGE COUNTY TOURISM

"It has been noted," the winery says on its website, "that the clergy population in the area grew substantially during this period."

Amen! I'll drink to that.

For more information, visit www.brotherhood-winery.com.

★ ★

The World's Largest Kaleidoscope
Mount Tremper

Remember kaleidoscopes? As kids, we used to peep through them until our squint muscles hurt, dazzled by the twists and turns of the colorful objects trapped in an obscure space at the end.

Well, Mount Tremper, in the heart of the Catskills, is home to the Guinness-stamped World's Largest Kaleidoscope!

It's housed in an old animal-feed silo, sixty feet tall, with a giant pyramid of mirrors at the top. A video of brightly colored patterns and pop-culture images is aimed through the opening at the top and reflected through the mirror-mid.

The kaleidoscope opened in the late 1990s, but it has that retro 1960s feel. In one of the ten-minute shows, the faces of Native Americans, Lincoln, Nixon, Elvis, Marilyn Monroe, and others flash through the scope, punctuated by images of American flags, trains, and marijuana leaves.

The giant scope seats—er, stands—twenty people, though the best seat in the house is actually on the floor.

Lying there, I felt like I should be wearing a headband and tie-dye and saying things like "Far out."

The silo-scope is attached to a barn-turned–upscale resort called Emerson Resort & Spa. The groovy vibe of the kaleidoscope is totally mismatched with the posh self-importance of Emerson Resort, making it feel a little like the hippy gardener at a Hamptons estate.

This place is so money, it should come as no surprise that you exit the world's largest kaleidoscope into a huge kaleidoshop, which has everything from three-dollar scopes to fine-art scopes priced in the thousands.

Sitting in the corner like Tom Thumb is the World's Smallest Kaleidoscope, a little one-inch wonder displayed in a ring box. Another cool item is a groovy coffee table with a kaleidoscope on each corner for group scoping.

★ ★

The shop was cool, but I couldn't help but be disappointed with the World's Largest Kaleidoscope. I guess what I really wanted was giant beads and gallons of colored oils in an esoteric tumbler overhead instead of Lincoln and weed.

You'll leave with some pain in your neck and squinting muscles, perhaps also your pocketbook, but hey, check another "world's largest" off your bucket list!

The World's Largest Kaleidoscope is on Route 28 in Mount Tremper.

For more information, go to www.emersonresort.com or call (877) 688-2828.

It used to store animal feed; now it houses Lincoln, Nixon, and Elvis. Far out!

★ ★

Vroom! Vroom! Vroom!
Newburgh

Newburgh is famous for being the headquarters of the Continental Army during the American Revolution and as one of the first cities to get an Edison power plant.

But now, it's about to be known for something else—motorcycles!

Gerald Doering and his son Ted have opened an 85,000-square-foot museum devoted to motorcycles, called Motorcyclepedia.

Adding the –pedia sounds like a tall order—a dare, even—but if anyone can live up to that, it's the Doerings.

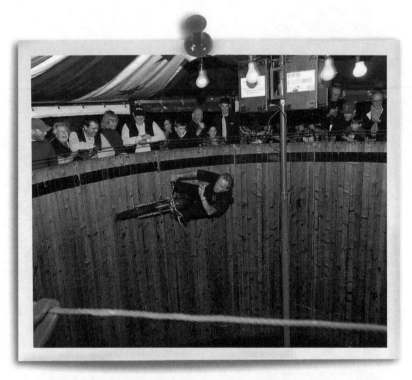

And this over here on the left is the "Wall of Death." What did you expect from a motorcycle museum, a diorama?
COURTESY OF MOTORCYCLEPEDIA

The collection consists of over 400 motorcycles from 1897 to the present. (Did you even know they made motorcycles in 1897?!)

Gerald's first bike was a 1929 Indian Scout that he bought in 1947. And, even though the Indian brand is no longer around, he has what he calls the Indian Time Line—an Indian bike from every year they made 'em except the first, when they put together only three.

The museum boasts that it has motorcycles for any kind of fan, "ranging from the 1915 Iver Johnson to the recreation of the Captain America chopper from Easy Rider to the amazing creations of Arlen Ness."

They also have a 1964 Harley-Davidson that Doering says was used in the presidential motorcade when President John F. Kennedy was shot—that same bike was later called into service in the Oliver Stone film, *JFK*.

Of course, there are photographs, posters, and other memorabilia that you might expect, but you might not expect this interactive exhibit—the "Wall of Death."

The *New York Times* described it as "a cylindrical carnival attraction in which daredevils raced faster and faster around a steeply banked track, eventually achieving a horizontal position."

For more information, put on your helmet and drive over to www .motorcyclepediamuseums.com.

UFO Sightings and an Alien Parade
Pine Bush

The rural hamlet of Pine Bush has many dairy and horse farms, and one of its biggest claims to fame was that it was known as the "Butter Capital of the World" in the early nineteenth century. But it has another claim to fame that you might not know about—it's often referred to as the UFO Capital of the East Coast.

The paranormal activity has been going on since at least the 1960s, though the region went through a hyperactive period in the mid-1980s and 1990s. And it's not just sightings of Unidentified Flying

★ ★

Objects: There have also been reports of strobe lights in the sky, inexplicable orbs of light, strange creatures, encounters, and even abductions.

"I had things that I couldn't explain," says Bill Wiand, a computer network specialist in Pine Bush who is also the coleader of the United Friends Observer Society (UFOs). "I saw a lot of different things in the sky. Lights in the sky. Flying saucers," Wiand says.

He says he also had interactions when he was younger with "little people" he couldn't explain—they were small, seemed to be made of a cartilage-like material (not really bones), and just floated, defying gravity.

"People would tell me it was because I lived in Westchester—it was the guys who took Rip Van Winkle!" he says, referring to the famous Washington Irving character who goes for a walk in the mountains with his dog and falls asleep for twenty years.

The crescendo of paranormal activity resulted in masses of people known as "skywatchers" wandering out at night to look to the stars and see what they could see. This coincided with an acceleration of development in this rural area—houses and businesses were going up everywhere. Sometimes the crowds of skywatchers were so big they disrupted traffic or prompted complaints of trespassing. So, in the late 1990s, the police actually outlawed skywatching, threatening anyone caught trespassing or parking with the intention of skywatching with jail time and/or fines.

The activity, perhaps due to development or the change in legal status, has died down in the past decade. But now, thanks to the recession, it is revving up in a different way. The town is embracing its unidentified flying claim to fame and holds an annual Pine Bush Area UFO Festival and Parade.

"It was a way to put us on the map for economic reasons—for tourism," Wiand says. "It's very hard to get people to visit the area. We do have a couple of wine trails, but people don't go all that often. Now that the recession is here, people are looking for family things to do."

Greetings! Take me to your diner.
PHOTO BY PETER MOSEN

For true believers, one of the best gathering spots is the Cup & Saucer Diner (get it, saucer?!) to swap stories. But the Pine Bush Area UFO Festival and Parade offers something for everyone. For believers, there are lectures by UFO and abduction scholars, and a screening of *Adventures of an Earthling,* a documentary about one woman's UFO adventure in Pine Bush in the 1990s. For the rest of the events, whether you believe in UFOs and aliens or not is irrelevant—all you have to believe in is fun.

There's a parade, filled with all kinds of people and kids dressed like the caricature little green aliens with big black eyes, but also an "Alien Hide and Seek," where Alfie the alien hides in various local businesses. When you spot him, you get a ticket. You get the right amount of tickets, and you get a coupon for a free ice-cream cone. You can also attend an Earthlings & Aliens Ball, a Cosmic Chili Cook-Off, and an "Out of This World" car show.

Wiand is among the true believers in something being out there, but he says he knows not everyone takes them seriously.

"Yes, people make fun of you—it's OK," Wiand declares. "Most of us have gotten past that state years ago—we're very tough."

For more information on the Pine Bush Area UFO Festival and Parade, visit www.ufopinebushfestival.com or look them up on Facebook. For more information on sightings, activity zones, and other UFO news, go to www.pinebushufo.com.

Psssst. I've Got Some Dirt.
Pine Island

Before I tell you this next story, I should warn you that it's a little bit dirty. Oh, and please don't cry.

The hamlet of Pine Island, in the town of Warwick, was once known as the "Onion Capital of the World."

That's because 12,000 years ago, the valleys were filled with a glacial lake that melted into a swamp. When Polish immigrants arrived one hundred years ago, they settled in Pine Island because the valleys

You can see this dirt from space!
COURTESY OF ORANGE COUNTY TOURISM

and fertile soil reminded them of home. They drained the land, revealing "black dirt," rich soil that was perfect for growing onions. The dirt is literally so black, you can see the "Black Dirt Region" from space!

Another curious fact is that there isn't any oxygen in the muck, as the farmers call it, which slows decomposition. As a result, this area has one of the highest concentrations of mastodon remains!

"We find Indian arrowheads, cow bones," says onion grower Chris Pawelski of Pawelski Farms. "Mastodons are dime a dozen," he adds. During my visit, the Pawelskis popped open a big, blue Tupperware tub, revealing what they believe are the remains of a 12,000-year-old moose elk!

It's like going to a natural history museum and farmers' market all at once! Do Black Dirt onions taste better? Try them for yourself at the Warwick Valley Farmers' Market (www.warwickinfo.net/farmersmarket), on Sundays in the summer and fall.

Some farms, such as the Rogowski Farm (www.rogowskifarm.com), which grows 250 different types of produce, hold their own daily markets. Farmer Cheryl Rogowski, who writes "The Black Dirt Blog" and hosts weekly a radio show on WTBQ, sometimes holds culinary classes in the farm's kitchen. She's also been nationally recognized for innovative programs such as English-language classes for the farm's migrant workers.

Perhaps you want to leave the preparation to the pros. Area restaurants that use local produce include the Crystal Inn, Landmark Inn, and Old Forge Inn. If you're not hungry just yet, try a hot-air balloon ride to get a bird's-eye view of the black-dirt region and work up your appetite!

For more information contact Orange County Tourism at www.orangetourism.org or call (845) 291-2136.

A Little Joy in Your Hike

Pine Island

Andrea Colman and her daughter Elizabeth were on vacation in Utah when Elizabeth accidentally left her newest prize possessions, two little doggy dolls, in one of the stores. She was about six years old then, so this was devastating. She went to the car sobbing.

Andrea told Elizabeth that she must've lost them for a reason. They weren't really hers to begin with. She was just holding on to them until some kid who really needed them—maybe a kid whose parents had just divorced—found them. She always taught her daughter that you should give to the universe and it will come back to you.

Later that day, they were hiking off-trail in Zion National Park. They stopped to take a picture when Andrea noticed something dangling into the frame that was ruining the shot.

Lizzy's little bundle of walking joy.
PHOTO BY ANDREA COLEMAN

She said, "Lizzy, what is that? A dish rag?"

Elizabeth replied, "Oh my gosh, it's a doll!"

The doll was lovingly hand-stitched with the words "walking joy" embroidered on it. They were touched by this gesture of a stranger. That day, they knew it was meant for Elizabeth.

Since then, they've made a couple dozen "walking-joy dolls" and left them in the woods to bring joy to someone else.

The dolls are made without sewing, using fabric remnants, twine, raffia, twigs—whatever materials they can find. Sometimes they sit down at the dining room table, other times they just tuck a few pieces of fabric and twine in their backpack and make them right there in the woods.

The only requirements are that there is no sewing involved and that the doll is made with love. "It has to be so beautiful, you don't want to give it away!" Andrea says.

Andrea shares that her favorites are the ones that they don't draw faces on. That way, "the person who finds it can imagine the emotion," Andrea says. "If they're having a good day, they can have a happy, laughing doll. If they're having a bad day, it could be a commiserating doll."

So, the next time you find a little surprise in the woods, maybe it's a friendly greeting from Andrea and Elizabeth. And maybe—just maybe—you'll leave something nice for the next person.

A Castle as the Ultimate Storage Solution
Pollepel Island

For years, train passengers have been elbowing their travel companions in amazement as they spot what appears to be a castle on an island in the Hudson River just north of Cold Spring.

No one knew too much about it, so the curiosity generally ended there. Well, let me tell you the story of that castle.

It was built by Francis Bannerman VI in 1901. Bannerman ran what may have been the first Army-Navy surplus store. He sold helmets and military gear, rifles, revolvers, cannons—you name it. He ran the business from Brooklyn, and later expanded into Manhattan.

After the Spanish-American War in 1898, Bannerman bought his biggest supply of military surplus, including a large stock of black powder. His neighbors in Brooklyn weren't happy. They said, "Fugheddaboudit! You're not storing that stuff here! One false move and we all go sky high!" (OK, that was a loose, dramatic reenactment of what they said.)

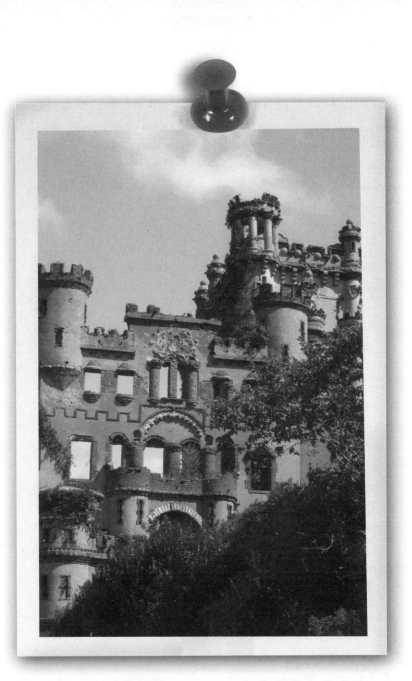

A castle fit for a queen . . . or a keg of gunpowder!

★ ★

So, Bannerman did what any of us would do: He bought an island and built a castle on it to house his munitions!

He modeled it after European castles, reflecting his Scottish heritage. He also made some interesting architectural choices: The towers of the castle are smaller at the bottom and wider at the top, giving the illusion that the castle is bigger than it really is. No one knows why he did it, perhaps to make the building more imposing to passersby.

After Bannerman's death in 1918, his wife and sons took over the business. Two years later, the "powder house," used to store that gunpowder supply, exploded. No one was killed, but the castle suffered some structural damage. According to accounts of the incident, the blast was felt from Poughkeepsie to Peeksill. (And by my account, you could hear the big, fat "I told you so!" all the way from Brooklyn!)

A massive fire in 1969 destroyed most of the buildings on the island. Firefighters had rushed to the scene, but when they realized no one was in danger, they let the fire burn itself out. Some spectacular ruins remain.

The island is now owned by New York State, but a group known as the Bannerman Castle Trust began operating public tours there in 2003.

Boat tours to Bannerman Castle depart from Newburgh and Beacon. For more information visit www.bannermancastle.org. For tours, visit www.prideofthehudson.com or call (845) 220-2120.

Carving His Place in History
Prattsville

There's an odd set of small, white objects set into the rock high above Route 23, just outside of Prattsville.

It's been called "New York's Mount Rushmore," but quite honestly, it looks like someone got tired of all the knickknacks in his living room and, for kicks, decided to bolt them to the side of the striated rock!

There are a couple of busts, a horse, a tree, a wreath, a scroll, and, like a broken toy found behind the sofa, an arm wielding a hammer.

When we said you should write your life story, we thought you knew that we meant on *paper*!

This is Pratt's Rock, a three-dimensional biography of not a living room, but Zadock Pratt, a wealthy entrepreneur and congressman. The story goes that, one day in 1843, he was approached by a beggar. Pratt, a firm believer in hard work not handouts, asked the man what his trade was. When the man replied that he was a stonecutter, Pratt put the man to work, carving his life story into the cliff.

(The Zadock Pratt Museum on Main Street in Prattsville says this legend about the beggar is probably not true. It's more likely that he hired a number of skilled stonecutters who worked on and off over a period of several years.)

★ ★

Pratt owned the largest shoe-leather tannery in the world (well, until he cut down all the hemlock trees in the Catskills). So, the tree is a hemlock and the horse represents the animals that carried the bark to the tannery. There's the Pratt coat of arms and a wreath containing the names of his children. One bust is, of course, Pratt; the other, his son George, who was killed in the Civil War. Who knows what that arm and hammer represent. Perhaps it was the manual labor involved in tanning leather, or maybe it was just an early example of product placement. (Keep your life story fresh with Arm & Hammer!)

Actually, an inscription offers some insight: "This hand for my country."

Pratt had intended to be buried in the cliffside, but the tomb, which you enter through a doorway carved in the rock, leaked. So, that's now just a nice little stopping point; Pratt is buried in the town cemetery. However, he did bury six of his favorite horses and dogs at the site, down near the picnic tables.

Pratt's Rock Park is open to the public. It's a gorgeous little hike: Switchbacks take you up the 500 feet to the monument and the top offers spectacular views of the Schoharie River across the street.

For more information visit www.prattmuseum.com or call (518) 299-3395.

Someone Must Be Hungary!

Rock City

Wow. That's one big fork in the road.

Literally, at thirty-one feet tall, it's the world's largest fork!

The fork, located at the intersection of Routes 308 and 199 in Rock City, is jammed straight into the ground, as if the Jolly Green Giant was eating a salad of trees and grass and stabbed his fork down for a second while he ran to the bathroom.

The back of the fork officially says the "punny sculpture" was made by Stephen B. Schreiber, president of the Rock City Arts Council.

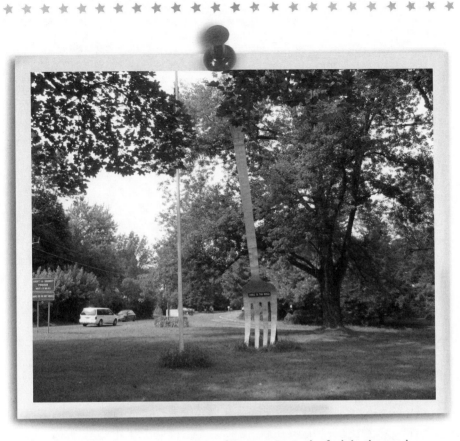

OK, when you get to the fork in the road . . .

But Schreiber, a local real-estate entrepreneur with his tongue planted firmly in cheek, told the *Poughkeepsie Journal* in a 2003 interview that he did it as a joke.

"I didn't think they would let me leave it there," Schreiber is quoted as saying. "Nobody has said anything."

So, there it stands. The world's largest fork at a fork in the road. A joke that just keeps on . . . ahem . . . sticking it to you!

When you're taking your companion's picture, try to play along and be a punny guy. Say something like: "Hey, your nose is running and your feet smell!" Or, maybe stick with the food theme and try this one, compliments of www.punoftheday.com:

★ ★

"I like European food so I decided to Russia over there because I was Hungary. After Czech'ing the menu I ordered Turkey. When I was Finnished I told the waiter 'Spain good but there is Norway I could eat another bite!'"

Once you're all punned out, you can make the big decision everyone faces when they come to a giant fork in the road: Are you going to Rhinebeck or Red Hook?!

It's a Pickle Party!
Rosendale

When Eri Yamaguchi came to visit her friends in America, she told them she wanted to have a "pickle party."

"We didn't have a clue," say Bill and Cathy Brooks, "but we could always throw a pretty good party!"

More than a dozen years later, the Brooks are still throwing annual pickle parties, now known as the Rosendale International Pickle Festival. The festival aims to expand people's culinary and cultural horizons "through the simple, but alluring, PICKLE!"

Here, you'll learn they can pickle just about anything—carrots, onions, mushrooms, beets, garlic, olives—even lemons! They can also make anything out of actual pickles, from pickle soup to pickle chili, pickle pizza, and—wait for it—deep-fried pickles!

The festival is truly international, with a Japanese tea ceremony, traditional German dancing, and an African drumming performance mixed in with the bluegrass. "From sushi to sauerbraten" and "kimonos and lederhosen," the festival boasts, there's something for everyone.

Amid all this cultural-horizon expanding, the festival truly is a family affair, and events such as the pickle-eating, pickle-juice-drinking, and pickle-tossing contests, have a "Sure, I'll try that!" feel to them. A lot of kids compete in all the events, and I can tell you that I didn't find a single professional-circuit pickle eater in the bunch!

These pickle people have a pretty good sense of humor, too. There were, of course, the T-shirts, such as "Pickles—get hooked! They're

KAPOW! It's Spacey Tracy's deep-fried pickle truck.

the real dill." And, let's not forget *the accessories.* Tracy Krawitt, owner of Spacey Tracy's Pickles and maker of a mean fried pickle, sported dangly pickle-chip earrings she bought through Pickle Packers International.

Mike Mongeon, the "chief brine brewer" of Mike's Grenades, named his pickles after ammunition because of their "shape and burst of flavor." He also brings his Picklemobile for a prop at the festival. He uses it in Adirondack sled racing, so he can—you had to see this coming—"slide down the hill in a garlic dill."

All pickle puns aside, the food is extraordinary. Don't forget to check out winners from the pickling contest. Awards are given for best pickles, best relish, best green beans, and best chutney, as well as for specialty items such as watermelon-rind pickles, pickled heart-shaped beets, and pickled carrots with cinnamon and cloves.

Suddenly, I look around, and the whole world looks like one, great, big pickling opportunity!

For more information visit www.picklefest.com or call (845) 658-9649.

Mr. Fite's Opus
Saugerties

From the rubble of an abandoned bluestone quarry near Woodstock rises a six-and-one-half-acre stone sculpture that *Architectural Digest* once described as "one of the largest and most beguiling works of art on the entire continent."

It is a series of swirling rock formations that form steps, paths, tunnels, and platforms, topped by a nine-ton monolith. The massive formation is comprised of a series of flat rocks, tightly stacked, one on top of the other, by one man.

That man was Harvey Fite, a self-taught artist and former professor at Bard College. He initially created it as a place to display his bulbous, Picasso-esque sculptures of people. But the pedestal formation became so stunning in and of itself, it began to overpower Fite's sculptures, and he was mature enough at that point to realize you listen to your art when it grabs you by the scruff of the neck and says, "This is not right!"

I say he was "mature enough" because it took him thirty-seven years to lay down all of those rocks! He'd bought the quarry in 1938 for a measly $250 after it became worthless when concrete came along and replaced bluestone as the primary material used to make sidewalks.

He called it *Opus 40* because, he joked, composers had an easier time of naming—well, numbering—their work! And, by the time he named the piece in 1972, he'd been at it for several decades (so, you add these two . . . hum hum hmm . . . carry the one . . .) and estimated that it would take a total of forty years to complete.

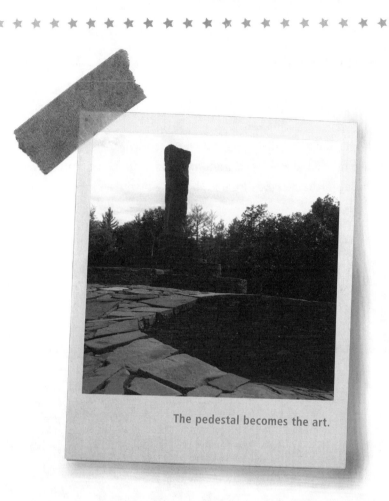

The pedestal becomes the art.

Sadly, or poetically, however you want to look at it, Fite never made it to forty years. He died three years short of that goal when his lawn mower jammed and tossed him over the edge of the quarry.

He was seventy-two years old and died at the hand of his beloved masterpiece, which, as an artist, isn't too shabby.

Today, you can take a self-guided tour of *Opus 40* in all of its massive glory, including the unfinished wall and pile of bluestone where Fite's work abruptly ended. There's also a Quarryman's Museum that Fite built to display traditional quarryman's tools.

For more information visit www.opus40.org or call (845) 246-3400.

★ ★

Go Ahead, Wig Out!
Schenectady

I'll bet you have always wanted to know where Gene Simmons buys his makeup.

Well, it's out of the frying pan and into . . . Schenectady!

I have no idea where the lizard tongue came from but I can tell you that those star-framed eyes from his band Kiss were all Schenectady.

Hey, it's the Fruit of the Loom guys—minus the guys!

★ ★

The makeup came from a shop called The Costumer, which typically specializes in renting costumes for high-school musicals.

The owner, Kathe Sheehan, is a former teacher who directed high school, college, and community theater. She and her husband Jack, who passed away in 2006, saw a void and decided someone needed to make quality costumes, makeup, and props available for the kids. "This led us to 'change hats' and become costumers," Sheehan said.

Now, after providing makeup and costumes for the famous rock band, The Costumer not only outfits high school students but also "every Kiss tribute band that comes down the pike!" says Deborah Trowbridge, store supervisor at The Costumer.

You know? I think that's one retail line I wouldn't mind waiting in!

They also rent or sell costumes to commercial production companies, reality TV shows, MTV, *Saturday Night Live,* and everyday people looking to up the Halloween ante or dress their groomsmen as Beefeaters.

"We do a huge Internet business," Trowbridge says. "We ship Santa Clauses, Easter Bunnies, high school mascots—you name it."

It's a gigantic warehouse, with thousands of characters mingling on the racks. There's the gang from *West Side Story* stepping and snapping next to the fringe-shaking fabrics of *Thoroughly Modern Millie.* Hey wait, was that a ketchup costume trying to get close to Miss Millie? I think she's got bigger aspirations than you, buddy!

There are knights and hippies. Showgirls and princesses. Kings and Fruits of the Loom. Oh, and Elvis is definitely *in* the building.

Awesome! You can't see me right now, but I'm totally sticking my tongue out as far as it will go—like the rock star I know they can dress me to be!

For more information visit www.thecostumer.com or call (877) 218-1289. Tours are available.

★ ★

That's Schenecitalia!
Schenectady

So, you've been to Italy and it's ruined you for the food they pass off as Italian here in the United States.

Great news! We've got your Italia right here. No, not in Little Italy, in, um . . . Schenectady!

At the Villa Italia bakery in downtown Schenectady, the pastry recipes were handed down to owner Bobby Mallozzi from his grandparents, who owned a bakery in Italy. "Every recipe is from Italy—what my grandmother made," Mallozzi says.

What really sets this bakery apart and makes you think you've died and gone to Italian heaven is that most of the ingredients in the pastries actually come from Italy, like the chocolate-covered cannoli shells and the flavoring for the gelato. "You can tell the intensity is different," Mallozzi explains.

Just about everything, right down to the $300,000 refrigerated display cases Mallozzi had custom-made, came from Italy. I'm sorry, no. I meant right down to the three cabinetmakers he imported from Italy to put that display case together!

Even the paper napkins on the table . . . yep, from Italy!

"We're just trying to bring something unique to the table," Mallozzi says. "The flavors, tastes, and smells you get from products [in Italy] are different than the ones you get domestically," he explains. "The majority of the bakeries in this country are all buying from the same place."

You might be sitting in your cubicle, asking no one in particular, "Schenectady? Really?" Look, if you're not up for the trip, don't worry about it. That just means more for Chuck Mangione, Dom DeLuise, Ray Romano—all fans of the Schenectady bakery—and the rest of us!

Villa Italia is so popular that they actually advise you to try not to come on Fridays and Saturdays, and at Christmastime, they have a police officer directing traffic in front of the bakery!

Mmmmmm. Can you smell that? That, my friend, is a Sicilian cannoli shell.

For more information visit www.villaitaliabakery.com or call (518) 355-1144.

Aquatic Days Are Here Again

Schenectady

The sign on top of Jumpin' Jack's Drive-In says SKI SHOW EVERY TUESDAY 7:00 P.M.

Wait, what year is it? Is Fonzie going to be in this show?

You might think that it has to be either 1950 or a theme park in Florida for a human pyramid on water skis, but in July and August, you can see one every Tuesday night in Schenectady—for free!

Schenectady is home to the US Water Ski Show Team, a dedicated group of about thirty-five skiers who compete in team waterskiing and, between practices, put on shows for the locals, complete with spangled costumes and set to music.

"It's the closest thing you can get to a Broadway show on water!" says Kara Pangburn, a member and former president of the ski team.

If you've ever tried dancing, you know how difficult it is on land to hold your leg out in front of you. (If you haven't, take a moment to try it now.)

During a show, you'll see a "ballet line" of synchronized skiers, each on a single ski. They start with one leg pointed out front and one arm curved gracefully in the air. Then—don't blink—they flip away from the rope, using a swivel ski, so their foot is pointed behind them, holding the rope. It's like the aquatic Rockettes!

A team of barefoot skiers creates a stunning wall of water to dazzle the crowd. The jumpers do spectacular acrobatic spins and flips—as if gravity hasn't already been defied!

The strap-double acts offer up lifts straight out of a ballroom-dancing championship, only on water and being pulled by a boat! The ropes are connected to a strap around the men's waists as they hoist their partners overhead, sometimes even inverted! In some acts, there may be ten or more couples on the water at the same time.

Then Tuesday comes . . . we'll have some fun. . . .
Ready to entertain you!

The big finale is the human pyramid, the ultimate display of strength, grace, and teamwork, which can be anywhere from three to four tiers tall, involving up to twenty people.

Well, the boat picks up two, three, and four. . . . When the clock strikes five, six, and seven . . . we're gonna rock . . . gonna rock . . . gonna rock it all aquatic tonight!

Shows are held on the Mohawk River, behind Jumpin' Jack's Drive-In snack shack on the Scotia side of the river. For more information visit www.uswaterskishowteam.com or call (518) 346-7405.

★ ★

The Elephant Hotel

Somers

At the intersection of routes 100 and 202 in Somers is a three-story building that has "Elephant Hotel" in big letters on the front and a monument of an elephant in the front yard.

What is this, some kind of elephants-only hotel? Where pachyderms pack it in for the night?

Nope. This building has been a hotel for humans, meeting place for menagerie/circus owners, a stagecoach stop, a dance hall, a bank, the town clerk's office, and a museum, but never a hotel that housed elephants.

Its name is a nod to Somers's circus past. It was built between 1820 and 1825 by Hachaliah Bailey, who is not the "& Bailey" in the Ringling Bros. circus, but was one of the first Americans to tour a menagerie of exotic animals. (In fact, he predates the Ringling Bros. and was said to be a role model for the famous carnival barker P. T. Barnum.)

This Bailey, a farmer-turned-circus showman, started his menagerie in 1827 with an elephant known as Old Bet. He'd transported his share of cattle, so moving a menagerie was no sweat. Soon, other menageries began sprouting up around the Somers area, earning it the nickname, "Cradle of the American Circus." In fact, a lot of homes in the area have some oddly large rooms—something that was necessary when you were boarding a menagerie!

Bailey built the Elephant Hotel as a memorial to his beloved elephants. Old pictures show a few elephants did visit the hotel as promotional stunts, but to my knowledge, none ever spent the night!

Today, the Elephant Hotel houses the town clerk's office, the Somers Historical Society, and the Museum of the Early American Circus, which is a small but worthwhile stop.

But please, leave your luggage in the car.

The Elephant Hotel hasn't been an actual hotel since the town bought it in 1927. Nonetheless, "we still sometimes get folks arriving in the town clerk's office, or at a town board meeting, with suitcases,

★ ★

wanting to book a room in the hotel!" says Terry Ariano, curator of the circus museum.

For more information visit www.somershistoricalsoc.org/museum .html or call (914) 277-4977.

Maybe they need a monument to remember, but I'll never forget!

All Together Now
Stone Ridge

Being a teacher in a one-room schoolhouse was a lot like being one of those entertainers who spins plates.

You had to juggle twenty to thirty kids, spanning at least six different grades, making sure everyone stayed in line. That would be enough to drive anyone to dri—no, no, no! According to the "Rules for Teachers" posted at the Kripplebush Schoolhouse when it opened in 1857, you weren't allowed to drink, smoke, or get "shaved in a barbershop." (Scandalous!)

Class! School is in session!

Teachers were allowed some recess time, though. The rules stated that male teachers were allowed one night per week for "courting purposes," two if they went to church regularly! Female teachers, however, were dismissed for getting married or engaging in "unseemly conduct." (Well, I never . . .)

The Kripplebush Schoolhouse, which held classes until 1951, is now a museum, offering all kinds of insight—and entertainment—about what it was like to work and study in a one-room schoolhouse. Today, thanks to a dedicated corps of volunteers, the museum is set up exactly as it would've been if school were in session, with chalkboards, iron-legged desks, a watercooler—even an outhouse key. The rules are posted on the back wall.

Arlita Perry, who attended school here in the 1940s, says having all the grades together was tricky, but it worked. Older kids helped younger kids. Students did their homework while other lessons were going on. That way, homework never had to come *home* with you!

She recalls the moral lessons from penmanship class, with classic one-liners such as "Always do your best" and "Beauty is as beauty does!" And, with just one room, the reward for being good was obvious: time outside this educational sardine can. "If you were good, you could clap erasers outside!" Perry says.

The Kripplebush one-room schoolhouse museum is a wonderful walk back in time, when you *could* put all those kids in a room without mayhem ensuing and one man or woman could keep all the plates spinning, as long as he didn't do any drinking or barbering and she didn't engage in marriage or unseemly conduct!

The museum is located at 204 Kripplebush Road, off of Route 209. It's run by volunteers, so the hours are limited to Sunday from 2:00 to 4:00 p.m. June through September, or by appointment. For more information visit www.ulster-web.com/schoolhouse or call (845) 687-9229.

Just Like Old Times

Sugar Loaf

The proliferation of superstores like Wal-Mart has driven small mom-and-pop shops out of business, but one little craft hamlet has stood the test of time.

Sugar Loaf is an artisan community of more than fifty shops and restaurants, offering handmade goods such as soap, candles, folk-art pillows, and wood-carved and leather items. The hamlet is surrounded by apple orchards and horse farms, and the shops are located in barns and buildings from the eighteenth and nineteenth centuries. The Barnsider Restaurant, for example, is housed in what used to be the general store.

In the mid-1700s, when the village was formed, this was where farmers came to buy supplies and trade horses. By the 1800s, there was a wagon maker, a carpenter, a blacksmith, a tannery, a cheese factory, and other businesses.

Its preservation is credited to two men, Walter Kannon, who owned a barn-siding business, and Jarvis Boone, a wood-carver. When the craft-revival movement swept America in the late 1960s, these two decided to establish Sugar Loaf as a craft community, and soon attracted other artisans. By 1971, the hamlet's population had doubled in size.

What makes it truly unique is that, like their predecessors, these artists and craftspeople not only work but also live in the hamlet.

A lot of wood-carved signs are made with machines now, but Jarvis Boone's son, Clay, still does all his carving the old-fashioned way, by hand. "There's character in a hand-carved sign that you don't get with a machine," Boone says, while working on a huge, wooden dining table that is for a firehouse in New York City.

Character, I understand. But when you're doing it by hand, wouldn't you be worried you'd mess up and cut off part of the design?

"We never make mistakes," Boone says, "but occasionally we have to redesign."

Walking down the streets of Sugar Loaf, you don't find yourself asking a passerby, "What time is it?" but rather, "What YEAR is it?!"

Israeli-born Yaron Rosner was working as a photographer in France when he met his wife Kiki. He decided to turn his soap-making hobby into a business, but decided to set up shop in Sugar Loaf because there was more room here for a family than in Paris.

Well, soap, surely *that* would be easier to do with a machine?

"No machines," Rosner says firmly. "Part of the quality of soap is in small quantity. Salad for six tastes better than 600!"

For a complete list of shops and directions, visit www.sugarloaf newyork.com.

Just Follow the Bubbles

Tannersville

As you drive down Main Street in Tannersville, it looks like the whole town is playing one big game of Pictionary.

There are cartoon soap suds painted on the Laundromat and liquor bottles on the shutters of the village liquor store. Wine and cheese icons offer a taste of what's to come at the Last Chance Restaurant, and a picture-book laundry line of clothes dangles from the front of the Clothes Line boutique.

The buildings are painted in eye-popping shades of squeeze-mustard yellow, aqua, lime green, and cherry.

What's going on here? Did the village get an extreme makeover from Nickelodeon?

The village did get a makeover, but it was inspired by Elena Agostinis Patterson, an artist who moved here in the mid-1980s with her investment banker husband. Patterson got a little tired of the humdrum look of her house, so, she painted it orange, yellow, periwinkle, and green.

"When I painted my house, it was based on the 'Painted Ladies' from San Francisco," Patterson said, referring to a famous row of Victorian homes in San Francisco, painted in all kinds of crazy colors.

"But my house was totally modern and didn't have all the gingerbread trim and all that funky stuff that the Painted Ladies had," Patterson said. "It still lacked something."

So, she decided to paint pictures on the shutters depicting what was going on in that room. So, there are dentures on the bedroom shutters (har har) and a toothpaste tube on the bathroom shutters!

Well, before long, people started veering off of Main Street to check out the house like they do a decked-out yard at Christmastime.

Meanwhile, the sleepy little village of Tannersville was trying to figure out how to jump-start its tourism industry—and the local economy—which had languished since the automobile and airplane came along and whisked the once-thriving tourism industry off to more exotic, faraway places.

Let's see, cheese + wine + martini + fork . . . I
like what's going on in here!

Patterson had a bright idea: What if they could recreate her formula across the whole village and drive that gawking traffic onto Main
Street?

So, she pitched her idea to the mayor, who thought it was a great
plan. Today, there are about a dozen businesses that have gotten a
Patterson-inspired makeover, and Tannersville is billed as "The Painted
Village in the Sky."

Patterson currently owns several boutiques called Chaos NY and is writing a children's book based on her story called *Ms. Flamboyant Paints the Town*. She's also still got the urge to paint stuff.

"I'm trying desperately to get the people who own the telephone poles to give me permission to paint them. There are millions of them in town!" she exclaims.

Tannersville is on Route 23A in the Catskills. I'd be more specific, but honestly, you'll know it when you see it!

My only question is: If you lived in Tannersville, what would be painted on *your* shutters?!

For more information on the Tannersville project and what Patterson is painting now, visit www.chaosny.com.

Ham from Uncle Sam

Troy

We all know the iconic image of Uncle Sam: that tall hat, white goatee, and finger pointed straight at you to let you know that he wants YOU for the US Army.

What a lot of people don't know is that Uncle Sam was a real guy!

His name was Sam Wilson. He was a meatpacker from Troy who shipped rations to US troops during the War of 1812. The soldiers would receive these packages stamped "US." When someone asked who it was from, they would jokingly reply, "It's from Uncle Sam!"

The "US" stamp became an indicator of top-quality meat inspected by Sam Wilson. Soon, the Army stopped accepting any meat that wasn't passed through Uncle Sam.

The face of the famous finger-pointing Uncle Sam, used on recruiting posters during both world wars, was actually modeled after the artist, J. M. Flagg, not Sam Wilson. The gesture came from a similar British Army recruiting poster featuring not a white-goateed guy but a guy with a handlebar moustache that looked like it belonged on one of the Village People.

Sam Wilson is buried in Oakwood Cemetery in Troy. A statue of him stands in downtown Troy. Everything from the bowling alley to the parking garage is named after him, and, for the past thirty-four years, the city has held an annual parade in his honor.

I'm not saying you have to go to Troy or anything; it's just something I want YOU to know.

Beware of "Collectors" at Halloween!
Ulster Park

If you've ever watched a horror movie and thought, "This just isn't scary enough being on my couch. I wish I could be in the horror movie," then head to Ulster Park for the Headless Horseman Hayride and Haunted Houses. It's so big it's like Disney World, only with chainsaws, fake blood, pitch-black, and blood-curdling screams!

This Halloween horror fest is unlike anything you've ever seen. It starts with a haunted hayride. As you chug along the one mile of open farmland in the dark of night, you'll come upon a town with some strange occurrences. Two men stand over a woman, who levitates and then poof! She vanishes into thin air. A bartender serves up a severed head. A murderous mortician opens a box to display his preserved bride-to-be, who never made it to the altar but will remain with him forever.

In the pitch-black interludes between these houses of horror, with your legs dangling off the side of the hayride, "collectors" might chase after you, revving their chainsaws as they look to add your body parts to their collection. And suddenly, the moment everyone's been waiting for: The Headless Horseman emerges from the darkness for one final spine-tingling ride.

With your heart still pounding, you'll get dumped into a labyrinth corn maze. Good luck finding your way out! Ah ha ha ha!

The maze ends in a series of haunted houses. Creepy characters pop out of walls, a head sits on the counter, a vampire swoops overhead, and someone is following you. . . . "Your eyeballs look tasty!" he whispers.

"It's the scariest thing I've ever done in my life," one visitor said. "It gets worse as you go along!"

More than two hundred actors are recruited to scare the crap out of you during this Hollywood-style fright fest, which was named the number one haunted attraction in America by *Hauntworld* magazine two years in a row. It's all the brainchild of Mike Jubie, a former Kingston detective with a penchant for the macabre.

Allow a few hours for the whole thing, as there are also four food-court shacks, several gift shops, and a not-to-be-missed sideshow act and female sword swallower.

It's not for children under eight years old or the faint of heart, so consider yourself warned!

It's expensive as haunted houses go—about forty dollars per person—but it will certainly give you something to talk about on the car ride home. Just stop digging your nails in so hard when you're telling the story, OK?

The Headless Horseman Hayrides and Haunted Houses are held weekends in September and October in Ulster Park on Route 9W. For more information visit www.headlesshorseman.com or call (845) 339-BOOO (2666).

Something Is Up
Warwick

Ask anyone in Warwick, and they know about "the doors." No, I'm not referring to Jim Morrison's rock band, I'm talking about a curious decorating choice at the Landmark Inn restaurant.

"People know," says owner Michael DiMartino. They'll be in the bar, then drag their friends into the dining room saying, "'You have to see the doors!'" he says.

Um, the doors?

Let me start at the beginning. The inn was built in 1778, with a dining room added on by then-owner Gordon Richardson in 1954. Richardson's wife Cynthia got a little ahead of herself and booked

★ ★

Those are really doors on the ceiling, aren't they?
Well, I guess it saves you in insulation, eh?!

the dining room for a wedding before it was completed. The bride-to-be was horrified when she came by for a walk-through, declaring: "There's no way I'm getting married in this place with the paper ceiling!"

Richardson was a pretty eccentric guy, so he came up with a creative solution. The Red Swan Inn, where he'd tended bar, was being torn down. So, he salvaged dozens of doors from the old inn, and nailed them to the ceiling of his dining room!

The bride, incidentally, did wind up getting married there, in the place—not with the paper ceiling, but—with all the doors on the ceiling!

Richardson had a pretty odd sense of humor, DiMartino says. If you came into his restaurant wearing a tie, he'd cut it off and tack it to the wall! And, there is a dinghy on top of the awning over the bar. Still, no one knows exactly why he chose to put the doors up instead of Sheetrock. Alcohol may or may not have been involved. "There are a lot of hammer marks where they missed," DiMartino says. "Some have four nails in them, some have fourteen!"

In the psychedelic 1960s, Richardson painted the doors every shade of the rainbow, including gold, and some had murals done by his daughter. One of the subsequent owners painted the doors a nice, tasteful shade of brown, which remains today.

"Parents like to scare their kids," DiMartino says. "It's the same joke all the time: 'Hey, you never know who's gonna come through that door!'"

The Landmark Inn is at 126 Route 94, near the intersection of 17A, in Warwick. For more information, visit www.landmarkinnwarwick .com or call (845) 986-5444.

A Divine Pipe Dream
West Point

Military accommodations tend to be pretty sparse, but not at the West Point Cadet Chapel.

This Gothic chapel, on par with some of the most spectacular cathedrals, is home to the world's largest working organ in a religious structure.

The West Point organ, built in 1911 and subsequently enlarged, is the size of about fifteen good-size church organs put together, says Grant Chapman, curator of organs at West Point.

There are at least 23,500 pipes, which run the length of the massive chapel—on either side of the altar, wrapping around both side bays, even over the door at the far back entrance. Those are called *trumpet en chamade* (meaning "pointing at you") pipes, Chapman says, and,

These are just a handful of the more than 23,500 pipes in the West Point organ.

by my layman's estimate, they're what you might expect to greet you at the gates of Heaven!

"A big organ like this has no speakers," Chapman explains. "Everything runs on air!" Though, "the intention is not to be louder, but richer."

There are four keyboards on the organ, with 874 "stop controls" (each one controls a different set of pipes), 244 notes to be played by hand, and thirty-two notes for the feet!

Craig Williams, who is only the fourth organist the academy has hired, says that periodically an aunt will ask if she can play the organ for her niece or nephew's wedding. "They sit down and say, 'That's not my church organ!'" Williams says. "They take one look at it and say, 'What am I doing here?!'"

"Most organs don't have a gong crash," Williams explains, referring to the buttons below the keyboards, which are mostly percussion and special effects.

Williams says the organ can be overwhelming even for him at times, but mostly, it's inspiring. "There are almost an infinite number of possibilities," he goes on. "If there's a sound in my head, I know I can make it happen on this organ."

The sound that comes from the West Point organ, echoing through the halls of this divine Medieval-like fortress, is unlike anything you've ever heard. I don't care how deep or shallow a person you are, it will find your soul and touch it, before sending a ripple up your spine.

Sunday church services are open to the public, as are special concerts held in the chapel. For a schedule visit www.usma.edu/chaplain and click on "Events."

The Forty-Year Drip

Woodstock

When most people get a drip, they call someone to fix it right away. Not Barbara and Dennis Moss—they've had a drip going for the past forty years and counting!

It's a drip candle that was started by the Mosses' friend Kenny in his Manhattan apartment in the 1960s. You know how it goes. One candle melts down and you just jam another one in there, thinking, "I'll clean it later."

Four inches of wax on the table later and Kenny still hadn't gotten around to it. By that point, in 1969, Dennis was opening a candle shop down the street. Kenny, seeing his window of opportunity, asked Dennis if he wanted this mound of a drip candle. Dennis said, "Sure, why not?"

So, they cut off the legs and put the wax-covered tabletop in the window.

When they moved the shop up to Woodstock a few years later, they took Kenny's drip-candle table with them. "It's like a mascot or something," Barbara says.

You know what, Kenny? At this point,
don't even worry about it.

★ ★

They haven't moved the candle since 1971 and have continued to add candles to it. Today, that tabletop has an eight-foot mountain of wax on top of it!

The Mosses call it "The Mountain."

In a fitting tribute to its '60s roots and home in Woodstock, this is a rainbow-colored mountain, with knobby drips of red, white, yellow, aqua, purple, pink, and neon green wax, with peaks at the top like a castle.

The candle mountain is magical for kids, who like to look into all the little nooks and crannies for hidden figurines, like the white-bearded dude playing guitar, the boy on the unicycle, and the bear on a blue surfboard.

It's all about peace, love, and wax, man.

Visit "The Mountain" at the Candlestock candle shop at 16 Mill Hill Road in Woodstock. For more information go to www.candlestock .com or call (845) 679-8711.

New York City

5

New York City & Long Island

Wild Parrots in Brooklyn and a Naked Cowboy in Times Square

The Empire State Building, Statue of Liberty, and Broadway are some of New York's finest gems, but there's so much more to discover in this massive urban jungle that spans well beyond 42nd Street to the tippy top of the Bronx and the far reaches of Queens, Brooklyn, and Staten Island.

New York City is a wonderful cacophony of cultures that can transport you to faraway lands, from the lively Russian supper clubs in Brighton Beach, Brooklyn—Tonight, is dancing girls!—to the hookah cafes on the block known as "Little Egypt" in Astoria, Queens.

Of course, we've got plenty of Americana, too, from the competitive Christmas-light extravaganza in Brooklyn's Dyker Heights to the man whose pants precede him, the Naked Cowboy in Times Square.

There's more wildlife here than you'd expect, from Pale Male, the famous red-tailed hawk who calls Fifth Avenue home, to the cluster of green monk parrots that mingle with the pigeons in Brooklyn.

We pride ourselves on education here in New York. For all you would-be Wallendas, there's the New York Trapeze School. If you're more the nail-up-the-nose type, well step right up to Coney Island's Sideshow School and get your freak on!

Are you ready to see the real New York?

Long Island

King of New York

Pop quiz: What county is New York City in?

Even if you're a New Yorker, that's probably a tough question. You may only have learned the county you live in when you registered to vote. Here, people identify themselves more by borough than by county.

Your first guess might be that New York is in New York County. Well, that's partially right. Each of the five boroughs that comprise New York City is in a different county, and Manhattan is the only one in New York County.

Two of the boroughs—the Bronx and Queens—share the same name as their county, residing in Bronx County and Queens County, respectively.

So, ninety-nine bottles of borough on the wall, that leaves us with two more to go, right?

Brooklyn, contrary to what you might expect, isn't in Brooklyn County. (I wonder how many people write that on their voter registration forms!) It's actually in Kings County. And Staten Island, the third tenor of the boroughs as it's often forgotten, is in Richmond County.

Here's how it went down. The Dutch, in 1646, were the first to settle the area we know today as Brooklyn, and they named it Breuckelen, after a town in the Netherlands. But about twenty years later the English arrived and got all up in their business. They told the Dutch to fugheddaboudit.

Brooklyn, true to its tough reputation, kept its name. But when New York was divided into counties, the English daddios named it Kings County, after their king at that time, King Charles II of England.

Queens was named for Charles's wife, Queen Catherine of Braganza.

Staten Island (seriously, you forgot about it, didn't you?) kept it all in the family, and Richmond County was named for one of Charles's numerous illegitimate sons, the Duke of Richmond. Who, incidentally, is said to be the ancestor of both Princess Diana and Camilla Parker Bowles, the now Mrs. Prince Charles.

Think you can remember it now?!

Did You See Saw Lady?

New York City

In the bustling Times Square subway station, there's a strange sound. It's angelic. It's otherworldly.

Woo woo woo woo eee ahh oh oooh . . .

You can't quite put your finger on it. A violin? No, wait. An opera singer. Hold on a sec. Is it even . . . *gulp* . . . human?

Jaded New Yorkers might stop you right there and caution that it's probably some subway huckster with a tape recorder and dancing puppets, so either get your buck out and tip him, bub, or keep it moving.

Finally, 257 eyebrow-raised New Yorkers and a flash mob of Japanese tourists later, the source is revealed: A slim woman with long, brown hair. But she's not singing. She's got a bow—but wait—that's not a violin. It looks like a saw! A real-life, build-you-a-house, chop-you-some-firewood household saw!

Her name is Natalia Paruz. Born in Israel, Paruz came to New York, where her professional dance career was cut short by an accident. Her parents took her on a vacation to Austria to cheer her up. It was there that she heard a saw played for the first time. Moved by the experience, when she returned to New York, she picked up her landlady's rusty old saw and well, the rest, is, as they say, hist-saw-ry.

She's played with orchestras and been featured on commercials. She's played big concert halls, including Lincoln Center in New York and Verizon Hall in Philadelphia—known for its top-notch acoustics—but she credits the New York City subway as having the best acoustics in the world. "I don't know," Paruz says. "Maybe it has something to do with all the concrete!"

Playing in the subway, Paruz says she's met all kinds of people—rich, poor, homeless, and thieves. "You just can't get that in a concert hall!"

Paruz goes underground about three days a week. Catch her at one of her favorite stops, including Times Square (42nd Street), Union

Natalia Paruz is armed, but not dangerous.

Square (14th Street), and Lexington Avenue (59th Street). Check her out online at www.sawlady.com, where she has CDs for sale and a performance schedule.

And every July, she hosts the NYC Musical Saw Festival (www.musical sawfestival.org) where she gathers about a dozen saw players from all over the world, including India, Japan, and Germany. They play everything imaginable on the saw, from classical to bluegrass and pop music. There's even been a comedy duo!

Oh, and in case you're wondering, you post-9/11 skeptic you, Natalia's saw is toothless and not considered a deadly weapon. (And yes, she once had to explain this to the police.)

The Da Vinci Code of Toothpaste

The Bronx

Woodlawn Cemetery in the Bronx has some of the most famous graves in the world.

There are jazz greats like Miles Davis and Duke Ellington, and the father of the blues, W. C. Handy. There are more monuments to *Titanic* victims here than anywhere else in the United States. There are also many household names, including R. H. Macy, J. C. Penney, and F. W. Woolworth. There are six former New York mayors, as well as master developer Robert Moses, who was famous for wrapping New York parks in highways. (He is, appropriately, buried next to an on-ramp to the Major Deegan Expressway.)

The sprawling 400-acre city cemetery, which was designated a National Historic Landmark in 2011, has all the charms of its rural counterparts, with rolling green hills, dappled sunlight through the treetops, and even a waterfall.

But the real reason to visit the cemetery isn't its famous residents or idyllic setting. The secret to its charm lies in the people that you've never heard of and the stories their tombstones tell.

John Goffe Rand, an American portrait painter who invented the "artist's color tube," the squeeze-out tube that paint comes in, is here and his headstone is, appropriately, shaped like an artist's palette and paint tube. This invention had an even greater cultural impact when they started putting toothpaste in those tubes.

You can also read the sad yet charming story of George Spencer Millet, who died at age fifteen. His tombstone reads: "Lost life by stab in falling on ink eraser, evading six young women trying to give him birthday kisses in office of Metropolitan Life Building."

You can get lost in all the stories. "It's your own little Da Vinci Code trying to figure out what they [the family] meant when they designed each tombstone and mausoleum," says Susan Olsen, Woodlawn's historian.

The Da Vinci Code of toothpaste revealed in the tombstone of John Goffe Rand, "inventor of the artist's color tube."

There are guided tours, though a little-known secret is that the security guards tell the best stories, albeit less accurate. There's a life-size statue of a bride, Clara Sulzer, who guards will tell you slipped on her gown and died on her wedding day. In fact, the cause was appendicitis before the wedding.

Before you leave, be sure to do an air toast to Jerry Thomas, father of the cocktail, who's also here. And next time you're squeezing the last drop out of the Crest, shout out to the paint-tube guy.

For more information go to www.thewoodlawncemetery.org or call (877) 496-6352.

We're Not Going to Take It, but Yes We're Lying Down

On the Woodlawn Cemetery plot of artist Patricia Cronin and her partner, Deborah Kass, is a larger-than-life (literally) marble sculpture of the couple lying in bed, in what has been described as a postcoital embrace. It is as striking as Michelangelo's *David* but with a tenderness that is a sharp contrast to David's sideways can't-be-bothered look.

As you take in the sculpture, titled *Memorial to a Marriage*, you can become consumed by its sweetness and love. Before you go embarrassing yourself by asking, "Oh, how did she die?," try, if you will, to think outside the . . . casket. The couple is very much alive, thank you very much.

So, why a sculpture for the living in a resting place for the dead? Cronin explains that, as a gay couple, she and Kass share as many legal documents as the law will allow—wills, health-care proxies, powers of attorney—but those papers are "all about the end of our lives." She wanted to create "the most elegant official object" she could think of to address the issue. And, since the government seemed so fixated on the death part, why not a cemetery? (Cronin also explains, for the historically challenged, that before museums, art was found in cemeteries.)

Instead of being one of those artists eternally griping about The Man and The System, Cronin worked the system. Oh yeah, government? I'll see your death and raise you two lives. And so, while Cronin is off in Rome on her next project or picking out a new sofa with Kass, the sculpture is out there diligently, day after day, on the front lines of the gay rights movement, touching visitors with the ordinariness and beauty of their relationship.

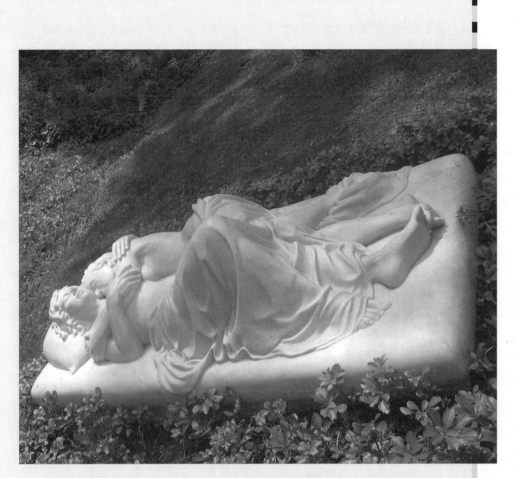

Shhhhh. Can you hear what they're saying?

There are also several smaller versions of the sculpture that tour the country, traveling soldiers who lie down in museums from coast to coast, quietly making their statement, without ever having to get out of bed. The version at Woodlawn is on all of the cemetery's walking tours. Or, see it online at www.patriciacronin.net.

A Brooklyn-Style Welcome
Brooklyn

If you've ever been to Brooklyn, you know what it is to have Brooklyn style and Brooklyn attitude.

If you've ever driven to Brooklyn, they set you straight from the get-go.

At key entry points on the expressways, overhead signs say things like WELCOME TO BROOKLYN: BELIEVE THE HYPE and WELCOME TO BROOKLYN: HOW SWEET IT IS!

There are about a dozen of these signs, part of a campaign by Brooklyn Borough President Marty Markowitz.

Nobody loves Brooklyn like this guy, who calls himself "Mr. Brooklyn." Oh, and he's earned it. Markowitz was the guy with the megaphone on the Brooklyn Bridge during the Blackout of 2003, greeting

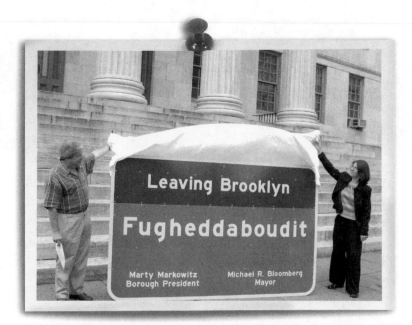

Only a true Brooklynite would know how to spell "Fugheddaboudit!"

melting Brooklynites with a resounding, "Welcome home to Brooklyn!" In the freezing cold of the December 2005 transit strike, he was back on the bridge with that megaphone, cheering, "We'll get through this!"

Markowitz even launched a tourism campaign for Brooklyn—yes, *that* Brooklyn—to show off the borough's assets, such as the Coney Island amusement park and beach and the borough's cultural cornucopia of restaurants. Check it out at www.brooklyntourism.org.

In Markowitz's opinion, "You shouldn't be leaving Brooklyn for almost anything." So, if you even *think* about it, he's got a street sign for that, too: LEAVING BROOKLYN—FUGHEDDABOUDIT!

For a listing of the locations of the Brooklyn signs, visit www.brooklyn-usa.org/Press/2003/july21.htm.

Little Green Invaders in Brooklyn

Brooklyn

Little green creatures have invaded Brooklyn. They gather in groups of fifty or sixty, building elaborate colonies, with landing strips and lookout posts. They have a sophisticated communications system that seems almost human. They laugh. They argue. They dispatch warnings. And sometimes, they appear to be conspiring.

But don't go opening an X-File or calling the paranormal experts. These invaders aren't here to take over.

They are monk parrots, also known as Quaker parrots. They have a green robe of feathers, which makes them monk-like, and a ruffled gray chest, for that dash of Quaker style. They are native to Argentina. The story varies as to how they found their way to Brooklyn, but the long-standing theory is that they were being shipped to JFK Airport around 1968 when the crate broke apart. A man named Vinny may or may not have been involved, but if you like your kneecaps, you'll leave it at that.

You may think of parrots as delicate, tropical birds that couldn't survive the winter in New York, but these tough guys came from the

A rumble in Brooklyn
PHOTO BY STEVE BALDWIN, BROOKLYNPARROTS.COM

mountains of Argentina, so they're used to the cold and actually thrive here year-round.

You'll find them on the athletic field of Brooklyn College—they've built condo-style nests up in the stadium lights—or in nearby trees and fire escapes. They huddle in groups of two or three to stay warm in the winter. Another major colony has set up shop in the huge Gothic-style entrance gate to Green-Wood Cemetery. You might even find them mixing it up with the local pigeons at dinnertime.

Make no mistake, though, these Brooklyn birds take crap from no one. At the first sign of a predator, their charming banter turns to an "Eeeee! Ack! Ack! Ack!" sound that the *Washington Post* once described as like "metal scraping metal." They're supersmart and extremely strong, so they'll go after that predator, a little winged army zigzagging through the sky. You don't mess with a bird from Brooklyn.

"They're gutsy little creatures," says Steve Baldwin, who runs a website devoted to the parrots, called www.brooklynparrots.com. To watch them go up against a predator, it's "like a game of chicken between a motorcycle and a tractor trailer," Baldwin says.

To learn more about the parrots, check out Steve's website, which includes photos, videos, and even a song he wrote for them, "Ballad of the Brooklyn Parrots." Or, join him on a "Wild Brooklyn Parrot Safari," held on the first Saturday of each month.

Daily Commute: Brooklyn to Crete
Bay Ridge, Brooklyn

George Kortsolakis grew up on the Greek island of Crete (pronounced "kreet-y") and came to New York in 1955. He spent years working as a tailor to the stars, everyone from Frank Sinatra and Mrs. Frank Sinatra, as Kortsolakis refers to them, to Paul Newman and prizefighter Mike Tyson. (For the record, Kortsolakis has both ears intact. I checked.)

When Kortsolakis retired in 1990, he turned to his garden, a small swatch of roughly seven by twenty feet, between his house and the sidewalk. He dreamed of returning to Crete, so one day, he built a seven-foot-long replica of Crete right there in his garden! He added moss for grass and pieces of slate down the middle for the main road. Chunks of concrete stand in for Crete's mountains. Turquoise aquarium rocks represent the sea. There are dozens of houses, churches, cars, boats, tiny people, and farm animals—even a representation of Kortsolakis's childhood home.

"This is one of a kind!" Kortsolakis proudly declares in his thick Greek accent, happy to explain his masterpiece—and the history of

Crete—to passersby, pointing out the clock in the back under the shell-spelled banner CRETE TIME.

"Up in the mountains, you see here?" he says pointing. "These are the kri-kri, jumping goats that you find only in Crete."

Also represented are mythical figures such as Icarus ("eek-a-russ"), who glued feathers together with wax to fly, and Alexander the Great's sister, who drank forbidden water, leaped into the ocean, and became an immortal half-fish half-human.

Kortsolakis is out there every day, before dawn, and well after dusk, always thinking about what he can add next. "The island was

Welcome to George's Crete. Please watch your step and enjoy your stay.

too dark," Kortsolakis explains. "It needed lights." So, he recruited an electrician to help him make streetlights, tiny white lights covered with clear pen caps.

Kortsolakis built a temple-like structure of Plexiglas trimmed with gold-painted molding to protect his island from the elements, then added rope lights on the ceiling for stars. He rigged systems for simulated weather patterns. "I put rain inside. Snow inside. I make stars inside. It's a beautiful thing . . . looks exactly like Crete," he says.

"He's always dreaming up things that don't exist with household objects," says Magda Capurso, one of his daughters, while Kortsolakis stands nearby, planning his next Cretian wonder.

"We're very proud of him," his wife Flora adds.

"I still have a lot of work. I never finish. Next, I have to put in the sun and the moon," says Kortsolakis, now over eighty years old. "I'm going to work until I die. When I die, then I stop."

Tonight, Is Dancing Girls!
Brighton Beach, Brooklyn

When you think of Russia, a few things probably come to mind: Vodka. The KGB. Furry hats. An accent that's fun to impersonate.

Well, here are a few more visuals: Men in tight pants and cabana wear. Women in nude unitards with strategically placed sequins. Bongos. Plumage.

Where might you find this star-spangled Russia?

In Brighton Beach, Brooklyn, a seaside community that's sometimes referred to as Little Odessa because of all the Russian and Ukrainian immigrants. The restaurants, fruit stands, and Russian-language signs seem to instantly transport you to the land of furry hats and funny accents.

You are still wondering about sequins, yes?

One of Brighton Beach's most transporting experiences is its lively Russian supper clubs. In Russia and other eastern European countries, such clubs are a posh experience. In Brighton Beach, these fancy clubs

Everybody, tequila! I mean, vodka.

under the elevated subway tracks make the experience more like a campy low-budget Vegas act.

Most are banquet style, which means you'll eat like a king in a grand ballroom while a steady stream of entertainment—and vodka—flows. The elaborate spreads often involve a couple dozen dishes—everything from beef tongue to blintzes—for about fifty-plus dollars per person.

At the National (273 Brighton Beach Avenue), the music and costumes change quicker than you can say, "More vodka, please!" At one performance, strategically placed sequins starred in a "Tequila!"

number, which was equal parts lady jumping out of a cake, Julie Andrews twirling an umbrella, and Robert Palmer video. The show-girl numbers were punctuated by soloists, including a stocky Russian crooner in a brown velvet jacket and amber-tinted J-Lo shades and a well-endowed, bustier-clad blonde in silver eye shadow.

"We have gypsy show!" says a manager at Odessa (1113 Brighton Beach Avenue), who adds that the show's music is in a variety of languages. A dishwasher at Rasputin (2670 Coney Island Avenue), describes the show there as "a human zoo," with performers in animal costumes and pop music. "There is toro [bull]. There are dogs," he says. "Las Vegas–type thing." And at Primorski (282 Brighton Beach Avenue), an employee sums up the show this way: "Very good music. Believe me."

To get to Brighton Beach, take the B or Q train to the Brighton Beach stop. Or, get a preview of the dancing girls and appetizers online: www.restaurantodessa.com and www.rasputinny.com.

You have very good time. Believe me.

Is It Hot in Here, or Is It Just Me "Sweating Gravy"?
Coney Island, Brooklyn

By now, you've probably heard of the great American Fourth of July tradition, the Nathan's Hot Dog Eating Contest in Coney Island, Brooklyn.

Now, don't go rolling your eyes. Competitive eating is a wildly entertaining sport—oh yes, I said "sport"—complete with star players, a league, and a national federation that signs them to contracts. There are announcers who call the shots and offer stats, and the sport has its own vocabulary. It's like the NFL, only with a much greater chance of a player puking.

Sorry, my bad. The first rule of eating club is you don't say "puke." Or "vomit" or "hurl," for that matter. You say "reversal." As in: "For Joey Chestnut, reversal is not an option at this point!" And, so you know, reversals *do* happen, but not as often as you'd think, according to George Shea, the P. T. Barnum of the sport and chairman of the International Federation of Competitive Eating.

The IFOCE, based in Manhattan, puts on about eighty eating contests per year worldwide. You can pretty much eat your way to fame with any number of foods, though only the top few competitors eat their way to fortune. Takeru Kobayashi, who won the Nathan's contest for several years running, is one of the sport's top earners. He's also held titles in hamburgers, bratwurst, and cow brains.

It's a man-eat-dog world out there
PHOTO COURTESY OF IFOCE

American Joey Chestnut finally became top dog on July 4, 2007, eating sixty-six hot dogs in twelve minutes, and went on to become the top-ranked eater in the world by IFOCE count. He's won the Nathan's hot dog–eating contest at least five times and holds titles in at least eighteen other foods, including asparagus, jalapeño poppers, Philly cheesesteaks, pork ribs, and shrimp wontons.

There's Sonya "The Black Widow" Thomas, weighing in at just over 100 pounds, with nearly thirty titles behind her small belt, including the ladies' hot dog–eating title at Coney Island, as well as wins in chicken wings, baked beans, and oysters, among others. Eric "Badlands" Booker, who subsidizes his eating earnings by selling CDs of himself rapping about eating, holds the corned-beef hash record and, according to Shea, "sweats gravy." (Meat events, apparently, are the most sweat-inducing.)

As for training (what, you thought it was just show up and eat?), the most common technique is to drink large quantities of water to stretch the stomach's capacity. Or the buffet-water combo. Thomas estimates her stomach can hold eighteen pounds of food; Kobayashi, more than twenty pounds.

To learn more and brush up on your eaters, check out www.ifoce .com. There's also an indie league, www.competitiveeaters.com, which declares itself "Home of Picnic Style Rules."

May you have many happy returns, but never a reversal.

Where the Mermaids Mambo
Coney Island, Brooklyn

Everyone, it seems, has their day. There's Mother's Day. Father's Day. St. Patrick's Day. Presidents' Day. Even the fools have their day.

But what about the merpeople? They get no love from Hallmark. None.

Well—and this isn't the first time you'll find yourself saying this— thank goodness for Coney Island! They understand that it ain't easy being half-lady, half-fish!

Coney Island holds a Mermaid Parade every year in late June. The ladies get all decked out in their best tails. Some walk, some ride floats. Some ride bikes. Some even walk on stilts.

Even the guys get into it. A father dressed as a fisherman pulls his merdaughter. There are Mambo mermaids and Egyptian mermaids. French (mer)maids. There's a mer-bride, and a mer-momma-to-be-maid. There are pirate mermaids, belly-dancing mermaids, and even hula-hooping mermaids. They're joined by crabs, lobster, and other glittering sea life. Marching bands, tambourine bands, and even a kazoo band.

Gawker.com describes it this way: "For many participants, the parade is the one day where they can let their freak flag fly. That counter guy from your deli? He was there, wearing blue briefs and a cape. The topless ladies came in twos and threes, painted in rich blues and bright reds, like the daughters of Miranda, Disney's Ariel, and Mystique from *X-Men.*"

(It's worth noting that the "topless ladies" have strategically-placed stars, seashells, and other sequined items to ensure that they are not violating any public nudity laws, but it's a fine line and they swim right up to it!)

The parade, led by the "Permanently Unelected Mayor of Coney Island," Dick Zigun, and a celebrity King Neptune and Queen Mermaid, kicks off on the Coney Island boardwalk and winds through the streets, where awards are given out for best costume. In the final leg—or fin—the Queen leads the masses of merfolk down the beach, where she cuts four ribbons—one for each season. The parade ends in the ocean, where all the costume parade-goers jump in and toss fruit out to sea as an offering to the gods. Mayor Zigun holds up a giant key, and the ocean is unlocked for the summer swimming season.

That night is a Mermaid Parade Ball complete with live music, burlesque, and sideshow acts.

For more information walk or swim to www.coneyisland.com/mermaid.shtml.

Aw, look at the mer-baby!

New York City Garbage

New York City is arguably one of the finest food meccas in the world, and New Yorkers will be the first ones to tell you that—whether you like it or not!

So, it's amusing that one restaurant in the city, Daddy-O, has imported a delicacy from Rochester—the garbage plate.

Actually, it's not called a garbage plate—that would be trademark infringement. It's called "the plate"—though, if you order a "garbage plate," no one will correct you.

Like the Rochester original (see page 45), this plate consists of two hamburgers or two hot dogs (including the option of white hots! See page 42), with macaroni salad, potatoes (Daddy-O's are cubed), and spicy meat sauce on top. The big difference here is that the Daddy-O's version feels a little more New York-ified, a little more fussy than the down home chop-it-all-up/fry-it-all-up version you get in Rochester. The potatoes keep to their side, the macaroni keeps to its side, the burgers or dogs lay neatly on top, covered in a blanket of meat sauce and drizzled artistically with spicy mustard.

Still, if you're from Rochester, you'll enjoy this little shout-out to your hometown, and if you're not, but you've always wondered what a garbage plate is, here's your chance to experience the garbage in all of its delicious glory for yourself.

If you're wondering how New York came to import a Rochester special, that's because Daddy-O owner Phil Casaceli is from Rochester. (He's also, by the way, a Pittsburgh Steelers fan and has a signed helmet from Terry Bradshaw behind the bar.)

Of course, everything is more expensive in New York City so this "plate" is going to cost you fifteen dollars—more than double what the original garbage plate goes for in Rochester.

In addition to the "plate," white hots, and love for the Steel Curtain, Daddy-O's is also famous for its tater tots (some say the best in the city), specialty cocktails, and outstanding selection of scotch (more than thirty single malts).

Daddy-O's is at 44 Bedford Street (at the corner of Leroy Street). For more info, visit www.daddyonyc.com.

Even the "garbage" is fancier in the big city.

★ ★

Step Right Up, Freak
Coney Island, Brooklyn

Sure, we all say we're freaks from time to time, but how many of us have a certificate to prove it?

If you aren't quite ready for the face tattoo but would like to make your freak status official, you're in luck. Coney Island, home of the famous Coney Island Sideshow, with sword swallowers and fire-eaters, has a sideshow school where they'll teach you all kinds of tricks—and make your freak status official.

You'll learn fire eating, snake charming, sword swallowing, and how to drive a nail into your nose, which, in the biz, is called the Human Blockhead.

Wait just a minute. That stuff is all fake, right?

"The fun thing about sideshow is that half of it is fake and half of it is real," says Todd Robbins, a longtime sideshow performer and former teacher at the school. "The irony of it is that which you think is fake is probably real and what thought was real is probably fake."

The old lady-in-the-box-punctured-by-swords trick, for example, "looks impossible until you get up there and look in. There's a way to twist yourself around the blades," Robbins explains.

It's all "based on principles of physics and anatomy," he says, and mastering the risk factors. Of course, there are exceptions like glass or lightbulb eating, which is—literally—a crapshoot. You wait a couple days and hope that everything comes out all right.

To be sure, the teachers won't teach you anything that risky. Their number one priority in class is safety. Outside of class, however, is a different story. Robbins says he has been known to attend a party, drink his martini, and then eat the glass.

That, my friends, is how they roll in Coney Island.

Sideshow School isn't cheap: It costs $800 for four or five classes, but you will leave there with some great party tricks—and unemployment insurance. Should you ever lose your job, just stand on the street corner and hammer a nail into your nose for money.

Move over, bearded lady. There's a new freak in town.

For more information, check out www.coneyisland.com/sideshow_school.shtml.

The Lights of Dyker Heights
Dyker Heights, Brooklyn

When my friend asked me if I wanted to go on a pilgrimage to Brooklyn to see the Christmas lights, I quickly agreed, visions of fun light-gazing trips with my mom dancing in my head.

And then, I spotted the life-size Mary and Joseph wearing wigs.

And all I can tell you is: These aren't your mother's Christmas lights. Frankly, these aren't even the lights of that crazy guy who lives on the way to your grandmother's house.

Oh no.

These are the lights of Dyker Heights.

In the Dyker Heights section of Brooklyn, McMansions fill the blocks, with sweeping staircases, topiaries, and decorative gates. And at Christmas, there's only one way to describe what goes on here: It's "keeping up with the Joneses" on cra—Christmas.

Stepping out of the car, we were greeted by the wig-clad, Nativity-going mannequins, flanked by signs advertising Christmas-decorating services—one for the lights, the other for the Nativity scene. Here, residents pay professional contractors up to $20,000 to deck out their homes for the holidays.

At that price, it goes without saying that there are lights on pretty much everything. Keep your children and pets in sight at all times during the ODS (Official Decorating Season).

Gothamist.com called it, "An over-the-top illuminated love letter to Con Edison," the electric company.

There are armies of plastic angels. Rows of lawndy canes. Carolers and Clauses. Sleighs and snowflakes. Wreaths the size of a Manhattan apartment.

One house features dancing dolls spinning on pedestals. Another has cherubic ice-skaters in snowsuits—bearing an eerie resemblance to

★ ★

Bring it on! It's Christmas in Brooklyn, baby!

Oompa Loompas—frolicking with furry polar bears. Another has a full-scale diorama of *A Christmas Carol,* complete with soundtrack.

It's not hard to figure out which house belongs to the "Joneses" that everyone's trying to keep up with. That's 1145 84th Street, between 11th and 12th Avenues. The centerpiece of that display is a twenty-five-foot, casually posed Santa, flanked by two thirty-foot-tall toy soldiers, rearing horse statues, and giant carousels that spin. You can climb the stairs, but a rope will keep you from actually walking up and sitting on Santa's lap. Not that you'd want to.

Standing beneath casual Claus, both dazzled and terrified, it felt more like the Hollywood set of a horror movie than Christmas in Brooklyn. I half-expected Jack Nicholson to jump out with an ax. At one point, I swear I saw the shrubbery take an aggressive stance. Up on the balconies, dancing reindeer seemed to mock my fear of the festivity.

The "light district" stretches from 83rd to 86th Streets and 11th to 13th Avenues in the Dyker Heights section of Brooklyn.

You can do a self-guided tour or call up Tony Muia, host of the Travel Channel's *A Slice of Brooklyn,* who offers a "Christmas Lights & Cannoli Tour," a bus tour that leaves from Manhattan. For more information, visit www.asliceofbrooklyn.com/christmas.html.

Life, Liberty, and the Pursuit of Hello

Greenwood Heights, Brooklyn

Millions of people visit the Statue of Liberty each year. She is one of the most recognizable icons in the world. There she is in the New York Harbor, torch to the sky, saluting America in all of its liberated glory. What most people don't know is that, across the harbor, on Brooklyn's southwestern shore, someone is waving back. And she's been doing it for more than eighty years.

She is Minerva, the Roman Goddess of Wisdom. She is made of bronze, roughly seven feet tall, and she resides in Green-Wood Cemetery on Battle Hill, Brooklyn's highest natural point, and the site of the first and largest battle of the Revolutionary War. She's loaded up with all her Roman warrior-goddess gear, including a helmet, but her left arm is raised in a friendly wave to her old pal, Lady Liberty.

Despite its historical significance, we all would've forgotten about the battle that took place here. The truth is, we lost that battle—and nearly lost the war at that point—and who wants to dwell on defeat? (It would be pretty hard to sell star-spangled paper plates and ballpark franks in July had we not actually won our independence.) But Charles Higgins, who made his fortune selling Higgins India ink, thought the

★ ★

Hey, Lib! How's the weather over there?

battle was pretty important and wanted to make sure that we didn't forget. So he had Minerva built, and he donated her to the people of Brooklyn.

There is no disputing that Minerva, built more than thirty years later, was intended to face the Statue of Liberty. But the Statue of Liberty is another story. Some say she faces France, who gave her to us. The official statue website says she faces the harbor to greet incoming ships.

But Green-Wood Cemetery has always maintained that she's facing Brooklyn, and Battle Hill, as a way of recognizing the starting point of our liberation.

"If she's facing France, I guess that's possible," says Green-Wood Cemetery Historian Jeff Richman. "You'll have to stand behind her and see if you can see the Eiffel Tower in the distance!"

The amazing thing is that in New York City, with all of its revised zoning laws to clear the path for ever-skyward buildings, the view between the two ladies of liberty remains unobstructed. One building between the old gals had threatened to block their greeting, but the builders agreed to cut out a corner so as not to interrupt.

And so, Minerva, and the Statue of Liberty, now 126 years old, will forever exchange greetings, like a couple of old ladies on the way to the market.

The next time you're visiting the Statue of Liberty, mugging for the camera in your green foam crown, gaze across the harbor and give a shout-out to Minerva. Better yet, visit Green-Wood at 500 25th Street in Brooklyn (www.green-wood.com).

The Dancing of the Giglio
Williamsburg, Brooklyn

Every summer, just as June is melting into July, there's a street festival in the Italian part of Williamsburg, Brooklyn, near Our Lady of Mount Carmel Church. It has all of the usual street-fair fare—refreshments, cotton candy, and carnival games—and, of course, Italian special-ties. But twice during this festival, something extraordinary happens. Out from between the carts of Italian sausage and deep-fried zep-pole emerges a towering spire, five stories tall—and it appears to be dancing.

The spire, which has a priest and twelve-piece brass band at the base, weighs about five tons and is carried by 125 men down the street. It is the Giglio. (And no, it has nothing to do with J-Lo.) As the band plays an eccentric medley comprised of Italian classics, "The

Dancing in the streets.

Star-Spangled Banner," and even "The Rainbow Connection," the burly men, with cutoff sleeves, headbands, and backward baseball caps, carry the immense monument with lightly padded steel beams resting on their shoulders. Lieutenants on each side call out orders to *la paranza,* the lifters, and the entire regiment is overseen by one man, the capo. Bobbing, swaying, and turning it as they go, they pause every few minutes to wipe the sweat from their brows and take a swig of beer from the sidelines, the Giglio version of the Gatorade shot at a marathon. The crowd stands in awe.

The Dancing of the Giglio, as the feat is known, is a tradition that was brought to Brooklyn more than 100 years ago by immigrants from the southern Italian town of Nola near Naples. The Giglio, which means "lily" in Italian, is topped with a statue of San Paolino, or Saint Paulinus, the patron saint of Nola. As the story goes, the Huns invaded Italy nearly 1,600 years ago and Paolino, a lawyer-turned-priest, escaped with the children of the town to protect them. Upon his return, he soon realized that he'd missed one boy, who was captured. Paolino offered to trade himself into a life of slavery in exchange for the boy's freedom. When Paolino himself was finally freed, the people of Nola greeted him with bouquets of lilies. The town made this an annual tradition, carrying the lilies into the town square on big poles.

Brooklyn's Giglio is part of a two-week festival that celebrates both Our Lady of Mount Carmel and San Paolino. It begins with *La Questa,* when volunteers hand out bread in the neighborhood to remember San Paolino's sacrifice of all his worldly possessions. There are also Giglio dances in Harlem and Long Island.

The Metropolitan Museum of Plastic Forks

Williamsburg, Brooklyn

Dave Herman was the kind of New Yorker who kept his old sub-way tokens. He was also the kind of guy who took it a step further and displayed them in the window of his street-front apartment in

Williamsburg, Brooklyn, along with other New York paraphernalia, like his collection of Statues of Liberty.

Passersby would stop and ponder the odd window museum. Pretty soon, they started stopping to chat and even offering their own collections—everything from Ceramic ETs to Chinese menus—for display.

You might not think of the one or two Chinese takeout menus tucked in that drawer in your kitchen as artifacts, but put 10,000 of

That's a lotta Liberty!

them together, and you've got a collection, my friend. You know what they say—one man's junk is another man's . . . museum.

Not surprisingly, after about three years, the tiny museum with a grand name, the City Reliquary, outgrew Herman's apartment, and he and a handful of friends started renting a public space around the corner.

The museum's permanent collection consists largely of New York artifacts such as an old subway door and trolley tracks from Brooklyn (which, incidentally, are the reason the Brooklyn Dodgers got their name because the kids would always be dodging the trolleys). But you'll also find a stuffed pigeon, a subway paint chip, and artifacts-in-the-making such as a plastic fork from Nathan's Famous hot-dog stand in Coney Island. "New is the old of the future," Herman explains. The rotating community collections, on loan from locals, can be anything from argyle socks to unicorn figurines, dipsticks, and yes, Chinese menus.

Oh, and for the record, the Transit Museum at Grand Central Station is now selling those old subway tokens (set of five, dating back to 1953) for twenty-five dollars!

If you're inspired to start a collection, the museum has a vending machine with starter kits, which include a small Statue of Liberty and a gift pack of soil samples from all five boroughs.

The City Reliquary is located at 370 Metropolitan Avenue in Brooklyn (718-782-4842; www.cityreliquary.org). The museum is often limited to weekend hours, so call ahead to make sure it's open.

The Fangs Come Out

East Village, Manhattan

From *True Blood* to *Twilight,* vampires and blood-sucking thoughts seem to be everywhere these days. If this whole vampire craze has you running your tongue over your canine teeth wondering, *What if I had fangs?* . . . then I know just the guy for you.

Father Sebastiaan is a professional "fangsmith" (you didn't even know that was a real job, did you? Well, now you do), which means he will create a pair of custom-made fangs for you that fit right over your teeth.

We're not talking about costume-shop plastic fangs that fall down and steal your vampire mojo as you try to say, "I want to suck your blood." No, Sebastiaan is trained in dentistry and, you might say, has dentistry in his blood—his grandfather and aunt were both dentists. So, these are dental-quality fangs that slide on like caps.

(And for the record, most modern-day vampires don't drink blood. So, you're going to need to work on a few new pickup lines when you get your fangs.)

Sebastiaan got into the whole vampire thing (actually, in the vampire subculture it's spelled "vampyre") reading Anne Rice's vampire novels at the age of nine, which turned into an interest in the whole Goth subculture. When his grandfather passed away, Sebastiaan tinkered with his grandfather's dentistry tools and made himself a pair of fangs that he wore all kinds of places, like at the shoe store he worked at in New Jersey called, appropriately, Wild Pairs. That might seem like an odd job for a fang maker (hey, everyone's gotta start somewhere) but, in fact, that is where he made his first connection with someone in the NYC club scene as well as a dentist who took him on as an apprentice. (He couldn't ask his grandfather, he says, because "he would've looked at me as if I had two heads!" Nope, one head. Two fangs, though.)

He, ahem, cut his teeth, you might say, in the fang-making business while working at the famous NYC nightclub Limelight making fangs for club kids.

Now, he's a full-time fang maker (not just at Halloween), splitting his time between New York, New Orleans, and France. He hosts The Endless Night Vampire Ball (www.endlessnight.com) in New York and similar masquerade-type balls around the world. He is also the author of several books, including *Vampyre Virtues: The Red Veils,* offering one hundred words for vampires to live by.

The fangs, which cost ninety-nine dollars a pair plus tax, are made of the highest quality dental acrylic and pop over your existing teeth like a cap. They come in a variety of styles and degrees of sharpness, from the ladylike Lilith to the supersharp Beast and his own signature Sabretooth. There are also pop-culture styles, including the Lost Boys, Underworlds, and True Bloods. (There are no Twilights, however—if you've seen the movies, you know those vampires don't have fangs. He did, however, once make a set of fangs for Ashley Greene, who plays Alice in the *Twilight* movies. "She said she was really disappointed because she couldn't wear fangs in the movie!" Sebastiaan says.)

Fangs are sharp—after all, that's what you're paying for—so you have to be careful not to cut yourself on your own teeth.

It's OK to drink or smoke with the fangs on, but Sebastiaan advises against eating with them.

"My rules are: No sleeping, no eating . . . but sex, absinthe, and rock & roll are highly encouraged!"

Vampires. They're so sexy, aren't they?

His New York "office" is located in the Halloween Adventure Shop at 104 4th Avenue in the East Village, though he's not there year-round. To book an appointment, e-mail father@sabretooth.com. For more information, visit www.fathersebastiaan.com.

The Human Car Wash
East Village, Manhattan

New York is home to some of the best spas in the world. But why would you go for a froufrou spa treatment when you could simply get a beating with an oak-leaf broom, have a couple of ice-cold buckets of water dumped over your head, and then jump in a forty-five-degree pool?

Europeans and Russians have long used extreme temperatures—hot steam and cold pools—as a way to detoxify their bodies. In Russia, there's even a group called *morzhy*, or walruses, that jump into frozen rivers and lakes in the middle of winter.

You can sample it for yourself at the Russian and Turkish Baths, the oldest bathhouse left in New York and a year-round gathering spot for the Polar Bear set. The idea is to toggle between hot and cold, starting with heat.

There are four rooms for heat, but the most popular is the Russian Room, where a huge oven heats 200 giant boulders to make dry, intense heat. With temperatures over 200 degrees, you'll actually grab one of those ice-cold buckets of water and dump it on yourself—multiple times. You take breaks by sitting in the hallway, jumping in the cold pool, or hitting the Swedish shower, which blasts you with cold water from all sides.

"You know, *shvitz*," the Yiddish word for sweat, "then cold pool, shvitz, then cold pool," explains Aron, an antiques dealer from Brooklyn who brings his own oak-leaf broom, known as a *Platza*. He and his friends—like Frank, who's been coming to the baths for forty years—take turns in the Russian Room, whacking each other with the brooms.

"The only way I can describe it, it's the closest you can get to God—spiritually, mentally, and physically," Frank says.

You can make up your own routine at the baths, with input from old pros like Frank and Aron, but there are two things not to be missed: the cold pool and the Platza. As you lay on the top shelf of the Russian steam room with a wet washcloth over your head, a Platza specialist will literally beat you with a broom made of oak leaves. Then, you sit up and they "whack you a couple times in the head," says Dmitry Shapiro, who runs the place with his brother, Jack. To be clear, it doesn't hurt. It's meant to intensify the heat. "You take detox to a new level," Dmitry says.

Platza, which comes from the Yiddish word for shoulders, "opens the pores, penetrates more heat," Aron explains.

"It's like a human car wash," Frank adds, which is an apt description, particularly when you're holding your breath and hot, wet leaves are coming down on both sides of your head.

It's certainly not the pampering you get at a spa. Just the thought of someone at the spa hitting you over the head with a broom sounds absurd. But when you walk out, your skin will feel like that of a

★ ★

newborn baby. "You're not necessarily going to look prettier when you come out" with bright, pink skin, Dmitry explains, "but you're going to feel better."

And when you're done, one of the charms of the baths is sitting around in the lounge/cafe, chatting in your standard-issue robe and rubber slippers while downing a fruit juice or Russian beer.

The Russian and Turkish Baths are at 268 East 10th Street. For more information, visit www.russianturkishbaths.com or call (212) 674-9250. Most days are coed, but some days are ladies only or men only so call ahead.

Would you like wax or just the wash?

★ ★

Clickety-Clack, the Walls Whisper Back

Midtown Manhattan

In Grand Central Station, thousands of commuters whiz by every day, filling the marble corridors with a cacophony of clacking heels and cell-phone chatter as they make a mad dash for the next train.

But down below the main concourse, on the subterranean food-court level, people are whispering. A young girl runs into a corner and says softly, "Can you hear me?" On the opposite side of the corridor, diagonally, her friend quietly exclaims into the wall: "Yes, I can hear you!" and both run off giggling.

The girls are replaced by a father with his son on his shoulders. "I love you, Mommy!" the boy whispers into the wall, before meeting up with his beaming mother. A young man leans into the same wall, egged on by his friend. On the other side of the corridor, an attractive woman is startled when the wall whistles at her unexpectedly.

This is the Whispering Gallery, one of the charming secrets of Grand Central Terminal. It is located right outside the Oyster Bar. There are no signs pointing out the gallery's exact location, but a steady stream of people darting in and out of the whisper spots lets you know you've found it.

Here's how it works: When you talk directly into the corner, the sound travels up and over the domed ceiling, covered in impervious Guastavino tile, and down the other side. To your friend on the other side, it sounds as if your voice is coming from a speaker tucked behind the tile about arms-length overhead. Or, depending on how you're standing, the sound may seem to come from elsewhere around you. I nearly jumped out of my skin thinking my friend, who was a good thirty feet away from me, was right behind me whispering in my ear.

Since the tile isn't absorbent, and there are no vents, rugs, or other sound-escaping or sound-absorbing items, there's no place for the sound to go but up and over, a spokesperson for Metro-North Railroad explained. And even though you're on opposite sides of the corridor, the people buzzing through the corridor can't hear you. No one knows

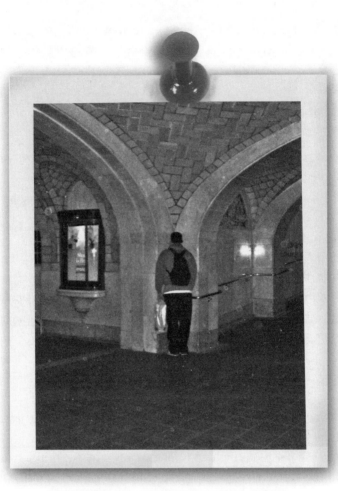

I'd like two cheeseburgers, an order of fries . . .

why the secret-communication ceiling was created, but it's been that way since Grand Central was built in 1913.

According to employees at the Oyster Bar, it's not just for idle chatter. The Whispering Gallery is a popular spot for marriage proposals. They're smart guys—that's one transmission you wouldn't want to get lost in a subway vent! All you have to do is make sure you have the right woman on the other side.

For a self-guided tour of Grand Central that includes the Oyster Bar, Whispering Gallery, and the "Kissing Room," among other highlights, visit www.grandcentralterminal.com/info/walkingtour.cfm.

Night of a Thousand Gowns

Midtown Manhattan

The hair is big. The gowns are big. The dance numbers are big. And most of all, their hearts are big.

This is the Night of a Thousand Gowns, an annual charity drag ball at the Marriott Marquis hotel in Times Square and one of the biggest events of the year on the gay society calendar.

It's put on by the Imperial Court of New York, a chapter of the International Court, and features dinner, dancing, Broadway-style entertainment, and an auction of fabulous things. (We're talking MAC Cosmetics, Swarovski-crystal bling, and yes, a portrait of Liza Minnelli.)

The guests wear lavish gowns, many of which they've made themselves (if you're six foot five, you may not fit into Miss USA's hand-me-downs), sequined cocktail dresses, leather numbers, or tasteful tuxedos.

The purpose of the event, aside from showing off your rhinestones and shaking your tail feathers, is to raise money for charity. At $325 a head, the ball raises thousands for a variety of charities including Broadway Cares/Equity Fights AIDS and PFLAG (Parents and Friends of Lesbians and Gays).

The ball includes awards for outstanding achievement in the gay community and offers a chance to brush satin-gloved elbows with celebrities—everyone from Boy George and Cyndi Lauper to cabaret star Dirty Martini and PBS personality Clover Honey.

The crown jewel of the event is the crowning of a new emperor and empress, chosen for his and his extraordinary fund-raising efforts. The royal couple reigns for one year as ambassadors of the court.

★ ★

"It's like Broadway," says CJ Mingolelli, a Manhattan and Fire Island real-estate agent. "There's the passing of the crown. Each emperor and empress has an entourage. . . . It's kind of outlandish."

In case you're wondering—which, I know you are—CJ and his partner favor tuxedos. But they love the spectacle of it all, as well as the chance to see friends and raise money for a worthy cause.

The event is held in late March or early April, but tickets sell out fast. For more information visit www.icny.org.

The emperor and empress, surrounded by their gorgeous man court.
PHOTO BY JOE SAPORITO FOR NEWYORKQNEWS.COM

Retrospective: My Sock Collection

Have you ever been standing in the middle of your living room, looked around, and wondered what it would be like if someone in the year 2158 were giving a guided tour of this now-historic spot?

"Over here on the left, is Jim's sofa. You can see the indentation in the cushion where he sat most nights watching television. On the right, a pile of newspapers that he kept meaning to get around to reading . . ."

Amazingly, someone had the foresight to do just that: preserve homes from 150 years ago on Manhattan's Lower East Side.

It's called the Lower East Side Tenement Museum, and what you'll find on the tour is far more than a nineteenth-century butt print. You'll learn—and feel—what it was like for immigrants struggling to make it in America in the late 1800s and early 1900s.

Today's New Yorkers love to complain about *that time they lived in an apartment so small they could shower and stir a pot of spaghetti at the same time,* but the New Yorkers you'll encounter at the Tenement Museum would've considered such living a luxury. For them, coin-operated gas lighting and heat, indoor plumbing, and shared toilets were a treat. Before that, they used candles and went to the bathroom in the backyard.

On the tour, you'll get to know a few of the tenants of 97 Orchard Street, including Nathalie Gumpertz, a single mother from Prussia who ran a dressmaking business out of her tenement to support four kids after her husband went to work one day and never came home.

Unfortunately, Julius Gumpertz wasn't the only husband who vanished in the wake of the Panic of 1873 as severe economic depression gripped the nation. There were so many that the local newspaper had a "Missing Husbands" section. No one knows for sure if men like Julius died or simply buckled under the pressure and ran

Thanks to the heavy iron, this is the kitchen, laundry room, and gym.
PHOTO COURTESY OF BATTMAN STUDIOS

away. But as one woman pointed out on the tour, "If they ever did come home, their wives would've killed them!"

You can take a virtual tour of several tenement apartments at www.tenement.org. Or, you can stop complaining about your desk job for five minutes, turn off your computer, make a pit stop at your indoor bathroom (don't forget to wash your hands under the running water), and head over to 108 Orchard Street—across the street from the preserved tenement building—where tours begin. Tours cost twenty-two dollars. For more information, visit the website or call (212) 431-0233.

The Naked Cowboy
Times Square, Manhattan

If you've been to New York's Times Square, chances are you've seen the Naked Cowboy, pointed, and giggled. Any attempts to look away are generally futile.

For the uninitiated, the Naked Cowboy (aka Robert J. Burcke II of Secaucus, New Jersey) is the guy singing in the traffic divide at 45th and Broadway, wearing only a cowboy hat, boots, a guitar—and tighty whities with "Naked Cowboy" emblazoned on the butt.

He's not going to be up for a Grammy anytime soon, but then again, few people pretend they stopped by for the singing. Nonetheless, the Naked Cowboy's briefs are overflowing with . . .

Confidence.

The Cowboy will tell you he's the third top attraction in New York (after the Empire State Building and Statue of Liberty) and likens himself to Christ, Buddha, and Copernicus. "I, myself, am God Almighty!" the Cowboy declares.

When he's not in Times Square or at the gym, you'll find this urban cowboy reading the work of great philosophers such as Nietzsche and Emerson, self-help guru Tony Robbins, and, uh, himself.

That confidence and greatness translates into lyrics for the Times Square set such as: "If you really wanna live / feel the way I feel / you've got to whip out! / your balls . . . of . . . steel," and "The homophobes say I'm a queer / but I like chicks and beer . . ."

You can find him in Times Square most days—even cold winter days—though the Cowboy does occasionally "tour" other cities. In the early days, that meant him showing up someplace and playing in his underpants until he was either thrown out or arrested, which, for the record, was forty-nine times. Today, he's gotten a bit more recognition for his craft. He's been in a dozen commercials, including one for the Super Bowl, and may soon have his own underwear line at a chain store near you.

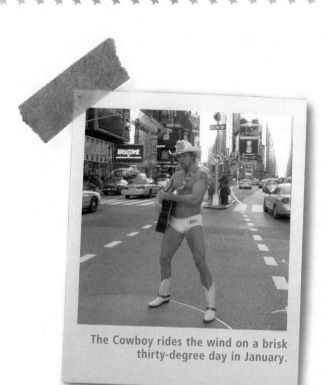

The Cowboy rides the wind on a brisk thirty-degree day in January.

Once, a tourist asked the Cowboy: "Why do you do this?" He replied: "Because if I don't do it, it won't get done. You're not going to do it, are you?"

No, Cowboy, probably not. Thanks for taking one for the team.

The Cowboy's business, like his confidence, grows every day. Now you can get married by the Reverend Naked Cowboy (ceremonies start at $499) or start your own Naked Cowboy or Naked Cowgirl franchise.

You can buy a copy of his self-published book, *Determination: Legend of the Naked Cowboy,* for $16.99 on Amazon. On his website (www.nakedcowboy.com), you can buy all kinds of Cowboy gear, from hats to T-shirts and even a pair of those signature briefs—just in case, y'know, you feel like air guitar-ing Naked Cowboy–style in your living room.

★ ★

Seriously, You Would Look Great in a Unitard
Tribeca, Manhattan

So, you've passed the point in your life where running off and joining the circus is a viable option. No problem. Step right up!

Tucked between the Hudson River and the West Side Highway is the New York Trapeze School. In the summer, the trapeze rig is all out in the open, so you can feel like you're really flying over Manhattan. In the winter, they put the rig in a tent.

Imagine yourself climbing up the ladder in your shiny sequined unitard, like the new kid on the Flying Wallenda block. OK, OK. You

Turn this city upside down at the New York Trapeze School.

don't have to wear a unitard. (But it's fun to picture yourself in one, am I right?)

Standing on top of the platform, in your modern athletic wear, that top-of-the-roller-coaster giddiness will come rushing back. Your adult sensibility may interrupt with a gut-level alert of "Retreat! Retreat!" But your inner cheapskate will remind you that you've already paid sixty bucks for this experience, so just jump already.

As you fling yourself off the platform—twenty-three feet in the air—you might scream. You might laugh. You might cry. But you're gonna freakin' love every minute of it.

Dangling upside down, trying to muster the courage to try a flip, you'll realize that this is *much* harder than it looks. In an inverted moment of epiphany, you'll completely understand why the pros make such dramatic "Ta-da!" poses when they're done. You'll also make a note to self to clap much louder for these guys the next time you're at the circus.

Throughout your high-flying act, you'll have breathtaking views of the Statue of Liberty, World Financial Center, and the Hudson River. And you'll always have the bragging rights that you once performed in New York City!

Visit http://newyork.trapezeschool.com or call (212) 242-8769. Prices range from thirty-five to sixty-five dollars per class. During the busy summer months, sign up in advance because classes book up quickly.

A Celebrity Who Eats Rats

Upper East Side, Manhattan

In New York City, it's hard to stand out. But one high-flying Manhattan resident has managed to do just that. In a town full of celebrities, he *is* a celebrity. His love life and run-ins with the law have been chronicled in the tabloids. He's inspired a documentary, has his own website, and is hounded by the paparazzi *constantly.*

His name is Pale Male, and he is a red-tailed hawk. His story might not have drawn more than a passing mention if he lived in a treetop

Great dinner, honey. The pigeon is delicious!
DONEGAL BROWNE, PALEMALEIRREGULARS.BLOGSPOT.COM

in eastern Pennsylvania. What rocketed this carnivorous leading man to fame was the fact that he built his nest on the twelfth-floor ledge of a Manhattan apartment building. And not just any building: This one was on Fifth Avenue, which is dotted with names like Tiffany and Trump, and boasts other famous residents such as Mary Tyler Moore and Paula Zahn. Usually, in this town, it takes more than a few twigs to land such a prestigious address!

When Pale Male gets hungry, he heads to Central Park, which has a lot of wide-open spaces for hunting up squirrels and pigeons to bring back to—you guessed it—Mary Tyler Moore's house.

He's drawn bird lovers from all over the world, but, like all celebrities, not everyone is a fan. (It may have something to do with the fact that his dinners are soaked in blood, not béarnaise sauce.) In 2004 he was temporarily evicted with then-lover Lola (she passed away in 2010) after outspoken residents such as Zahn and her then-husband had had enough of the unwanted attention and leftover carcasses from dinner that spilled onto the sidewalk below. But the bird lovers united—staging rallies and even circulating a 10,000-signature petition—and before too long, the birds were back in town.

Pale Male and Lola were together from 2002 to 2010. He has had several lady loves since then.

You can visit Pale Male in person, or check him out online at fan sites including www.palemale.com and www.palemaleirregulars .blogspot.com. The pictures are stunning, and the commentary is wildly entertaining. A March 21, 2012, post on palemaleirregulars about Pale Male mating several times a day with a new lady named Zena, included this caption: "Obviously Pale Male is doing a dynamite job because Zena is looking a bit cross-eyed, don't you think?"

Mary Tyler Moore, following Elvis's lead, has left the building, but Pale Male still lives at 927 Fifth Avenue.

A Night at the Museum
Upper West Side, Manhattan

If your kids loved the movie *Night at the Museum,* where the animals and historic figures at the American Museum of Natural History come alive at night, then guess what? They can spend a night at the museum, too!

One to two times a month, the American Museum of Natural History hosts a "Night at the Museum," where more than 450 kids and their parents can spend a night at the museum. That includes a flashlight tour of some cool parts of the museum—from the Hall of Human Origins where they keep the monkeys (make sure you know where your keys are!) to Dinosaur Hall, where you'll get to stand under a

Good night, dum dum!
COURTESY OF AMERICAN MUSEUM OF NATURAL HISTORY

sixty-five-million-year-old Tyrannosaurus rex like "Rexy" from the movie, who ran around the museum like a dog!

It also includes an IMAX film or space show, a live animal show, a snack, and bedtime stories. The night ends with everyone tucked into their sleeping bags in the Hall of Ocean Life, under a ninety-four-foot-long blue whale suspended from the ceiling, or in the Hall of African Mammals or Hall of Planet Earth.

This unforgettable "night at the museum" lasts from 6:00 p.m. to 9:00 a.m. and costs $129 per person. For more information, visit www.amnh.org/kids/sleepovers or call (212) 769-5200.

What to Do with a Spare Island
Roosevelt Island

New York City is really a collection of dozens of islands. And, back before modern medicine, how did New Yorkers deal with contagious, sometimes deadly diseases? They shipped them out to another island! Imagine that: OK, this here is Plague Island. And this over here is Crazy Island. Got it? Good. Now go.

Roosevelt Island, which the Indians used to call Minnahononck ("It's nice to be here") Island and the Dutch called Hogs' Island, is a thin swatch of land in the middle of the East River between Manhattan and

Roosevelt Island's former smallpox hospital is an eerie green beacon in the night.

★ ★

Queens. Because it was close to Manhattan but still isolated from the wider population, it became a favorite parking spot in the nineteenth century for the sick, crazy, and incarcerated.

Today, the island is popular with a loyal following of yuppies and diplomats, many of whom work for the United Nations, which is located a short tram or subway ride away across the river in Manhattan. They love their condos and that small-town feel in the middle of the big city. But at the southern tip of the island lies a macabre reminder of the island's sordid past.

It is the ruins of the former smallpox hospital, built in 1856 by James Renwick, who is famous for his less-contagious work, St. Patrick's Cathedral. It's an imposing Gothic structure, with vines creeping through the pointed windows like ghosts of plagues past. At night, it's lit from below with an eerie greenish light, as if the building were doing some sort of Blair Witch impression, compliments of the lighting designer for the Statue of Liberty.

You might think that living on an island steeped in years of disease, madness, and crime would be a bit of a bargain. Not true. Residents pay New York prices to live here, and over on Manhattan's eastern shore, residents pay a premium for a "view" of, well, a creepy hospital.

Ahhhh, New York. We're all a little bit crazy, aren't we?

Rent-a-Hookah
Astoria, Queens

Admit it: You dream of Arabian nights, though you're not exactly sure what that means. It just sounds exotic.

If you don't have the 1,500 bucks for a flight to Cairo and picking up some Sabra hummus at the grocery store isn't quite exotic enough for you, here's a way you can get a taste of the Middle East—literally.

Head to Steinway Street in Astoria, Queens, between 28th Avenue and Astoria Boulevard, often referred to as Little Egypt because of all the Middle Eastern cafes, restaurants, and shops.

★ ★

Take a stroll on Steinway; stop in for a hookah.

Wearing your jeans and sneakers, *you* may feel like the foreigner when you see some of the local women in their *hijab,* or head scarves. Just act like you left yours at home and press on to one of the block's many cafes, such as the Egyptian Coffee Shop, Egyptian Cafe, or Casa Lounge.

For less than ten dollars, you can rent a hookah for a few hours, with your choice of flavored tobacco. A hookah is a water pipe, usually made of brass and glass, which stands on the floor. Charcoal lights the tobacco and the smoke is filtered through water, which makes it light and airy—nothing like cigarette smoke. Attached to the pipe is a hose with a disposable plastic mouthpiece, through which you inhale the smoke. The tobacco often comes in fruit flavors such as apple, strawberry, cherry, and mango.

Now, a hookah may *look* like a bong, but to be clear, what you'll get in a hookah is tobacco and not an illegal drug. If some of you are disappointed by this, I offer no apologies. Remember, we're trying to have fun here, not get arrested.

While we're going over protocol, you should know that most authentic hookah cafes don't serve alcohol, as it's against Muslim custom. So don't get all frat boy on me and order a beer. Instead, try the Turkish coffee. If you simply must have alcohol, there's an Irish bar, Sissy McGinty's, on the same block.

For a little souvenir from your hookstravaganza, you can buy a hookah or brass lantern from one of the shops on Steinway. Strategically place the item in your living room to help steer the conversation at your next cocktail party toward "that time you smoked the hookah."

After Wrestling, These Pianos Hit the Sauna
Astoria, Queens

From a classical concert at Carnegie Hall to Billy Joel's world tour, have you ever wondered where those gorgeous grand pianos come from?

You might guess that they are created at a big factory in China where a small, goggle-clad man presides over a massive machine that drops in each key with robotic staccato before it glides down the conveyer belt.

In fact, most concert grands are made by Steinway & Sons at a small factory right here in Queens, land of the Mets and Archie Bunker. There aren't giant robotic machines. Rather, each piano is made (tech geeks, cover your eyes for this part) *by hand.*

Actually, it's more like 600 hands. It takes about 300 people to assemble the 12,000 parts that comprise a Steinway grand piano. And it takes one year to make.

You can take a tour of the Steinway piano factory, which is like Willy Wonka's Chocolate Factory for the Chopin set. There aren't Oompa Loompas, but there is a full cast of characters and some surreal sets the piano encounters on its journey. There are the burly rim benders, who wrestle eighteen sheets of hard rock maple into that signature piano curve and then clamp it down with a piano-size vise.

Hey, buddy, can you throw some water on the coals?

There's a "sauna room," where the piano goes for a little R&R after all that wrestling, and a "belly room," where rows of women at long wooden tables toil over small parts with miniature hammers. There are men shaving keys and stringing strings. True to Wonka form, a lacquer waterfall recycles the runoff after each coat of gloss.

And then, the finale, when the piano gets its voice. Voicers poke, prod, soften, harden, and balance each note to perfect pitch. A voicer's office has all the usual cubical fare—staplers, pens, pictures of their kids, and so on—but a few key differences: There's a rolltop door like a garage, and a huge piano parked in the middle!

Upon exiting the factory, you'll notice a pile of wood in the parking lot. But don't even think of snagging some for your winter kindling—what may look like a "scrap" heap to you is actually piano wood left out to dry for a year and could be the Piano Man's next grand!

Steinway & Sons offers factory tours once a week, but only seasonally and the tours fill up quickly, so book in advance. For more information go to www.steinway.com or call (718) 721-2600.

What the Jetsons Left Behind
Corona Park, Queens

In 1964, space was the new frontier and *The Jetsons* showed us how to make a sandwich when we got there. The World Trade Center was merely a blueprint, and the Beatles announced to the world that they wanted to hold your hand.

The 1964–65 World's Fair, held in Flushing Meadows Corona Park in Queens, was a portal to the future, as envisioned by the likes of various countries, states, and major US corporations. GM's "Futurama" exhibit showed us we could live anywhere—even on the moon. IBM dazzled visitors with a 500-seat hydraulic stadium and high-tech presentation to explain that computers were our friends and not to be feared. (HAL came along a few years later and nearly ruined it for us all.) Disney brought the diorama screaming—well, more singing and frolicking—into the twentieth century with the debut of the animatronic "It's a Small World" ride. Wisconsin offered the world's largest cheese, and Belgium introduced the world to its culinary future: the Belgian waffle.

When the fair ended, many of the exhibits were carted off to other cities or countries, but there are a few curious hangers-on that remain in Flushing Meadows Corona Park. The most famous is the Unisphere, the world's largest globe, which is made of stainless steel and stands twelve stories tall. You might recognize it in the opening credits of *The King of Queens.*

The Unisphere is pretty well preserved, but not so much for the New York Pavilion, a roadside oddity visible from the Grand Central

**It was once the "Tent of Tomorrow,"
and now, it's a reminder of the past.**

Parkway. Huge columns support a spiky metal circle with wires
stretched like bicycle spokes. During the fair, it was covered in a colorful canopy and housed New York's "Tent of Tomorrow." Nearby are
the crumbling remains of three giant fair-observation decks, which
once featured futuristic pill-shaped elevators. Several movies were
filmed here, including *Men in Black*.

The Queens Museum, located inside the park, is home to a
9,335-square-foot panorama of all five boroughs of New York City
that was one of the fair's most popular exhibits. You can't take a simulated helicopter ride over the "city" anymore, but it's still pretty cool.

Today, there isn't much evidence of *The Jetsons* in Queens, except
for two very tall curiosities outside the Hall of Science—two 100-foot-
tall rockets, an Atlas and a Titan 2. (Don't worry, the fuel tanks have
been removed.)

On the number 7 train to Queens, a little boy looks out the window. "Look, Daddy, a rocket!"

That's cute. As for me, I'm still holding out for the jet pack.

Franny from the Block

Floral Park, Queens

Bing, bong. Stand clear of the closing doors, please. Honk honk! Waieeeeeeeeerrrrrrrrowaieeeerrro! Hey, watch it, buddy! Taxi!

Ah, the sounds of the city.

Er er er er errrrrrrrrrrr!

Wait, who was that last guy? He wasn't from New York, right?

Actually, that rooster *is* a New Yorker, and he lives on a farm in Floral Park on the far eastern border of Queens. When you get there, you'll find him wandering the roads of the farm, so don't drive like a New Yorker lest you run over him, OK?

The farm has been around since 1697, and holds the distinction of being the last working farm in New York City. It sits on forty-seven acres, which in New York City terms is like an entire neighborhood.

The farm was in private hands for many years, before the state bought it for the Creedmoor Psychiatric Center for produce—and therapy. It was about to be shuttered in 1973, but the local townfolk rallied to save the farm, and it's now a museum.

But don't let the museum part fool you: They've got 250 hens that produce eggs and a beehive that makes honey, both of which are sold at the farm. Plus, nine goats, seven sheep, two alpacas, two geese, and two brown Swiss cows, named Franny and Dolly.

They also grow and sell a variety of fruits and vegetables including lettuce, tomatoes, peppers and pumpkins, plus flowers for making bouquets and a vineyard, where they make their own wine!

The location is a favorite for television, film, and magazine crews. Both *Sex and the City* and *Law & Order* have filmed here. The next time you see a bridal magazine spread set on a farm, check the credit! That farm may very well be in New York City.

**Do you have any idea how many times I've heard
"Why did the chicken cross the road?!" If I had a nickel . . .**

You don't have to be Sarah Jessica Parker to get into New York's farm; anyone can stop by and say: "Well, howdy doo, Ms. Dolly?" There are guided tours on the weekend, and the farm is open for self-guided tours every day of the week.

The best times to go are during the fall, when the crops are in full swing. There are a variety of cool events, including an interactive corn maze—a maze of maize, if you will—plus pumpkin picking, an apple festival, and an American Indian Pow Wow.

For more information go to www.queensfarm.org or call (718) 347-FARM (3276).

★ ★

How Many Points for Queens?

Jackson Heights, Queens

The street signs in Queens are confusing enough—24th Drive, for example, is followed by 24th Road, which is followed by 24th Avenue, which *intersects* with 24th Street. But the street sign for 35th Avenue in Jackson Heights is even more confusing—it has subscript numbers after the *t* and *h* in 35th as well as after all the letters in Avenue.

What is this—some kind of Queens code? A secret formula?

Close! It's an homage to the board game Scrabble and its inventor, Alfred Mosher Butts, who invented it right here in Jackson Heights.

It was the early 1930s, in the middle of the Great Depression, and Butts, an architect, was unemployed. So, he decided to try his hand at inventing a board game.

He concluded that games fell into three categories: number games like dice and bingo; move games such as chess and checkers; and word games such as anagrams. His game, he thought, would combine the vocabulary skills of a crossword puzzle or anagram with the added element of chance.

He didn't just willy-nilly start writing letters on wooden pieces and assigning them random number values. He studied the front page of the *New York Times,* the story goes, to see how frequently different letters of the alphabet were used. He limited the number of *s* tiles so you couldn't just dominate the game by making words plural!

He initially called the game Lexico, then changed it to Cross-Cross Words.

Like many great inventions, the game wasn't an instant success. Butts tried to sell it to game manufacturers, but not one played the words *yes* or *buy.*

In 1949, game-loving entrepreneur James Brunot wanted to start manufacturing the game on a larger scale, so he bought the rights and agreed to pay Butts a royalty on every game sold. He left most of the game intact as Butts designed it but changed the name to Scrabble, which means "to scratch or dig frantically with the hands" (which, let's be honest, is how some of us play the game).

That first year of production, more than ten years after Butts invented the game, the first Scrabble factory, in Dodgingtown (Newtown), Connecticut, where Brunot lived, turned out 2,400 Scrabble sets—but his little operation lost $450 that year.

It wasn't until the early 1950s, when then-president of Macy's, Jack Straus, discovered the game while on vacation and ordered some to sell in his store, that the game's popularity exploded.

Today, Scrabble is in more than thirty million homes and more than 100 million sets have been sold worldwide. There are all kinds of Scrabble tournaments, including the World Scrabble Championship, which is held every two years in a different city around the world.

Meanwhile, back in Jackson Heights, Queens, a Scrabble club still meets at the Community Methodist Church where Butts perfected the game. And on 35th Avenue at the corner of 81st Street, a street sign quietly honors Butts and the game he created here, for a total of fourteen points.

Incidentally, while Butts was a master at lexicon analysis, he was, by his own admission, a terrible speller. His wife, Nina, was better at the game than he was and famously played the word "quixotic," worth twenty-six points, against him. Alfred died in 1993. The last line of his obituary in the *New York Times* read, "He admitted that she 'beat me at my own game,' literally."

The word Butts is only worth seven points in Scrabble, but his contribution to the world is priceless.

5Pointz for Queens
Long Island City, Queens

One of the most famous museums in Queens is Long Island City's PS1, a public-school-turned-funky-art-gallery that is now owned by the Museum of Modern Art.

Across the street, next to the elevated subway tracks of the 7 train, is a lesser-known art gallery with huge street cred. It's called the 5Pointz Aerosol Art Center, aka "graffiti mecca," and it is a

200,000-square-foot former factory building covered in graffiti. It's named for the convergence of the five boroughs of New York City (Manhattan, Bronx, Brooklyn, Queens, and Staten Island), but the graffiti you'll find here isn't just from New York, it's the work of some of the best artists from all over the world, including the Netherlands, Japan, Brazil, Switzerland, and New Zealand.

5Pointz isn't just a ragtag group of graffiti artists who show up and paint. It's a curated museum where all artists are welcome but painting is by appointment, according to a sign, which is, appropriately, spray-painted on a door. The curator is Jonathan Cohen, a graffiti artist known for his signature tag, "Meres One."

"Meres really started curating it and created an outdoor museum with no roof and no entrance," says Marie Flageul, an event planner who works with 5Pointz.

And, unlike most graffiti, which you find on dark sides of buildings or under bridges, this graffiti wraps around the building, which is a city-block long, hugging every corner and climbing all the way up to the top of the fifth story, where it towers over visitors in a way you have probably never experienced graffiti before.

The graffiti is constantly changing, as is the impermanent nature of the art form, though some of the better stuff can stay up for six months to a year, like the giant portrait of the late rapper Biggie Smalls by a graffiti artist from New Zealand. The art varies from traditional "tags," the artists' names in big, chunky graffiti letters, to cartoon-style gangsters, sexy comic book–style women, and giant compositions that look like album covers.

Some of the most famous graffiti artists in the world paint here, but they also let beginners try their hand with "burners"—small tags. Some artists of the younger generation marvel at being able to paint on the same "canvas" as their favorite artists. Even the old-timers love to paint here—and do it legally.

"It's awesome," says Walter Baus, aka "Breez," a graphic artist who broke a twenty-year dry streak with a painting at 5Pointz.

Jokers, rappers, ladies, and tags mingle at 5Pointz, the "graffiti mecca."

"People come from all over the world, and everyone gets creative, feeding off of each other," he says.

Baus's piece was a big "BREEZ" tag, with screws and wads of gum painted on it, an orange splash of paint in the background, and a gangsta-style guy on the side with a thought bubble that said, "EAZY BREEZY."

When you stop by, you never know who—or what—you might find.

5Pointz is at Jackson Avenue and Davis Street in Long Island City. For more information, visit www.5ptz.com.

The Mysterious Rock Man

Staten Island

One day about fifteen years ago, mysterious rock formations began appearing on Staten Island's south shore. The local paper, the *Staten Island Advance,* was on the case immediately. It brought in experts on demonic worship, who concluded that this was clearly the work of a Satanic cult. Textbook evil. They ran the story on the front page.

This outraged Doug Schwartz, an animal trainer and zookeeper at the Staten Island Zoo, for one very good reason: He was the one who built those rock formations. And he's no Satan worshipper.

Schwartz likes to pile the beach rocks, in rich earthy tones of brown and tan, as a way of showcasing nature's beauty. For Schwartz, personally, the rocks provide a spiritual, artistic, and emotional balance to his work at the zoo, which is all about science. And, he believes that art isn't something you keep to yourself, but something you share with the community.

He's been out there just about every Friday for about a decade, no matter the weather—rain, sleet, or snow. There are now dozens of the shoulder-high rock piles, known as cairns, on the beach, in what has been described as "New York's little Stonehenge." There would probably be more, but from time to time, as with Hurricane Irene in 2011, Mother Nature topples many of them over and Schwartz must start again. A path marked with—what else?—rocks and logs for benches offers beachgoers an opportunity to get up close and enjoy the art.

"I figured, well, if they see these things, they'll think somebody really cares about the beach," Schwartz says.

Some people know who he is—the man behind the rock formations—but others don't. There are still wild theories circulating that the cairns are some sort of vampire graveyard or a message to aliens. Schwartz likes the interactivity of public art, so he'll walk right up to visitors and introduce himself as the creator of the cairns. Often, they don't believe him.

Staten Island's mysterious rock man, revealed!

"I get this vague sense that people who meet me are sort of disappointed," Schwartz says. They expect him to be bigger—capable of lifting all those heavy rocks. Either that, or a crazy old man. "Perhaps wearing a loincloth with one eye open, gesturing to the heavens!" he adds.

In fact, Schwartz is very down-to-earth and has a great sense of humor about it all. "I'd love to call myself a mystic. Act it out with the whole loincloth thing," Schwartz says. "But the wife wouldn't allow it. So, I have to create a more vivid projection of spirituality."

He isn't breaking any laws, rearranging stones and concrete that were already on the beach, but in 2011, the State Department of

Environmental Conservation asked him to cease and desist—though there was no indication the order would be permanent. You can't stop the forces of creativity: Schwartz, and a few apprentices he'd picked up along the way, just moved down to another beach and started making

Staten Island Chuck

If you think Doug Schwartz, builder of the rock formations on Staten Island's south shore, looks familiar, it's because he's famous for something else.

Schwartz, who is a zookeeper at the Staten Island Zoo, is the handler for Charles G. Hogg VII, aka "Staten Island Chuck," New York City's very own winter-prognosticating groundhog.

Sure, some people are Punxsutawney Phil purists, following that other groundhog who hails from Pennsylvania, but the little-known secret is that Chuck has the better track record! Chuck has about an 80 percent accuracy rate, while Phil has about a 39 percent success rate in his prognostications.

Chuck basks in the limelight in February for Groundhog Day, meeting city dignitaries and making the media rounds. But the rest of the year, Chuck keeps a pretty low profile, just hanging out with Schwartz.

"In my day, I'll just do some of my regular work, then go in there and throw him a paper towel. Play with him and go back to work," Schwartz says nonchalantly, as if Chuck is just another guy in accounting.

sculptures out of discarded bottles and other items left on the sand, turning Staten Island's trash habit into something to treasure.

The cairns are located on the beach near Sharrott Avenue, just south of Hylan Boulevard, on Staten Island's southern shore.

And, while he's whisked around in limos for Groundhog Day interviews, on normal weekends, Chuck takes the bus like everyone else. He spends weekends at Schwartz's house, where he enjoys running around on the deck, playing tag, and hiding. "He has a whole series of games," Schwartz says. "He hops back and forth from front to back feet. When he gets really excited, he hiccups. If you've got a hiccupping groundhog, you know you're on the right track," Schwartz adds.

About a month or so after Groundhog Day, you're likely to find Chuck singing. Is he sad that his fifteen minutes are up? Upset that Matt Lauer doesn't return his calls anymore? Nah. He's just letting the ladies know that he's available.

Chuck got an upgrade in recent years, from the "cube" down the hall from Schwartz under the rain forest to his own Weather Station above ground.

Stop by and visit Chuck or "friend" him on Facebook at www.facebook.com/StatenIslandChuck. He's got over 4,000 friends and, despite an embarrassing incident a few years ago when he bit NYC Mayor Michael Bloomberg on Groundhog Day, his Facebook page says he "likes" Mayor Bloomberg.

Typical Chuck!

The Jeweled Gates of Staten Island
Rosebank, Staten Island

There have been many shrines built in the Virgin Mary's honor, but nothing quite like Our Lady of Mt. Carmel Grotto in Staten Island.

It's been described as "the city's most elaborate yard shrine" and "a fairy tale of a jeweled city." It looks like ruins from an ancient temple, or what the gates of Heaven would look like if they were designed by Antonio Gaudí.

It's a twisting and turning ornamental concrete wall, with one main altar in the middle. Set into the concrete structure, which is about twenty feet tall by fifty feet wide, are hundreds of smooth beach pebbles, as well as bits of blown glass, seashells, and even bicycle reflectors.

It all started with Italian immigrant Vito Russo, who built a small homemade shrine out of cardboard and tinfoil. Russo wanted to go bigger, so, one day in 1935, he convinced his buddies down at the Society of Our Lady of Mount Carmel to help him build a courtyard grotto. The construction workers handled the heavy stone blocks, sanitation workers gathered the pebbles, and a few of the guys worked at the glass factory down the street, which is likely where the blown glass came from. The men came from all over Italy, so the resulting architectural style is a mosaic of Italian styles.

"This was before television," says Mike DeCataldo, treasurer of the society, whose father and grandfather helped build the grotto. "So, the guys would come down to the town hall at night, drink wine, eat, and build things in the basement. That's just what they did back then."

The shrine is open twenty-four hours to offer a place for anyone and everyone—not just Italians or Catholics—to say a prayer or clear their head at their time of need—even if that time is 3:30 a.m.

People bring photos of loved ones, rosaries, flowers, or other objects. It's also become a popular place to leave that religious sculpture-turned-albatross you inherited when your grandmother died.

A peaceful place in Staten Island.

You know the one: It doesn't go with your decor, but you feel way too guilty to toss it.

"We don't throw anything away," DeCataldo says, to the collective sigh of relief from guilt-ridden Catholics the world over.

The grotto is located at 36 Amity Place in Rosebank, Staten Island. A good time to go is in July for the big feast, when you can hear these stories firsthand while listening to an Elvis impersonator and eating a piping-hot zeppole.

It doesn't get much better than that.

For more information, visit one of the longest URLs in the history of URLs: http://ourladyofmountcarmelshrineofrosebank.com/index.html.

The Tugboat Graveyard

Rossville, Staten Island

They stand there, tipped to the side or backs drooping, like a couple of drunken sailors.

But these guys aren't going to wake up tomorrow and continue about their business with a slight hangover. This is it for them. A couple of old souls trapped in shallow water, rusting away the time.

This is the Rossville Boatyard, where the pier crumbles off into slippery sand and a handful of old boats of all denominations—cargo vessels, tug ships, dredging barges—have come to their final resting place.

It's located off the southwestern shore of Staten Island, the end of the New York City line, just before the Outerbridge Crossing whisks the living off to New Jersey. It's a discreet enough place to just slump

Hey, George! Lookit these old-timers taking a nap. Whaddaya say we put one of their hands in water and see what happens?

over and hope no one notices, tucked between the now-retired Fresh Kills Landfill and the Arthur Kill Correctional Facility. The woods nearby are loaded with unwanted cars; a seaside cemetery hosts graves more than 200 years old. Here, graffiti artists hone their craft, and paintball players obliviously make their mark. The shops sell topsoil, tile, and concrete.

The water is shallow here, so you can get a really good view of the boats. Some urban adventurers have risked the busted-up pier to get a closer look, but you can see the boats from the shore. As you gaze through the tall marshy grass, Canadian geese gliding in and out of the wreckage, you can't help but wonder what tales they might tell if these old-timers could talk.

"Hey, Jimmy. Did I ever tell you about the time we were bringing in this aircraft carrier? One of these new guys—thinks he's a real hot shot—he falls straight off the edge! Took 'em two hours to get that kid back on the ship! I mean, those things are like 1,000 feet long."

Blink again, and they're asleep. Some appear to be dozing, others down for the count, as the tide washes in and out.

From the Mall to the Poorhouse

Willow Brook, Staten Island

How many times have you said something like, "Whoa, I'd better stop spending money or I'm going to wind up in the poorhouse!"?

We say such things absentmindedly, but the truth is, if this were 1902, that could actually happen.

One of the charming English holdovers in this country, which lasted well into the twentieth century, was the poorhouse, also referred to as the poor farm. Essentially, it was a place to sweep the poor out of sight from the rest of society. I have no idea why this was what we chose to keep instead of, say, the English garden or the English accent, which would've been pretty cool.

The New York City Farm Colony opened on Staten Island in the early 1900s. The idea was to have the poor be self-sustaining—growing

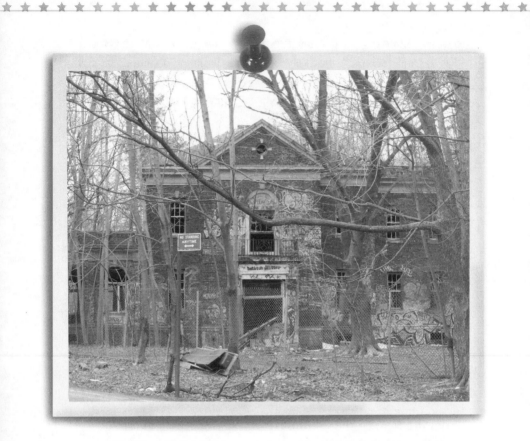

The historic district that was once the New York City Farm Colony.

fruit and vegetables, and tending to pigs and chickens—and to ensure that the rest of the community would never see them. Each person was assigned a set of work clothes and a small dorm room, not unlike prison. This particular farm colony did well in that department for a few decades, but there's one teensy-tiny problem with keeping a population isolated like that for an extended period of time: They get old. So, the facility quickly became a geriatric center, and the farming part petered out. The facility was eventually shut down in 1975.

Staten Island, which seems to have a problem with throwing things away (not only will you find boats left at sea, but cars and other unwanted items dumped in the woods), still has that poor farm, or what's left of it. Apparently, there were efforts to try to sell the land for residential development, but such plans got buried under a mound of red tape, and at some point, Staten Island just said, "Aw, what the heck. Let's make it a historic district."

And so, there it stands today, a series of decrepit buildings penned up behind a fence, tangled in a jungle of vines, trees, and trash. To look at this monstrosity, you might be inclined to think that the only "historic" things it's preserving are the fine art of graffiti and the cultural institution of the late-night teen party.

There are an abundance of photos online from urban thrill seekers who dared trespass on this tetanus-friendly site. They show rusty cots with mattresses askew, toilet bowls lying on the floor, piles of papers, and thirty-year-old laundry waiting to be claimed. It's as if the inhabitants were suddenly called away all at once, and never returned.

The ironic thing is that the Staten Island Mall is just down the street. It makes you wonder if shoppers ever realize that they're *literally* just a hop, skip, and a jump away from the poorhouse.

The Great Sphinx of Fontana
Bayport, Long Island

Not that it's terribly easy to steal heavy hunks of concrete, but just in case, a giant sphinx, an Egyptian symbol for guardian, presides over Fontana Concrete Products in Bayport, Long Island.

The twenty-foot-tall solid concrete sphinx was built in the early 1900s by Will Graham as a way of attracting politicians and movie stars to his hotel, the Anchorage Inn, in Blue Point, Long Island (which, incidentally, is also home of the tasty Blue Point oyster).

The inn burned down in the late 1920s, but the sphinx squatted the property for a few decades more. (It's probably not that easy to evict a concrete sphinx, whether he's paying rent or not.) But, in the 1970s, the jig was up for the squatting sphinx and he was bulldozed to make way for a new gas station.

Don't even think about stealing that bird feeder.

Louis Fontana, co-owner with his brother John of Fontana Concrete Products, was driving by and told the demolition workers to toss the 10,000-pound head on the back of his truck. He drove it back to Bayport, where he let the weary head rest for about seven years, before beginning restoration.

It took two years, but they rebuilt the body of the sphinx and it now keeps a watchful eye over all sorts of Fontana Concrete products, everything from paving stones to birdbaths and planters.

The inscription on the bottom of the sphinx reads: "She who climbs to the Sphinx's head, a millionaire will surely wed." But please, ladies, don't climb on the sphinx. Put on a pair of pumps and a little makeup instead, if you've really got your heart set on a millionaire.

The Great Sphinx of Fontana is significantly easier to get to than its more famous counterpart in Giza. It's located at 890 Montauk Highway in Bayport, just across the street from the 7-Eleven and Starbucks. Visit www.fontanaconcrete.com or call (631) 472-1600.

The East Coast Area 51

Camp Hero State Park, Long Island

You might want to put on your tinfoil hat for this next story.

Out on Long Island's eastern tip in Montauk, a popular summer spot for New Yorkers, is a former military base called Camp Hero, which is now a state park. Used during World War II, Camp Hero had all the usual fort fare—docks, hangars, bunkers, and barracks. But some say that a huge underground facility, located under the camp's giant radar, was subsequently used for secret government experiments.

The Montauk Project, as it's known, traces back to the 1943 Philadelphia Experiment, also known as the Rainbow Project, when the government was allegedly tinkering with radar invisibility and successfully made a ship invisible, though in the process removed it from the space-time continuum for fifteen minutes. As the story goes, several crew members were killed, and others were left with psychological damage.

The conspiracy theorists, several of whom are brilliant scientists and claim to have been involved with the experiments, allege that the government used the massive underground facility in Montauk to rekindle the time-travel experiment—opening a portal between 1983 and 1943—and to conduct other experiments in telepathy, mind control, and other equally bizarre subjects. They allege that homeless people were abducted for some experiments, and that young boys with heightened psychic abilities were able to materialize objects from their thoughts! Alien reptoids, a psychically generated Yeti, and a professional wrestler may or may not have been involved, but let's just leave it at that.

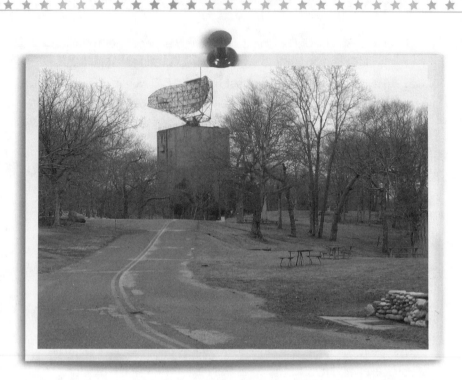

Site of a conspiracy theory, possible time
travel, and a lovely place for a picnic.

Today, there is no shortage of Internet sleuths who note the abundance of "do not enter" signs at the park as well as the generators,
cords, and other indications of activity at the allegedly decommissioned
site. Some even say that armed soldiers have shooed them away from
poking around.

The park is open to the public, so check it out at your own risk:
Drive past the boarded-up guard checkpoints, get up close to the giant
radar installation, or picnic in the abandoned military camp nearby.

To get to Camp Hero State Park, take Route 27/Montauk Highway
all the way to the end, just before you hit the ocean. Pack some sandwiches, chips, soda, and maybe some mini-Snickers. But don't forget
to wrap it all in tinfoil so you can make a hat.

All Hail the Queens!

Fire Island Pines, Long Island

Guy walks into a bar. (You've heard this one, right?)

He's wearing full drag. (OK, maybe not *this* one.)

The bartender says this isn't appropriate attire and refuses to serve the man/lady—m'lady.

M'lady returns home and tells the newly crowned (homecoming) queen what has happened. A few days later, the queen returns with an entourage. The bartender does the math. Drinks are served.

This is how the Invasion of the Pines, now an annual event, started thirty years ago.

Fire Island, on the southern side of Long Island, is a top summer spot for New York's gay community. Cherry Grove and the Pines are the most popular, but they couldn't be more different. The Pines, which came out of the closet in the 1950s, about twenty years after Cherry Grove, is home to a wealthy, conservative gay population that would never dream of dressing in drag. (Heck, some of its residents may still be rummaging around in the closet.) For its artsier sibling, Cherry Grove, anything goes. Gay, lesbian, straight, drag, leather— you'll see all the colors of the rainbow in Cherry Grove.

So you can imagine that, when the Grove's Teri Warren showed up in all of his glamorous lady glory for dinner at Botel, a Pines hotel, on July 4, 1976, the fireworks were flying. But when Homecoming Queen Panzi led the follow-up invasion, Pines residents were so surprised and entertained that they treated the ladies to a drink at the Botel's Blue Whale restaurant and bar, and a tradition was born.

And so, every Fourth of July, hundreds of men in all of their cross-dressing glory board a two-deck ferry in Cherry Grove and "invade" the Pines. They come in their best summer dresses, ball gowns, bikinis, big wigs, and of course, perfectly accessorized. Some dress as celebrities—Britney Spears and the Brady Bunch have appeared in past years—or in themed getups, like the Cherry Grove Airline Stewardesses and the beer stein–toting Heidi Hoes.

Once the boat reaches the Pines, the ladies strut that dock like a catwalk, to the delight of the shorts-and-sandals-clad Pines folk. They drink, they dine, they mingle. And just before Macy's kicks off its fireworks in Manhattan, the ladies return home to Cherry Grove, mission accomplished.

For more information check out www.fireislandinvasion.com.

The drag queens are coming! The drag queens are coming!
PHOTO BY MARCO HERRERA FOR FIREISLANDQNEWS.COM

The Man-Eating Lake

Legend has it that the spirit of an Indian princess lives in Lake Ronkonkoma in central Long Island. She drowned herself in the lake after the man she was to marry was murdered by a white man. It is said that each year she claims the life of one man as revenge.

There are many variations of this story and more than a handful of stories on the Internet from men who claim to have heard the voice of a woman beckoning them to the center of the lake—a very deep lake, once rumored to be bottomless—but managed to escape.

So, are men afraid to swim in the lake?

"Well, there's this one guy who comes into the bar," says Mickey Quinn, a longtime bartender at Parsnips Pub on the north side of the lake. "He says to me, 'Anyone drown yet, Mick?' If I say, 'No,' then he says, 'OK. Then I'm not goin' in.'"

Quinn, an Irishman who fashions himself a bit of a *shanachie* (Gaelic for storyteller), has a million stories about what's in that lake. A lot of cars, from days gone by when people used to try to drive across the ice, and at least one raccoon. (It's a long story, but the short of it is that the fuzzy little bandit was punished for eating kittens.) Few of his stories about the lake involve a lady. Well, except for that one about a date that ended with a moonlight dip and a misplaced car—but let's save that one for another day.

After more than a decade, surely Quinn has heard more than his share of tales from men who come into the bar, claiming to have been summoned by the lady in the lake, no?

"Well, maybe at four in the morning they heard something," he says, chuckling. "The girls get prettier at four in the morning, too!"

"Hey, did you hear about that new designer dog they got there?" Quinn asks with a sly grin. "Yeah, they crossed a bulldog and a Shih Tzu. You know what they call that?"

Hmmm. I guess it's not a dog zu, now is it?

Now That Is Fowl!

Flanders, Long Island

Long Island's eastern end is home to the Hamptons, a summer playground for the rich and famous. But let's face it, Long Island is for the birds.

To be more specific, ducks. Long Island, once home to a lively duck-farming industry, commemorates its fowl past with a building shaped like a big duck. It's located in Flanders, just down the road from the tony Hamptons.

The duck was the brainchild—or brainfowl, as it were—of duck farmer Martin Maurer in 1931. Inspired by a giant coffeepot he saw while on vacation in California, Maurer got the flighty idea that it might help his business if he made a big duck on the side of the road. So, he hired a local carpenter and a couple of theater-set designers to create the twenty-nine-foot-tall duck, which is appropriately called "the Big Duck." They used wood, mesh, cement, and Model-T taillights for the eyes.

"The duck is pure fun but nevertheless an important historic icon," says Barbara Bixby, curator of the Big Duck, who also proudly goes by the name of the Duck Lady. "It's a symbol of ingenious advertising, architecture, agriculture, and all-around Americana in the automotive age." (Say that one five times fast!)

Inside the Big Duck, Maurer used to sell his ducks. Today, thanks to the preservation efforts of the state, it's the home of a gift shop for duck-a-bilia—everything from Big Duck T-shirts to wind-up ducks and, of course, rubber duckies.

But make no mistake, the Big D's legacy is much more than bath-time fun. It spawned the architectural term "duck," meaning a building shaped like the products or services sold within, as well as a Duck Design Theory. Part of the DDT, coined by architect James Wines, goes, "Form follows fantasy, not function, for architecture that cannot offer fantasy fails man's need to dream."

Whoa! Now that's a mighty duck.

The duck sits on a thirty-eight-acre park known as Big Duck Ranch. The Friends of the Big Duck, a nonprofit organization, are working on opening a museum about duck farming on the site.

Stop by and see the Big D on Route 24 in Flanders, Long Island. For more information, call the store at (631) 852-8292 or visit www.big duck.org.

index

index

index

index

index

index

about the author

★ ★

Cindy Perman is a news editor at CNBC.com and author of the blog *There Must Be a Pony in Here Somewhere* (http://ponyblog.cnbc.com). Prior to CNBC.com, she worked at WSJ.com for nine years. Her writing has appeared in the *Wall Street Journal, USA Today,* and on Yahoo.com, among other outlets, and she has appeared on CNBC, MSNBC, and NBC's *The Today Show.* She has also done stand-up comedy at venues in New York City, including Comix and Gotham Comedy Club. She's had a lifelong curiosity about cool stuff in New York State, having grown up in Rochester, graduated from Syracuse University, and lived in the New York City area since 1994.